what people in charge say about
Smart Moves
for People in Charge

Pilots have very good reasons for using checklists prior to takeoff. The sophistication of modern aircraft and air traffic control has made kicking the tires and wiggling the rudder obsolete. In this book, I found the perfect checklists for business executives before they forge ahead. Here are the concrete steps for preventing the pangs of "gosh-I-wish-I-had-thought-of-that" remorse. Individual circumstances and personal experiences often encourage senior managers to fly by the seat of their pants. With this book at their side, haphazardness will be replaced by well thought out procedure. Thumbs up for *Smart Moves for People in Charge*. It should be in every executive's toolbox.

> —Helge H. Wehmeier, President and CEO,
> Bayer Corporation

Deep and Sussman have done it again! *Smart Moves for People in Charge* is high-octane fuel. It's so cleverly organized and well written that solutions to the problems I face as a change agent come to me more quickly and more powerfully than from other great management books. I read the book backwards first, then forwards. I now read one list at a time, depending on where I am and where I'm heading on the never-ending road to change.

> —Anthony J. Buzzelli, Partner-in-Charge of Audit,
> Deloitte & Touche

No one writes books with greater clarity and user-friendliness than Deep and Sussman. This one ought to be mandatory reading in every program that trains managers and supervisors on how to lead. Those who want to make "smart moves" in the hospitality industry need the wisdom in this book to positively "take charge."

> —Raúl Bustamante, General Manager & Director,
> Hilton International, Puerto Rico

Here at last is the practical advice I need to manage in today's world. What I like best is the way I can quickly retrieve so many valuable tips on such a broad array of management issues.

> —Bruce Hineman, Executive Director,
> National Council on Teacher Retirement

The keys to business success are people and common sense. This book shows how to handle the former and develop the latter, in a writing style that cannot possibly be misunderstood. Short, sweet, and to the point. It will be read by our Division Presidents.

—Tom McMullen, President & COO,
US Foodservice, Inc.

Smart Moves for People in Charge is full of thought-provoking insights that will jump start a meeting, a project, or your day.

—Daniel R. Madia, Senior VP of Administration,
Ketchum Communications, Inc.

Here is a book you will truly enjoy. What an exciting way to explore every vital area of improvement for the person in charge! This Deep and Sussman sequel to their marvelous book *Smart Moves* is a must-reference for any executive looking for help in solving the problems faced at, and near, the top.

—Alan Sweeting, Airline Station Manager,
Nassau, Bahamas

For the busy, impatient executive with a microsecond attention span, *Smart Moves for People in Charge* is a make-sense way to gain stimulating insights on demand.

—Bill Samuels, Jr., President,
Maker's Mark Distillery, Inc.

Smart Moves for People in Charge is the ultimate how-to book for people-oriented managers. It is jam-packed with quickly referenced and proven ideas on how to maximize the value of the most precious corporate commodity—people.

—W. Stephen Parker, Accounts Manager,
AgVet Division, Merck & Co., Inc.

A definite book to have available to become the successful and effective manager of the '90s, when change is inevitable and team-work is necessary.

—Earl Reed, Vice President,
Vencor

Smart Moves for People in Charge

Other Books by the Authors

Smart Moves: 14 Steps to Keep Any Boss Happy, 8 Ways to Start Meetings on Time, and 1,600 More Tips to Get the Best from Yourself and the People Around You

Yes, You Can! 1,105 Empowering Ideas for Life, Work, and Happiness

What to Say to Get What You Want: Strong Words for 44 Challenging Types of Bosses, Employees, Coworkers, and Customers

What to Ask When You Don't Know What to Say: 555 Powerful Questions to Use for Getting Your Way at Work

COMEX: The Communication Experience in Human Relations, Second Edition

Speaking Skills for Bankers

by Sam Deep

Human Relations in Management

A Program of Exercises for Management and Organizational Behavior, with James A. Vaughan

Introduction to Business: A Systems Approach, with William D. Brinkloe

Studies in Organizational Psychology, with Bernard M. Bass

Current Perspectives for Managing Organizations, with Bernard M. Bass

by Lyle Sussman

Communications for Supervisors and Managers

Increasing Supervisory Effectiveness

SMART MOVES
for People in Charge

---

130 Checklists to Help You
Be a Better Leader

Sam Deep and Lyle Sussman

Addison-Wesley Publishing Company
Reading, Massachusetts   Menlo Park, California   New York
Don Mills, Ontario   Wokingham, England   Amsterdam   Bonn
Sydney   Singapore   Tokyo   Madrid   San Juan
Paris   Seoul   Milan   Mexico City   Taipei

Many of the designations used by manufacturers and sellers to distinguish their products are claimed as trademarks. Where those designations appear in this book and Addison-Wesley was aware of a trademark claim, the designations have been printed in initial capital letters.

Library of Congress Cataloging-in-Publication Data

Deep, Samuel D.
    Smart moves for people in charge : 130 checklists to help you be a better leader / Sam Deep and Lyle Sussman.
      p.   cm.
    Includes index.
    ISBN 0-201-48328-9
    1. Leadership. I. Sussman, Lyle, 1944– . II. Title.
HD57.7.D48   1995
658.4'092—dc20   95-9571
                                       CIP

Cover design by Suzanne Heiser
Text design by Joyce C. Weston
Set in 10-point Sabon by Pagesetters

1 2 3 4 5 6 7 8 9 10-DOH-9998979695
First printing, August 1995

Addison-Wesley books are available at special discounts for bulk purchases. For more information about how to make such purchases in the U.S., please contact the Corporate, Government, and Special Sales Department at Addison-Wesley Publishing Company, 1 Jacob Way, Reading, MA 01867, or call (800) 238-9682.

CONTENTS

THREE Get the Word

FOUR Lead Your Team

SIX   Renew Your Organization

SEVEN   Stay Close to the Customer

EIGHT Control Your Organization

NINE Find Your Balance

INTRODUCTION

Being in charge has always been exciting and challenging. Today the excitement is even more thrilling and the challenge is even more trying. Massive shifts in technology, dizzying changes in market pressures, demographic transformations in the workforce, fresh demands from society, and customers as fussy as ever come together to put you in the center of the action.

We wrote *Smart Moves for People in Charge* to make sure that all this bedlam gives you imagination and not a headache. We want you to dream about and realize the possibilities for leadership today, not merely dwell on its difficulties. Where you encounter obstacles, we want you to have the tools to overcome them.

This book is aimed at people in significant levels of leadership and for those looking forward to such positions. While anyone in a supervisory capacity will benefit from the checklists, those who stand to gain the most carry titles like CEO, COO, CFO, owner, president, vice president, commander, director, chancellor, dean, general manager, partner, principal, department head, superintendent, division manager, plant manager, sales manager, bureau chief, store manager, and editor. They're in charge of corporations, small businesses, nonprofit organizations, government agencies, departments, associations, practices, institutions, schools, and hospitals.

Practical Tips, Usable Lists

In format this book is similar to our earlier business best-seller, *Smart Moves*, which provided practical tips in checklist form. The lists contain advice with a minimum of jargon and a maximum of practical value. Fans of *Smart Moves* will find the same appealing features in this version. You won't have to read page after page searching for a single nugget of wisdom. To the contrary, each page contains useful advice without lengthy anecdotes or wordy and theoretical treatises.

There are 130 lists in the book. All were written specifically for this edition. Even though some topics (reducing stress, managing time, writing clearly) are also included in *Smart Moves* and another book of ours, *Yes, You Can!*, we have rewritten them to reflect the special needs of top managers. For other lists, we have borrowed the expertise of colleagues whom we thank in our Acknowledgments. This material is original, having never appeared in any other form, other than in our training and motivational speaking.

As in *Smart Moves*, in many cases we've cross referenced the advice in one checklist with the advice in one or more other lists. Look for a number in parentheses after a checklist item. Consult the list with that number for more advice on a related topic. Sometimes you'll realize that you need to consider issues in more depth before you implement our recommendations. We hope you'll develop an appreciation of how widely you can apply this book's advice, and how it all ties together.

At the back of the book is an index. There we've listed the topics covered by our lists in alphabetical order. Almost all the common challenges people in charge face appear in this index, and we hope this way of quickly finding our advice will help you rise to those challenges.

Totally new in this book are the checklists appearing in all nine chapters titled "Twelve Quotes Worth Quoting About . . ." These provide that well-worded, insightful, or humorous phrase that can often unlock the door to wisdom better than we can. Read all 108 quotes. You may find that they start creeping into your conversations and speeches. You might post a few of them on the walls in your office. You might also find that you start practicing what they preach.

Our goal in writing *Smart Moves for People in Charge* was to present you with a comprehensive and portable encyclopedia of executive leadership. We hope we've accomplished that goal.

Sam Deep
Lyle Sussman

June 1995

FIVE WAYS TO USE THIS BOOK

We believe that the advice and the format of this book make it unlike any other book you've ever read. We also think you will want to use it in some special and unusual ways.

1. Read it from beginning to end.
You could start at list 1 and read straight through until you finish list 130. If you choose to read the book this way, don't do it in one or even two sessions. There is simply too much information to absorb in a short time.

2. Refer to it when a specific problem arises.
Use it the same way you would use an owner's manual, a dictionary, an atlas, or an encyclopedia. When you need specific advice, search the Table of Contents or the Index.

3. Keep it handy and randomly refer to it when you have time.
Keep it on your night stand at home, on your desk at the office, or in your briefcase when you travel. When you have time and are looking for a particular self-improvement tip, pick up the book.

4. Once a month reread all the quotations.
The quotations provide information, insight, wisdom, and in some cases humor. They should be reviewed and savored. Each time you read the quotations you'll learn more about yourself and your organization.

5. Make notes about lists that should be reread.
No two of our readers are exactly alike. A list that might be all right to one reader could be fabulous to another. After you've gone through the book once, note those lists that have special significance for you and warrant repeated readings.

1

BUILD YOUR EXECUTIVE POWER

When you're in charge, you make things happen. Through your person, your position, and your style you influence other people, both inside and outside your organization. This chapter will help you achieve that influence with the best results for yourself and for the people around you. Take a close look at the impact you have on your organization.

1 Fourteen Strategies for Making Better Decisions

Regardless of the organization or department you run, your success reflects your ability to make sound decisions. Some decisions are minor (furniture for the office), and others are pivotal (restructuring the corporation). It would be wonderful to have a genie sitting on your shoulder whispering "yes" or "no" every time you face a tough choice. If you can't find one, consider these strategies for increasing your success rate.

1. Recognize your personal decision-making biases.
Are you more emotional or more logical? Are you a "numbers" person or a "big picture" person? Do you jump to conclusions or weigh information *ad nauseam*? Do you look for immediate fixes or long-term solutions? Improve your decisions by understanding the person behind them.

2. Involve colleagues who see the world differently from you.
Improve your decisions by opening your ears and your mind to a perspective other than your own. Force yourself to listen to opposing views without becoming defensive. Test others' ideas before deciding on them. (31, 32)

3. Fight the temptation to solve today's problem with yesterday's solution.
We all develop habits and patterns of looking at the world. As a result, when a problem seems similar to one you faced in the past,

you're likely to handle it the same way as before. The world changes too fast to fall back blindly on old methods.

4. Solve problems with a win-win orientation.

Seek decisions that give as much value as possible to everyone concerned. Help others win, and they'll look for ways to return the favor.

5. Solicit information from individuals affected by the decision.

Regardless of how good a decision is, it will never work if employees fail to get behind it or, worse, if they sabotage your efforts. People who are involved in decisions are more likely to go the extra mile to make the decision a success. They may even point out solutions that you never imagined. (40)

6. Make sure you're solving the right problem.

Ask questions to probe the scope and nature of any problem you face. What are the symptoms of the problem? What are its root causes? What's the gap between where you are now and where you want to be? The answers to these questions will help you focus on solving the real problem. (33)

After months of customer complaints about shoddy treatment, a CEO elected to improve the training given to front-line employees. Immediately after the training, designed by an expensive consulting firm, complaints fell sharply. Six months later they were back to high levels. The reason? The real problem was the inconsiderate and heavy-handed supervision of those employees. The training had encouraged employees to treat customers better. But when the same poor supervision continued, the employees returned to their earlier levels of alienation—and poor service.

---

7. Consider as many solutions as possible.

Use your creative juices. Brainstorm alone or with a group. Generate as many solutions as you can before you evaluate any of them. When you do begin the evaluation process, ensure that each idea gets a fair hearing. Value each alternative for what's good about it before condemning its drawbacks.

8. Realize that even the best solutions may open the door to new problems.

Before you adopt a solution, look into the future to anticipate its consequences. Picture the worst-case scenario for a solution before you go with it. Get others to help you answer this question: "What can possibly go wrong with this plan?"

9. If you're using "hard data" as the basis for your decision, verify the numbers.

Numbers don't speak for themselves. Numbers are crunched by humans who have opinions about what they expect to find, so they're inherently biased. Don't get seduced by the supposed objectivity of numbers. Where do the data come from? How were they collected? What are the underlying assumptions or premises? Be hard-headed about "hard data." (101)

10. When you make a decision affecting others, share the reasoning behind the decision.

Some information is proprietary, extremely sensitive, or legally can't be divulged. However, if you can reveal information to those with a vested interest, do so. Your coworkers, suppliers, customers, and stockholders want to know the reasoning behind your decisions. When you don't meet their needs for information, they'll imagine their own scenarios and may cause a bigger problem than the one you just solved.

11. Think in terms of "satisficing," not optimizing.

The optimizing decision maker is determined to make the best choice in each and every situation. The "satisficing" decision maker recognizes that in an imperfect world there may be no such thing as the best choice. Rather, there are good choices and poor choices. Optimizers often wait too long to decide for fear that they don't have all the data. Optimizers often aren't flexible enough to alter earlier decisions when new data comes to light. Optimizers wouldn't consider implementing a good plan devised by employees when they know there's a better way—*their* way.

12. Ask lots of questions.

The key to making better decisions is getting better information; and the key to getting better information is asking better questions. The best questions are those that respond to the answers you get to your initial questions. These follow-ups are called "probes" because they enable you to delve into the issues. Such questioning also presents a good model to your people. (33)

13. Learn from prior decisions.
Go to school on every decision you make. Treat every crucial decision as a case study for personal development. With the last decision you made, what did you do well and what did you do poorly? Why? What will you do differently this time?

14. Ask for criticism.
Once you or your problem-solving group makes a decision, delay the celebration and the backslapping until you're sure you've done the right thing. Keep people around you who are strong enough to challenge your ideas so bad ones never make it out of your office. If necessary, say something like, "This idea won't be implemented until I hear at least three reasons why it might fail." Then listen.

Think of your decision as a beautiful statue you've designed for the people of a mythical town. You want to erect this statue in the town square where the people will praise its beauty and place flowers at its feet. However, before erecting the statue, place rocks in the hands of the workers who have helped you build it. Direct each of them to fire away at the statue. If after the pummeling the statue retains its splendor, it's ready for the square. If, however, you see some damage, you should repair the statue, completely recast it, or forget about it altogether.

---

2 | Ten Steps for Opening Yourself Up to Change

In a recent report the American Business Conference stated that, "One of the great problems associated with success and the achievement of great size is the risk that executives will behave as bureaucrats, not as creative thinkers." Are you as open to change and new ways of doing things as you need to be in today's volatile business environment?

1. Examine your history regarding change.
Which of these five postures toward change is most typical for you?

- Do you *avoid* change, not seeing or acknowledging the need for it?
- Do you often *resist* change and defend the status quo?
- Do you tend to *cooperate*, going along with justifiable change, even if reluctantly?
- Are you out in front as someone who *anticipates* and sees the need for change even before others do?
- Are you a leader in *creating* change, taking action to bring it about?

Those who will gain the most from this list are probably in the first three categories.

2. Identify the change most troubling you.
Consider one change at work or home that you feel yourself resisting. Possible business changes include merger, restructuring, downsizing, relocation, renaming of company, new hire, new assignment, new way of doing something, new board members, new boss, new team members, new schedule, new office, new technology, new laws or regulations, more work, less help, longer hours, retirement, going part time, being let go.

3. Be certain you understand the change.
Do you know exactly what this change involves? Has it been fully explained to you? What information do you still need in order to grasp the rationale for it, the role you need to play in it, and its implications for you, your employees, and your company? Find out.

4. Uncover the reasons for your resistance—the *losses* you fear.
People resist change when they believe they'll lose something as a result. Typically feared losses include control, security, prestige, self-esteem, ego, advantage, position, relationships, freedom, comfort, predictability, and wealth or money. Which of these are at the heart of your resistance?

5. Determine how much those losses may be imaginary or overblown.
On a sheet of paper, record any indications that the loss you fear will actually occur. What's its probability? Talk to someone else to be certain your eyes are open to reality. Do you have a history of overreacting?

6. Determine how much those losses, while real, can be lessened to make the change tolerable.

On that sheet of paper, record any actions you can take to reduce the probability of the loss occurring or to soften its impact.

7. Determine how much those losses may prove eventually to be advantageous to you.

On the same sheet of paper, record the potential each loss has for actually turning into an advantage—something you will someday value or at least tolerate without difficulty. Think back to once-feared changes that worked out for the best. Talk to others about apparent gains that you may not be allowing yourself to acknowledge.

8. Identify the pain of not changing.

After you've identified the potential pleasures that the change can bring, look at the potential pain of not changing. Will you pay a high price for resisting the change you identified in step #2 above?

9. Don't compromise your values.

After completing this analysis, you may be ready to cooperate with the change that's been concerning you. If so, make sure that such cooperation doesn't come at the cost of compromising your fundamental values and beliefs. Indeed, this analysis may have confirmed that you need to stand up and be counted as a conscientious objector to the change.

10. Take action.

Either publicly announce you'll back the change and support it through your actions, or declare your intent to increase your opposition. In the latter case, consider what you'll offer instead so as not to be seen as an obstructionist.

---

3   Twelve Ways to Keep Your Ego in Check

A philosopher once said, "Power corrupts and absolute power corrupts absolutely." When you're in charge, it's easy to get seduced by the power you possess and the deference others pay you. You're the boss, the top dog, *numero uno*, the head honcho. However, if you give in to the allure, you set the stage for your own demise. You create a barrier between yourself and your employees, and you put yourself on a pedestal from which you're destined to fall. One of the toughest balancing acts is to exercise power while maintaining humility.

1. Monitor the danger signs of a runaway ego.
If you answer yes to any of these questions, you may have an ego that needs to be reined in:

- Do your subordinates fail to confront you, even when you're wrong?
- Do employees cower in your presence?
- Do you like proving how powerful, smart, or impressive you are?
- Do you get angry and raise your voice when others challenge your ideas?

2. Realize that your success depends on the efforts of others.
You might think you're the star of the team, but without the team your star wouldn't shine so brightly. Your dream becomes a reality only if others have the interest and the ability to help you. Uplift your people, and they'll raise you onto their shoulders.

3. Remove self-serving and egoistic expressions from your language.
Listen to yourself speak. Starting today, cut your "I" statements in half. Increase your use of second person pronouns (you, yours) and first person plural pronouns (we, our, us).

4. Stop talking and start listening.
Use the ideas and suggestions of others. Let them express themselves and tell you what they're thinking. Recognize the value of their ideas. This simple strategy will not only help you keep your ego in check, it will also bring out information that could help you make money. (31, 32, 40)

5. Study the best "balancing acts" you can find.
Note the leadership and communication style of people in your profession and community who manage to wield power while maintaining humility. Emulate them. Reject negative models—those whose egos are bigger than any room they happen to be in.

6. Place your stature in context.
Look at a world map. There are over five billion people on this globe. How many of them know your name? Of the people that do, how many will have only positive things to say about you?

7. Identify your motives for self-aggrandizement.

Many people who blow their own horn do so out of insecurity. Others do so out of selfish ambition or envy of others. Whatever the reason, if an enlarged ego is getting in the way of managing your business, take a close look at yourself, perhaps with the benefit of professional guidance.

8. Learn to laugh at yourself.

Stop taking yourself so seriously. Whenever you say or do something foolish (and we all do), be the first to see the humor in it. Laugh at yourself in front of your colleagues, and they won't laugh at you behind your back.

9. When you've offended or embarrassed someone, apologize.

An apology is a two-edged sword, both sides of which cut in your favor:

- Apologizing causes you to humble yourself in front of others.
- Apologizing enhances you in the eyes of those who receive the apology.

10. Associate with many different kinds of people.

Stay away from executive cliques. Meet people with diverse backgrounds, opinions, and values. Don't spend too much time with any one group, lest you identify so strongly with them that you begin to look down on others. (85)

11. Serve the downtrodden.

Service to the needy is both humbling and uplifting. You can't retain much pride in being so successful when you meet less fortunate people and encounter their circumstances first hand.

12. Become a servant leader.

Don't overdo the "rank hath its privileges" bit. Cook hot dogs at the next company picnic. Pass out handouts at the next seminar. Make coffee for your secretary tomorrow morning. Ask employees what they need from you in order to succeed. Listen to what they tell you, tell them what you'll do about it, and deliver.

4   Twelve Tips for Enhancing Your Executive Presence

Some executives light up a room by walking into it, and others light up a room by walking out of it. Most successful people exude an aura that shows they deserve attention and respect. A few simple strategies can help you command that same positive regard.

1. Stay on top of current events.
To sound intelligent you must have something intelligent to say. Devour news magazines and newspapers. Track popular trends so you can speak in the language of the day. (35)

2. Improve your vocabulary.
It's next to impossible to have a polished, professional image with a deficient vocabulary. Pay attention to your use of English and be alert to usage errors. Attend a college course or professional seminar on communication skills. Read one classic book each month. Make liberal use of a thesaurus when you write. Learn one new word a day. Listen to great speakers, learn their rhetorical tricks. (17, 18)

3. Study positive role models.
Every time you meet someone who reflects power and style study that person. How does he or she act? Think? Speak? Dress? What do you see that will work well for you?

4. Whenever you feel intimidated or outclassed, fight the fear and project poise.
Inhale and exhale slowly and deeply. Focus on the strengths you've worked hard to develop. Remind yourself that everyone you have ever met has, over time, revealed weakness to you, and this new person will as well.

5. Engage in an objective self-appraisal.
Study yourself on videotape. Listen to the voice mail you send, or record yourself on audiotape. Ask for feedback from your colleagues. View yourself in a full-length mirror before you leave for the office in the morning.

6. Maintain proper hygiene.
Bad breath and offensive body odor may have a far stronger negative impact than the positive impact created by an expensive outfit. Carry breath mints with you. Carry deodorant in your purse or briefcase. If you plan to meet important people in the evening after work, make sure you look and smell as good at the end of the day as you did when the day began.

7. Focus on the three Cs: Control, Composure, and Confidence.
Executive presence isn't established by ranting, raving, shouting, or demanding. Rather, it's communicated in subtle ways—for example, by resolving a confrontation without having to prove that you have the most power in the room. Confidence, composure, and control are manifested in admirable personal actions, not in a formal title, the size of your office, or the price of your car.

8. Make important points with your voice trailing down at the end.
When your words trail down through a slight deepening of your voice and a drop in inflection, you nonverbally communicate assurance. You insert an implied exclamation point. When your voice trails up instead, you're inserting an implied question mark. (18)

9. Make sure your stage is set.
You project not only through what you say and how you say it, but also through the setting you create. (19)

- Consider the arrangement, decor, and order of your office. What does it say about you?
- Take a close look at your car. Would you want your most important customer to ride in it?
- Check the inside of your briefcase. What does it say about your organization skills?
- Glance down at your shoes. Do they indicate a well-groomed executive?

10. Understand timing.
Knowing when to say something is as important as knowing what to say. Study what great communicators do to capture the moment. Say what people want to hear when they're ready to hear it.

11. Maintain your stamina and health.
Control your weight by eating the right foods. Increase your energy, endurance, and muscle tone through exercise. Don't smoke and don't drink alcohol excessively. Maintain your health and looks through a positive attitude. Customers, colleagues, and employees gain confidence when they see that you're in control of your well-being.

12. Hire a personal coach.
Once you've finished this entire book, you'll probably have identified several ways you want to improve yourself professionally. You can embark on those initiatives on your own or you can retain a

consultant to act as a coach. A personal coach can help you see yourself as you are and recommend strategies for getting where you want to be. (83)

5 Eleven Strategies for Dressing Impressively

Clothes communicate a powerful message about you. If you want to improve the message, improve your dress. This rule transcends time, gender, and industry. Regardless of what kind of organization you lead, whether you're male or female, and whether you're under 30 or over 70, people expect you to *look* as if you lead the organization.

1. View your clothes as an investment.
You get what you pay for. While you may want to time your purchases to take advantage of sales, don't compromise your standards to get a bargain. Realize a return on your investment by spending a little more than your colleagues. Choose fabrics that resist wrinkles, wear well, and will look as good next year as they do today.

2. Choose classic styles over trends.
Trendy styles, however expensive (and they usually are), may be outdated before you see the purchase on your credit card statement. Your closet should be a repository of timeless fashion, not dated fads.

3. Develop a special relationship with one salesperson at one retailer.
A retailer who remembers you and values your business will want to meet your particular needs, fulfill your special requests, and give you price breaks. A salesperson who knows your style preferences, your flattering colors and cuts, and your uses for executive dress will serve you well as a personal clothing consultant.

4. Choose clothes that compliment your body type.
View your wardrobe as an exercise in strategic marketing. Advertise your physical strengths; camouflage your weaknesses.

5. Count accessories as part of your wardrobe.
Everything you wear makes a statement, including pocket handkerchiefs, scarves, belts, neckties, necklaces, pins, bracelets, cufflinks, earrings, watches, purses, and briefcases. An especially good or poor choice in an accessory can make or break the impact of

your outfit. Select items that enhance your clothing and help form a positive overall impression. Impress people with your style, not your wallet or your gaudiness.

6. Count shoes as part of your wardrobe.
At least 10% of the people you meet will look at your feet for a reading of your executive presence. These are the clues shoe watchers look for:

- Do your shoes match your outfit?
- Are your shoes in good taste?
- Are your shoes excessively worn?
- Do you keep your shoes clean and polished?

7. Clean and maintain your wardrobe.
A trusted dry cleaner and professional tailor will help you maintain your investment. Clean clothes look better and last longer. They send two important messages: that you have positive self-regard, and that you take care of the little things and therefore can be trusted with the big things.

8. Wear clothes appropriate to the situation and to the climate.
Function dictates dress. Some settings are formal, others are informal. Let where you'll wear it determine what you'll wear. Also consider the time of the year and the climate. If you're not sure how to include these factors in your decision, ask someone who knows.

9. Wear clothing appropriate to your audience.
Meet the expectations of people around you. Don't shock, disappoint, or embarrass them. Find out if there is a dress code for situations you're about to enter, and conform to it.

10. Throughout the day check yourself out.
Make sure you don't have stains, loose threads, fabric tears, or other embarrassing blemishes on your clothes. Have a colleague look you over before you walk into an important meeting or check yourself out in front of a full-length mirror.

11. Read a good book on executive dress.
If this list has whetted your appetite for more information on dressing like a person in charge, choose any of the comprehensive volumes that have been published on the topic.

6   Nine Sensible Ways to Socialize with Employees

As the person in charge you often walk a tightrope. You want to be accessible and friendly, yet you need enough detachment to remain objective. You want to be close enough to your people to understand their needs, yet not so close that you lose sight of your primary goal: providing value to the marketplace. Also, in an increasingly litigious society you don't want friendliness to be misperceived as sexual harassment or favoritism. When you walk this tightrope, you need a safety net.

1. Know the law.
Ask your attorney or human resource professional about the latest legal interpretations of sexual harassment and employment discrimination. They may surprise you.

2. Monitor your participation in events planned by employees.
If employees invite you to a social event, it's a good idea to make an appearance. If spouses or dates are invited, take yours along. It's an equally good idea to leave at a relatively early hour, before the intensity of social interactions reaches its peak.

3. Celebrate victories with social events.
Host an employee recognition dinner. Throw impromptu lunch-time pizza parties. Send your outstanding employees on all-expense-paid vacations.

4. Involve employees in the planning of company-sponsored bashes.
Appoint a demographically and ethnically diverse team of event planners led by a person you designate as the company meeting planner. Empower them to plan holiday parties, annual picnics, and other activities.

5. Invite suppliers and customers to your social events.
Although you may not want suppliers and customers at all events, their presence makes sense at one or two events a year. Employees who have talked to suppliers or customers only over the phone will now be able to put faces with names. You might also increase sales.

6. Make sure your events don't endanger employees.

Some believe that mountain climbing, white water rafting, and survival courses are effective strategies for team building, but they're physically risky. Don't impose your hobbies or love of the outdoors on your employees.

7. Link social events with community causes.

Seek employee volunteers to build playgrounds, serve food at homeless shelters, or renovate run-down housing. Get involved yourself. You and your employees will benefit, and so will your community.

8. Take employees out to lunch.

On a regular basis take different employees to lunch. It's a great way to find out what your people are thinking and a great way for your people to join you in an informal setting.

9. Serve liquor only if you control consumption.

Provide safe transportation home. Ask your attorney about the liability you face if one of your employees has a car accident after drinking at a company social function.

7 Ten Guidelines for Joining a Professional Organization

Your business and personal life will suffer if you become a perpetual joiner and organizer. Nevertheless, professional organizations can be a vital source of personal enrichment and professional development. Use the following guidelines to help you decide which to join.

1. If you hold a professional designation or degree, remain a member of that profession's association.

If you're a CPA, a JD, a CE, a DDS, or any other professional, it pays to keep your organization membership even if you no longer work in the field. You'll receive newsletters, announcements, and other information you can use for networking or business purposes. And you never know when you might want to become active in that profession again.

2. Look for a match before you send membership dues.

Associations are in the business of selling a service. What are they selling and what are you paying for it? How is this organization going to help you succeed? If they lobby for legislation, do their underlying values appear to reflect yours? List what you want in a professional association (e.g., networking, education, journals, conventions, prestige, group insurance, purchase discounts). Shop around to find the best match to your needs.

3. Choose associations with strong member education programs.
The best associations do much more than send you newsletters, ballots, and credit card applications. They focus on the education of their members. Join an association committed to making you smarter through seminars, videos, travel, or publications. If members are sometimes asked to give presentations at meetings, consider ways you might use these opportunities to share your knowledge or your company's experiences with colleagues.

4. Join organizations with a vibrant annual meeting.
A certain sign of the health and value of an association is the vitality of its annual meeting. Get attendance numbers for the past three years. Declining attendance suggests either the meetings are poorly run or the association is losing its relevance.

5. Talk to trusted friends in your industry.
What organizations do they and their associates belong to and why? What organizations have they quit and why? What organizations would they recommend and why?

6. Select an organization that serves others.
If you focus your energy only on promoting yourself, you may find the career finish line less rewarding than you expected. Associations with a philanthropic bent allow you to give something back.

7. Join organizations with an international presence and membership.
The world is shrinking. Organizational memberships should provide you with opportunities to reach across national borders and network with foreign executives.

8. Find out if your name will be sold on a mailing list.
Chances are your association will give your name out to other organizations or entrepreneurs looking to market their products. If you don't want your name divulged, say so at the time you sign up.

9. Once you join, learn when to say yes and when to say no.
Be as active in your professional organizations as *you* choose to be. You may be a dues-paying member who never attends meetings,

becomes a national president, or anything in between. Plan your investment of time and energy so that you and the organization have a win-win outcome. Never volunteer under pressure or out of guilt; the long-term results will probably frustrate you and disappoint the organization.

10. Recommend appropriate professional organizations to your subordinates.
Some of your direct reports may benefit from professional membership in the same way you do. When they join with you in the same organization, you develop the added benefit of common professional experiences and acquaintances.

8 Sixteen Ways to Make Better Use of Your Time

Time is your most precious resource. Once lost, it can't be replaced. Great executives become merely good executives when they don't use time well. Good executives turn into great ones when they apply each minute to its best purpose.

1. Bring your daily priorities into synch with your values and beliefs.
We achieve true happiness when we spend our day doing what is most important to us. Are you in touch with your priorities?

- Identify your values and beliefs about vital components of your life: faith, family, friends, service, work, security, knowledge, achievement, advancement, creativity, leadership, communication, leisure, possessions.
- List those values and beliefs in priority order.
- List the activities that consume your time.
- Compare the two lists. What do the contrasts suggest you should change to make your life more satisfactory and fulfilling?

2. Take a memory course.
Stop wasting time looking for things you have forgotten. Learn how to recall names, statistics, telephone numbers, and other critical information you should have at your fingertips.

3. Learn to speed read.
Keep up with the torrent of information top executives need to absorb.

4. Waste less time.

- Run more efficient meetings; discontinue unnecessary ones. (38)
- Protect yourself from unwanted visitors; find a hideout when you need uninterrupted time; use your secretary to screen out unnecessary calls.
- Don't contribute to conversations that aren't going anywhere— end them by silence or by walking away.
- Shorten appointments by 25% and force yourself to get just as much done.
- Stand up when you talk on the telephone; outline topics before you call.
- Learn how to type at least 50 words per minute.
- Clear your desk of distracting materials.
- Stop losing things—put them only where you know you'll look for them.
- Write answers in the margins of the letters you receive and mail or fax a copy back.
- Stop revising when the cost of redoing exceeds the value gained.
- Stop procrastinating—do that unpleasant chore right now.

5. Spend less time in crisis.
Don't be caught up in the tyranny of the urgent. Think twice before leaving an important task in favor of one that shouts louder. Many crises don't deserve the attention we give them. Plan more thoroughly. Question the assumptions behind your decisions, and fewer of them will come back to haunt you in the form of crises. When you're diverted from one function to attend to an emergency, take note of where you are in the original task and where your thinking appears to be taking you so you'll more quickly get back into it when the emergency subsides.

6. Spend less time performing routine tasks.
Routine tasks include record keeping, repetitive work, maintenance, responding to requests, and travel. The three best ways to reduce the routine in your work:

- *Automate* using improved technology.
- *Delegate* to assistants.
- *Eliminate* by not doing it; consider how you might use that time more profitably.

7. Spend more time strategically.
Examples of time spent strategically include planning, growing professionally and personally, creating something, achieving important goals, keeping others informed, and supervising, coaching, or teaching others.

8. Use a comprehensive calendar and priority management system.
A number of good systems are available, but they work only if you rigorously follow their prescriptions. Get your entire team to use the same system and you'll improve coordination.

9. Spend more time with people, less time with things.
As the person in charge, one of your primary functions is to maximize the value of the human assets under your command. Reallocate 10% of the time you spend in front of your computer, bent over paperwork, or meeting with people outside the company to be with your employees. (45)

10. Restore your energy.
You need to be in shape to attack your work with enthusiasm and passion so that you, your people, and your company get the most out of your time. Build your energy by eating less fat and more fruits and vegetables, by drinking plenty of water, by breathing deeply, by exercising briskly three or more times each week, and by getting the right amount of sleep. If your stamina has fallen off, see a doctor.

11. Improve your communication skills.
Speak and write with the determination *to be understood* so that you don't need to send the same message twice. Listen with the determination *to understand* so you don't have to ask unnecessary questions or make uninformed mistakes. (15–18)

12. Three times each day ask yourself, "Is this the best use of my time?"
When the answer is no, switch to a more meaningful task.

13. Take time to improve the quality of your life.
Play to stay young. Daydream to see more clearly the road to your future. Read to renew your mind. Help needy people to uplift your spirits. Think about the people you love in order to draw yourself more closely to them emotionally. Spend more time with the people you love to feel better about yourself. Laugh to restore your balance and reduce stress. Develop new skills to keep yourself in demand. Explore your spiritual side to understand life and to accept your limitations in it. (125, 126)

14. Reserve one hour each day for yourself.
During this time, which might be planned jointly with a loved one, do what you most enjoy doing and what recharges your batteries, not what the world tells you to do.

15. Find joy in the doing.
Don't have such an urgent need to complete tasks that you miss out on the delight of performing them. In other words, don't become so obsessed with time management that life becomes a frenzy of achieving one goal after another. You spend far more of your life *experiencing* than achieving. Learn to enjoy these experiences for their inherent pleasures, rather than for the rewards that may follow them. Liberate yourself to have fun as you work.

16. Find the joy in today.
John Lennon sang that life is what happens to you while you're busy making other plans. Don't get caught in the "future trap." Don't wait for life to get less complicated, demanding, or routine so that you can begin enjoying it. First, it may never get simpler, easier, or more exciting. Second, there's a lot of fun to be had living even the most complicated, demanding, and routine of lives—don't let one precious moment of life pass without living it to the fullest. Stop waiting for a better tomorrow; delight in today.

9 Sixteen Ways to Get More from Your Business Travel

Since extensive travel is a given for most top executives, you'll want to do all you can to make it a positive experience as well as a good use of your time. Here are a few ideas for making business travel more pleasant.

1. Find a travel agent you can trust.
Whether you or your assistant makes your reservations, shop around for a travel agent on whom you can rely to find what you need.

2. Check your travel insurance.
Don't buy unnecessary policies; remember to collect on the ones you have.

- Accident insurance is automatic when you pay for tickets with certain charge cards.
- Most homeowner's policies protect personal belongings during travel.
- Your personal car insurance often covers damages to rental cars.

3. Invest in a laptop computer.
Don't waste another minute in airports or on airplanes. Get a laptop that offers extended battery life and a fax modem.

4. Invest in a portable telephone.
Conduct business while stuck in traffic, or in a hundred other un-productive situations.

5. Combine trip purposes.
As soon as you know you'll be traveling to a particular city, think of all the other business you might conduct or people you might visit there. Check your address file for customers and prospects to call on.

6. Take work with you.
During the week before you travel, set aside those nonurgent tasks that you can do as well away from your office as in it. Include important reading material that you're not likely to get to otherwise.

7. Take a good book.
Read for enjoyment or for profit. In either case, reading helps you arrive at your destination mentally refreshed and poised for action.

8. Play audiotapes or compact disks in your car.
Keep up on the latest developments in management, learn a lan-guage, improve a particular skill, or simply relax with an audio book. Watch for close-out sales at your favorite bookstore or look

for audio books at your library. Carry a portable tape or CD player in your briefcase.

9. Stay in hospitable hotels.
Choose hotels known for exceptional customer service, especially those who cater to business travelers rather than tourists. Your hotel will be your base of operations; make sure it will refresh you.

10. Check out the information technology capabilities of your hotel before you check in.
Does it have a fax machine? Will you be able to hook up your laptop to the hotel's printers? Does it have phone jacks in your room to accommodate your equipment? Does it have fiber optic cable? Does it have access to a teleconferencing center?

11. Fax yourself a message when you need hard copy on the road.
There will be times when you're on the road and want a hard copy of a file in your computer but don't have a printer. Use your fax modem to send the file to yourself through your hotel's fax machine.

12. Fly on airlines that offer good service.
Some airlines are more sensitive to the needs of business travelers than others. For example, when you travel in coach, ask your travel agent to book you with airlines that offer the roomiest seating.

13. Eat wisely.
A recent study showed that traveling salespeople put on an average of five pounds per year, primarily due to bad eating habits. Snacks and high-fat meals are the biggest problems.

14. Travel comfortably.
Many middle-age back injuries are suffered by travelers who lug too much. Ship heavy materials in advance; check luggage on planes; get help from porters. Also, dress casually. You'll feel more relaxed and your business clothing will fare better in a garment bag than in a car seat, plane seat, or sliding in and out of taxis.

15. Dream.
Take advantage of being away from the onslaught of your office to pose what-if and why-not questions about your operation and to reflect on your career. Jot down your thoughts.

16. Sleep.

Take a refreshing fifteen-minute catnap on airplanes and in limousines about one-half hour before arriving at your destination.

10 | Ten Things to Do Before Meeting Foreign Executives

As technology and ease of travel shrinks the size of the world, you're more likely to conduct business in foreign lands or with executives whose names you don't know how to pronounce. You can no longer assume that your customers all speak English or that your business partners share your cultural heritage. While you needn't be a cultural anthropologist or foreign diplomat, you will command foreign executives' respect by increasing your cultural sensitivity before meeting them.

1. Find their home city on the map.

Most foreign executives know far more about the United States than you know about their country. Pull out an atlas and find where they live. Place their home city in geographic context. Compare its size to the cities you know well. Note the other important cities and sites of that country. Compare the country's area and population to familiar countries or states.

2. Master the pronunciation of names.

Find out how your guests pronounce their surnames as well as the names of their countries and cities. Use *their* pronunciations rather than Americanized concoctions.

3. Learn about their country's "PERSIA."

Do some research on the Political, Economic, Religious, Social, Intellectual, and Artistic contexts of their home country. Pay particular attention to how the country was established. Most people are proud of their country's history and will be honored that you took the time to learn it.

4. Learn cultural customs and taboos.

Every part of the world has a set of behavioral do's and don'ts involving tone of voice, word choice, body language, eating habits, menus, dress, use of titles, eye contact, courtesies, exchanges of business cards, volume of speech, and introductions. Call a local university that specializes in foreign studies or the foreign visitor bureaus that exist in many large cities. Read up on the country with briefing booklets published by the State Department or books from your library. If the importance of this meeting warrants, invest in a personal consultation with an expert on that country.

5. Contract the services of an interpreter, if necessary.
If foreign executives don't speak English and you don't speak their language, hire an interpreter. Choose a professional linguist, as opposed to a bilingual member of your staff. A professional interpreter can also serve as your cultural consultant. (24)

6. Get advice from others who work with executives from that country.
If no one in your personal network has such experience, contact your local CEO club, chamber of commerce, or foreign visitor bureau. You might also check with your local or state office of economic development.

7. Learn how foreign executives view and use time.
The U.S. business culture is relatively fast paced and formal, loading business meetings with agendas that leave little time for "shmoozing." Many other cultures are more laid back and view building a relationship as crucial to business goals. Americans expect a meeting to start pretty much on time. In many other parts of the world, announced starting times are little more than guidelines. What attitudes about time will you be dealing with?

8. Find out as much about these executives and their business as you can.
If this is a negotiating session, such knowledge will reveal clues to the needs the executives bring to the meeting and to the bargaining ferocity you might expect. For purely get-acquainted events, your research will form a common ground for dialogue. Regardless of your goal, the time you spend to learn about the company will flatter the foreign executive. (11)

9. Assess your prejudices.
Carefully analyze any personal biases you might bring to the encounter. Particularly dangerous are feelings of cultural superiority that will creep into your tone or body language. Any wrong moves you make should stem from ignorance, not prejudice.

10. Present a gift or memento of the visit.
Choose gifts that are tasteful and more thoughtful than showy. An artifact of your home city or state might be a good choice. Your state office of tourism can help with gift suggestions.

11 The Five Most Important Rules for Negotiations

When you're in charge, someone always wants something. Your best customer wants a lower price. Suppliers want you to buy more. Employees want raises, time off, or special considerations. In each case you must decide whether to give in, seek a compromise, or push hard for your needs. These are the rules that apply to any negotiation.

1. Know yourself.
Never enter negotiations without knowing the absolute most you're willing to give. Analyze leverage—the relative power you have to exert pressure on the other negotiator. Understand your personal strengths and weaknesses. Control your emotions; if people start to lose their cool, call for a break.

2. Know the other person.
Obtain as much information as you can about the other person's background, position, needs, and negotiating style. Focus on the reason and motivation behind that person's requests, not just on the requests. Listen and ask probing questions. If you're doing business with people from another culture, don't violate their cultural norms. (10)

3. If you want something, be prepared to give something.
Negotiations are a process of give and take, not just take. Look for win-win solutions. Move beyond "fixed-pie" thinking, in which you see anything that the other person gains as your loss; see how a successful negotiation will make the pie grow. Move from discussing "my goals" and "your goals" to discussing "our goals."

4. Never go up or come down without getting something in return.
Your negotiating hand strengthens any time you make a concession, so never give in without taking advantage of that strength. Say something along these lines: "OK, I'm willing to reduce our fee if your staff will type up the final report."

5. Develop strategies to exert leverage and break impasses.
"I'll be pulling back that offer in ten minutes." "This sounds like something I need to turn over to my lawyer." "What will it take to close this deal today?" "I'll give you this if you give me that." "Shall we bring in a mediator?"

12 Eleven Elements of Entrepreneurial Thinking

What do Bill Gates, Ted Turner, Debbie Fields, Ray Kroc, Steve Jobs, and Mary Kay Ash have in common? They're all entrepreneurs. They risked capital on business ventures—questionable at the time—and succeeded beyond their wildest dreams. You may not plan to gamble on an inventive idea, but you do want your leadership to be characterized by the same entrepreneurial spirit and energy as these corporate heroes.

1. Look for opportunities.
Use your mental and physical down time to ponder new ways to take advantage of your firm's distinct competencies and your special abilities. Pose why-not and what-if questions.

2. See gain where others see only loss.
View adversity as the opportunity for gain that it is. *Any* change in the status quo, whether good or bad, provides an opening that you can use to get better results. For example, losing your most valued assistant may give you the opening you need to reorganize your office.

3. View failure as education.
Great thinkers look on failures as lessons to be celebrated, not mistakes to be mourned. Debbie Fields of Mrs. Field's Cookies cites the two most important lessons she's learned in business: never giving up and never making the same mistake twice.

4. Get past your mistakes.
Entrepreneurs bear the pain of their errors only once. They recognize that poor judgment is something to learn from, not suffer from. They don't have the time to waste worrying about yesterday. They never characterize a mistake as a statement about themselves, but as a statement about their performance in a particular situation under a particular set of circumstances. They vow next time to change their performance, the situation, or the circumstances.

> One CEO had an idea for creating self-managed teams. His application of that idea was a complete flop. Employees resisted the plan from the beginning, and the assumptions behind the initiative were fatally flawed. In a subsequent discussion with a colleague, the self-managed team experience came up. The colleague remarked, "So you failed with self-managed teams." The CEO's response was, "No, we didn't fail with self-managed teams. We just learned one way not to implement them."

5. Keep an open mind.

You never know where your next idea for a new venture will spring from. Unless your eyes, ears, and mind are open, you may not see, hear, or realize that opportunity is knocking. The next time you want to say, "We tried that before" or "That'll never work," bite your tongue. Say, "Tell me more about your idea" or "Run with your idea for a while and keep me posted." (2)

6. Increase your tolerance for risk.

Entrepreneurs are risk takers. High achievers have sometimes mortgaged homes, cashed in life insurance policies, and even left high-paying jobs in order to pursue success. You may not have to change your life so dramatically to realize new opportunity, but expect to take chances along the way. You might have to place tremendous trust in someone, divert funds from a profitable operation, and otherwise put your reputation on the line.

7. Dream.

Walt Disney once said, "If you can dream it, you can do it." When he first saw the land on which he would build Disneyland, he could see the smiles on the parents' faces, hear the laughter of the children, and smell the popcorn popping. What's your dream? What does it look, sound, smell, feel, and even taste like?

8. Share your dream.

At some point you'll involve others in your "wild and crazy scheme"—which is exactly how many of them will characterize it. These people may be investors, owners, bosses, peers, employees, and customers. Calm down about your idea long enough to clear your head and to plan carefully how you'll get *them* excited about it.

Then bring them into your dream. Reveal it so that they see the sights, hear the sounds, smell the smells, feel the touch, and taste the tastes. (74)

9. Remain optimistic.
One thing the entrepreneurs mentioned above have in common is that they believed in themselves from the start and they never lost that confidence. Worriers, naysayers, and pessimists are rarely in the forefront of change.

10. Expand your knowledge.
Spend time with creative, educated, and inspiring people—especially those who like to talk about ideas. Ask lots of questions, read voraciously, continue your formal education, attend seminars, listen to audiotapes in your car, gain from your travel, and reflect regularly on what you've learned. (35)

11. Expand your creativity.
Think like a child. Play with ideas and experiment with new behaviors. Ask questions no one has asked before. Believe there's always a different and a better way. Daydream about your current tasks; look for new relationships among them. Do something for the sheer joy of it.

13 Sixty-Four Business Terms to Have on the Tip of Your Tongue

It's easier to conduct business when you know how to talk business. These are some of the most useful terms to store in your mental management dictionary. Once you've mastered the entire list, use it to educate subordinate managers.

1. Amortize: To write off an expenditure by spreading the cost out over time.

2. Benchmarking: Comparing the practices within your company to the very best practices in some of the very best companies inside or outside your industry.

3. Bottom Line: Derived from the bottom-most figure on a profit-and-loss statement, it refers to an organization's most important measure of success: profit, service, productivity, expense reduction, quality, or some other.

4. Break Even Quantity: The number of units that must be sold in order to cover the costs of producing those units.

5. Cash Cow: Any highly profitable product or service.

6. Cash Flow: The movement of money into and out of a company; not the same as profit and loss.

7. Centralization: Maintaining power and decision making at the headquarters or the top management levels of an organization. Highly centralized companies often have several layers of management between the CEO and front-line employees. See Decentralization.

8. Cost-Benefit Analysis: A method for analyzing alternative courses of action by comparing their costs with their benefits.

9. Cost Center: A department or function within a company that consumes revenue. See Profit Center.

10. Corporate Culture: The values, beliefs, norms, and rituals characterizing the practices within a given corporation.

11. Current Assets: The assets that will be used up, sold, or converted to cash within one year.

12. Current Liabilities: The debts that must be paid within one year.

13. Decentralization: Pushing decision-making power downward in an organization, enabling employees to have greater input into how things are done. Decentralized organizations have relatively few layers of management between the CEO and front-line employees and are often called "flat" organizations.

14. Depreciation: The process of using up or receiving the benefits of a durable asset, which must be shown on the balance sheet.

15. DIRFT: "Do it right the first time." One of the essential philosophies of total quality management (TQM).

16. Distributed Processing: System in which computers store and manipulate data at multiple locations. The main purpose is to keep the computing function close to the end user.

17. Focus Group: A small group (usually 5–10) of managers, employees, customers, or shareholders brought together for the purpose of revealing their insights concerning a company-related problem, challenge, or opportunity.

18. Fixed Costs: Costs incurred no matter how many units of a product are manufactured or sold or how many customers are served.

19. Inventory Turnover: Number of times a firm sells and replaces (turns over) its merchandise inventory in one year. Called "turn" for short.

20. Just-in-Time (JIT): An inventory system designed to minimize inventory control costs. Based on the principle that supplies arrive just before they are needed and goods are produced and delivered just in time to be sold.

21. Learning Curve: The amount of time its takes to become proficient at a given task.

22. Leverage: Borrowing funds so that the return on the borrowed dollars is higher than the interest paid to the lenders for those dollars.

23. Line vs. Staff: *Line* employees are directly involved in producing the product or delivering the service; *staff* employees provide support to line employees (e.g., the personnel department).

24. Liquidity Ratio: Calculated by dividing the value of current assets by the value of current liabilities. The greater this number exceeds one, the better.

25. Long Term Capital: Funding invested in fixed assets that determine the future direction of the company.

26. Loss Leader: An item sold at cost or below cost to attract customers.

27. MBO (Management by Objectives): A management philosophy based on the notion that employees should be evaluated more in response to their results than on how they attain those results. Subordinates establish their quantifiable goals jointly with supervisors, and performance evaluation follows a period of ongoing monitoring.

28. MBWA (Managing by Wandering Around): Getting out of your office to encounter employees where they work.

29. Marketing Mix: The combination of product or service, price, distribution, and promotion used to reach a given market segment.

30. Markup: An amount added to the cost of a product in order to determine a selling price.

31. MIS (Management Information System): Any system that gives decision makers access to information (typically involving computers).

32. Mission Statement: A written document specifying the purposes of the organization, its reason for existence. See Vision Statement.

33. Net Income: The difference between the inflow of revenue and the outflow of expenses.

34. Open-Door Policy: A practice enabling and encouraging employees to communicate to upper management on any issues of concern to them.

35. Operating Expenses: Costs that don't result directly from a firm's purchase or manufacture of the products it sells.

36. Outsourcing: Hiring temporary employees or outside contractors to perform tasks previously performed by permanent, full-time employees.

37. Overhead: The costs of running a business that go on regardless of level of activity and that do not contribute directly to productivity (e.g., rent, property taxes, insurance, utilities, salaries of those in staff positions).

38. Pareto's Law (80/20 Rule): The majority of outcomes stem from a significant minority of sources. For example, 80% of your sales typically come from 20% of your customers; 20% of your responsibilities consume 80% of your time.

39. Parkinson's Law: Work expands to meet the time allotted to it. In other words, tell people they have five days to complete a project and it will take them five days, even if they could have finished it in four had *that* been their goal.

40. Positioning: Development of an image for a product or service that differentiates it from its competition.

41. Product Life Cycle: The theory that all products and services pass through four stages: introduction, growth, maturity, and decline.

42. Profit Center: A department or function within a company that generates revenue.

43. Proxy: A person appointed to represent and vote for a stockholder at a stockholders' meeting.

44. Physical Distribution: Those activities required to move products from the manufacturer to the consumer.

45. Pygmalion Effect: High expectations for another's performance tend to result in high performance; low expectations encourage low performance.

46. Quality Circle: A group of employees who meet on company time to discuss strategies for improving company performance.

47. Real Time: Pertaining to processes that keep pace with an actual occurrence.

48. Re-Engineering: Process of designing organizations so that they focus on processes (what they do to serve customers) rather than function (job, titles, hierarchy, and function).

49. Retained Earnings: Portion of profits not distributed to stockholders.

50. ROE (Return on Equity): Calculated by dividing profits by the investments made to generate those profits.

51. Self-Directed Team: Group of employees assigned to a given function or project who complete the task with a minimum of (or no) day-to-day supervision. The team is given its goals by upper management and is granted a great deal of discretion in how it will achieve those goals.

52. SPC (Statistical Process Control): Use of statistical analysis to assure that manufacturing (products) or delivery (services) doesn't deviate from desired levels of quality.

53. Strategic Plan: Document articulating the short-term and long-term goals of an organization along with a plan for actions that will achieve those goals. Strategic plans are often renewed yearly by the senior management team of the organization.

54. Stock Option: Legal contract that gives the holder the right to buy or sell a given stock at a given price within a stated period of time.

55. SBU (Strategic Business Unit): Separate business units within one organization run as if they were independent companies.

56. Telecommunications: Combination of telephone and computer technology for a common communications system.

57. 360-Degree Feedback: Managers receive feedback on a survey of their leadership abilities from their bosses, their peers, their employees, and themselves. Results are often used as input to a plan for professional development rather than for evaluation purposes.

58. Time-Sharing: Process that allows many individuals to share limited resources. Time-sharing is typically found in mainframe and minicomputer environments, permitting the computing resources of these systems to be shared.

59. TQM (Total Quality Management): Comprehensive approach to product or service improvement in the organization. TQM is driven by a belief in the eternal opportunity for continuous improvement in the products and processes of an organization.

60. Variable Costs: Expenses that fluctuate depending on the number of units produced.

61. Virtual Corporation: Conducting business with a minimum of full-time employees through a combination of outsourcing and computer networking.

62. Vision Statement: A document of the aspirations and desirable future state of an organization, communicated to all those people who are expected to take part in its realization. It includes a statement of the values and beliefs that will guide the organization.

63. Zero-Based Budgeting: A method of budgeting that requires managers of departments or programs to justify them and their expenses every year.

64. Zero Defects: Production standards based on total conformity to quantifiable levels of performance.

14 Twelve Quotes Worth Quoting About Executive Power

1. If you think you can, you can. If you think you can't, you're right. —*Mary Kay Ash*

2. It takes twenty years to make an overnight success. —*Eddie Cantor*

3. By far the most valuable possession is skill. Both war and chances of fortune destroy other things, but skill is preserved. —*Hipparchus*

4. Every man who takes office in Washington either grows or swells, and when I give a man office I watch him carefully to see whether he is growing or swelling. —*Woodrow Wilson*

5. Anyone who stops learning is old, whether at twenty or eighty. Anyone who keeps learning stays young. —*Henry Ford*

6. We ought to be able to learn some things second-hand. There is not enough time to make all the mistakes ourselves. —*Harriet Hall*

7. There's only one corner of the universe you can be certain of improving, and that's your own self. —*Aldous Huxley*

8. You are the same today that you are going to be five years from now except for two things: the people with whom you associate, and the books you read. —*Charles "Tremendous" Jones*

9. If the only tool you have is a hammer, you treat everything like a nail. —*Abraham Maslow*

10. One must learn by doing the thing; for though you think you know it, you have no certainty, until you try. —*Sophocles*

11. The will to succeed is important, but what's more important is the will to prepare. —*Bobby Knight*

12. There is no disgrace in not knowing when knowledge does not rest with you; the disgrace is in being unwilling to learn. —*Benedetto Varchi*

2 SPREAD THE WORD

Communication skills set great leaders apart from good ones. If you regularly practice the skills taught in this chapter, you already appreciate the wisdom of that generalization. However, if your communication skills aren't what they need to be, this may be the most important chapter in the book to you.

15 Thirteen Tips to Write Right

This list will help you make your business writing clear, concise, correct, complete, and conversational. Use the first five steps below as you draft your written communication. Use the remaining eight steps to edit for the power and results that come from clear and concise writing.

1. Brainstorm on paper.
Thinking out loud on paper helps you focus your attention on the writing task and achieve excellence. That task involves a very small portion of the ideas that fill your head during a typical business day. Long before you're ready to create prose, jot down some words, phrases, acronyms, sayings, or your own form of shorthand. This reduces competition for ideas in your brain and delays organizing the ideas until you can be certain of the proper order of presentation.

2. Get others involved in your writing.
Swallow your ego and ask others for ideas about your topic before you start to write. Ask them what they think interests your audience and how they'd approach the same information. Once you've completed the first draft, ask others to review it before you polish. They'll almost certainly uncover errors, inconsistencies, and omissions you won't find yourself. Edit the final document yourself.

3. Write to express, not impress.

Your primary purpose in business writing is to communicate ideas. Fancy vocabularies and long sentences may impress English teachers and college professors, but they waste time and money in business. Use shorter, more familiar words that sound sincere and conversational, not formal and academic.

4. Sit on it!

After you've written something, let that piece of writing leave your mind completely. Putting it aside for a day allows you to come back and read the document with a fresh approach. Even if only for an hour, put your writing aside.

5. Strive for sentences that don't exceed 16 to 18 words.

Sentences 20 to 24 words long are typical in poor business writing and are throwbacks to college papers. Longer sentences are harder to follow and are almost always less precise. As a person in charge you don't have time to write long sentences, and your readers don't have time to read them.

6. Become more personal with your writing.

Use the personal pronouns *I, me, you, we,* and *us.* "It has come to my attention that . . . ," is long and drives readers away from the important message. Instead, be specific and say "I learned . . . ," or "Marketing tells me . . . ," or "Government studies remind us . . ." You might even state your news first, and then say, "We know this because . . ." Avoid using *we* for something *you* did or will commit to do in a letter signed by you.

7. Favor the active voice over the passive voice.

The passive voice forces you to use more words and lessens the impact of your sentences.

> Compare the following two sentences. *Passive voice:* "A change in company policy was approved by the Executive Committee." *Active voice:* "The Executive Committee approved a change in company policy." You can focus on the "change in company policy" and remain in the active voice by writing, "A change in the company policy received unanimous approval from the Executive Committee."

8. Avoid needless words or phrases.

Phrases such as "there is" mean nothing and add nothing to a sentence except length. Consider the following examples. *Poor:* "There is contained in the enclosed pamphlet an important message for all retiring employees." *Better:* "The enclosed pamphlet contains an important message for all retiring employees."

> [In general] if you cut [all of the] needless [and extraneous] words [completely] from your sentences, they will [almost certainly] gain [a great deal of] precision.

9. Beware of nouns ending in *ion, al, or ment.*

Say "I decided to buy the company," not "I made a decis*ion* to buy the company." Say "Marketing recommended we lower the selling price," not "Marketing made a recommenda*tion* that we lower the selling price." Say "We gave the plan a quick look," not ". . . a quick perus*al.*" Instead of "imple*ment*," write "start," "carry out," or "complete."

10. Avoid corporate power words and phony phrases.

Don't *utilize* what you can *use*. Don't propose a *paradigm* that's really a *model*. Don't *roll out* a new idea that you mean to *introduce*. Don't give a *caveat* when a *warning* would do. Don't be *cognizant* when you're *aware*. Don't *initiate* what you can *start*. Don't *ascertain* what you *learn*. Don't be *expeditious* when you can be *quick*. Don't make something *subsequent* when it is *next*. Don't *endeavor* what you should *attempt*. Don't *reiterate* what you mean to *repeat*. Use the most familiar, honest, and reader friendly terms you can find.

11. Avoid overused openings and clichéd closings.

"Per our conversation" comes across as formal, academic, and impersonal. "As we discussed" maintains the attitude of a personal touch. "If you have any questions, don't hesitate to call" can become "If you have any questions, please let me know." "If I can help in any other way, feel free to call" does better as "If I can help in any other way, please call me."

12. Use contractions.

Contractions can make your language more concise, friendly, and conversational. In business writing, they allow you to add a personal touch that helps get the results you're looking for. Shun contractions only in formal writing or for emphasis: "I cannot go" sounds more proper and emphatic than "I can't go."

13. Use grammar checkers.
Computers offer many ways to save time with your business writing. Using grammar checkers with your word processing package also avoids embarrassment. These checkers find misspelled words, incorrect grammar, improper usage, lengthy sentences, and negative tone. They also contain measures of the readability of your writing. If you don't use them, encourage your typist to run your writing through them before you sign your name.

16 Eleven Tips to Write Persuasively

Successful salespeople know that persuasion depends upon their ability to focus on the needs of their audience rather than on themselves. The same strategy will bring you success as a writer. Write with the knowledge that your readers ask two questions: "Why should I read this?" and "What's in it for me to cooperate with this request?"

1. Know your audience.
To persuade readers, understand their backgrounds, their learning styles, their communicating styles, and their information demands. If you were selling a car, you'd want to know whether the buyer is mechanical, status conscious, turned on by speed, looking for a comfortable ride, or determined to save money. You'd also want to know if you have a comparison shopper or an impulse buyer on your hands. In the same way, before selling your ideas on paper, dissect your readers.

2. Start strong.
Grab your readers' attention with your opening statement. Focus on their needs and immediately and actively involve them in the message.

3. Offer benefits, not features.
You might announce a switch to a health care provider that promises to make program administration easier. That means nothing to your employee readers. Instead, describe how the change benefits *them*. The *features* of the new program are lower costs, less paperwork,

and more doctors. The *benefits* employees will want to know about are reduced premiums, easier enrollment, and getting the doctors and hospitals they want.

The sentence, "We're proud to announce an exciting change in our company benefits package," focuses on the company. The alternative sentence, "All full-time employees will now receive an additional paid holiday based on their seniority," focuses on the employees. It gives them a reason to continue reading because they're immediately involved.

---

4. Be specific, not abstract.
Phrases such as "in the near future," "a workable solution," or "dramatic increases" lack impact. State the date in the near future, describe the criteria of a workable solution, and quantify the dramatic increases.

5. Don't overwrite.
Persuasive writing limits the amount of justifying, and thus the amount of writing, you must do. Excite your readers, don't tire them out. Use short sentences to emphasize important points. ("You will save money. We guarantee it.") Limit your paragraphs to four or five sentences. Use one-sentence paragraphs on occasion as attention-getters.

6. Use your readers' language.
Listen to the words your readers speak. Study the words they write. Use their language to your advantage. Echoing or mirroring the way your readers talk and write allows you to communicate in terms that they understand and that create a bond between you. For example, if your customers popularize a new term to describe your product or service, go with it yourself. Consider dropping the formal name and substituting theirs in all your correspondence with them.

7. Use the "you attitude."
Involve readers in your writing by using the words "you" and "your." "We need demographic information in order to determine the most advantageous approach to a company-sponsored car pool proposal." This sentence does not involve the reader. Try the follow-

ing. "You asked for a company-sponsored car pool program and we listened. Now we need you to complete the enclosed form telling us where you live." Yes, you used two sentences to say the same thing. In this instance, more becomes better because the "you attitude" included your audience in your writing.

8. Maintain a positive tone.

"This exciting new product won't be available until the first week of January" becomes "This exciting new product will be available the first week of January." Or, you can use the "you attitude" and write "You'll start receiving your orders of this exciting new product the first week of January."

9. Format with impact.

Use, but don't overuse, the font selection and sizing, **bolding**, and *italicizing* capabilities of your word processor to stress important points. Avoid using all UPPER CASE letters or underlining to highlight. Employ bullets or numbers to set off vital lists of information. Box in ideas that should be set apart or should receive special attention.

10. Give your text a professional look.

Many sophisticated word processors and printers let you use typographic symbols that improve the look of your letter, report, or manuscript. Here are three that are not available on standard typewriters:

- true open and close quotation marks (" ") as opposed to the more common straight quotation marks (″ ″)
- the em dash (—) used to set off an aside or change of subject as opposed to a single hyphen (-) or double (--) hyphen
- foreign language symbols and accent marks for words such as résumé

11. Ask for the sale.

People remember the first thing they read and the last thing they read. Use the last sentence to emphasize what you intend to do or what you want them to do. You won't be as persuasive by saying, "Do not fail to complete the enclosed forms and return them to the Personnel Office by June 30," as you would by saying it positively. "Please complete the enclosed forms and return them to the Personnel Office by June 30."

17   Fifteen Tips to Speak Precisely

Think about the most impressive executives you meet. Chances are they all share a common characteristic. When they speak, they speak with clarity and focus. Subordinates know exactly what's expected of them. Others know exactly what is being said. You too can elicit the same focused response to your words.

1. Analyze your audience.
Tell people what they need to hear in a way *they'll* understand. Too many speakers say what they want to say in the way *they* want to say it. Get the answers to these questions about your audience before you speak:

- How much do they already know about the topic? How much more do they need to know for their purposes?
- Which terms might alienate or confuse them? Which terms will paint the most vivid mental images for them?
- When will be the best time and what will be the best place to send the message?

2. Don't confuse precision and clarity with volume.
Clarity of expression does not increase with vocal intensity. Shouting and yelling may get your message across, but it sends other messages: that you have trouble controlling your emotions and that you intimidate people around you.

3. Don't confuse precision and clarity with redundancy.
Listeners tune out repetitive messages. Focus on saying it clearly the first time. If you suspect you haven't been understood, rather than repeating yourself, say something like, "I'm not sure I was clear in those directions; please tell me what you heard me say," or "How do you plan to handle any problems that arise?"

4. Strive to be understood.
Even though this is a list on precision, being clear in your communication is not paramount. Rather, your ultimate speaking goal is *to be understood*. It's possible to be perfectly clear with your speech, yet be misunderstood. So before you send a complex message ask yourself, "How can I say this so my listener can't possibly misinterpret it?"

5. Begin with a clear intent.
Clear messages rarely result from obscure thoughts. If you don't know what you want to say and why you're saying it, don't say it. Imagine your words are arrows aimed at a target. What is that target?

6. Improve your vocabulary.
You can't communicate precisely if you lack the vocabulary to produce precision. Learn one new word a day. Use that word immediately in writing and in speech. Keep a thesaurus by your side. When you encounter a word you don't understand, look it up.

7. Speak to express, not impress.
Choose simple and widely understood words over pretentious and obscure ones. Don't equate enhancing your vocabulary with learning those little-known words that challenged you on the SATs. Unfamiliar words only confuse and frustrate your listeners. If you announced that employees were "sclerous" in their attitudes toward change, how many listeners would know you found them to be *hardened* against change?

8. Paint pictures for your listeners.
Someone once said that the best orator is someone who can make people see with their ears. People remember the images you burn on their brains. Use examples, analogies, metaphors, and words that leave unmistakable impressions in your listeners' minds. A *cobra* is more vivid than a *snake*; a *canary yellow Corvette* is more memorable than a *car*; the goal of *exciting* your employees is more energizing than the goal of *motivating* them.

9. Use words that listeners feel as well as hear.
Words have both connotative (emotional) and denotative (logical) meaning. You heighten your impact and your precision when you create visual images that your listeners can feel, thereby intensifying the connotative meaning. "Thank you for your support" is not as powerful as "Thank you for standing beside me as we do battle in the marketplace."

10. Express quantifiable concepts with a number.
Don't ask for your call to be returned "as soon as possible" if you need the answer in ten minutes. Don't report that the meeting was

"well attended" if you can say that eleven out of twelve divisions were represented. Don't ask an employee to "put in more time" on a project if you know you want another three days.

11. Stop making vague references.

If you don't know what to call a person, place, or thing, find out its name before you start describing it. "YouknowwhoImean" and "Whatchamacallit" aren't in a directory or on a map. When you begin to state a series of ideas, search ahead in your mind for three of them. Don't get caught saying, "Our employees are interested in recognition, accomplishment, and stufflikethat."

12. Use jargon only if you're sure others understand it.

When you're speaking outside your company or industry, assume that you're speaking with people from another country. Talk about your products, processes, corporate functions, and industry standards in terms they'll understand. These are probably not the same terms you use with your closest associates.

13. Delete unnecessary utterances.

Unnecessary utterances ("uh," "uhm," "well," "you know," "OK," "like") take the crispness out of your sentences and make you sound uncertain of your ideas. Play back your voice mail messages to see which of these space fillers you may need to control.

14. Ferret out habitual word choices.

An executive who prefaces the answer to every question with, "Well, if you ask me . . ." will become a joke among employees. Another who begins every fourth sentence with "basically" will be tedious. Someone who affirms every query from subordinates with "That's a good question" will eventually be dismissed as patronizing.

15. Rid your speech of errors.

No one can be accurate all the time in speaking, but most of us can make a greater effort to avoid grammatical errors, pronounce words properly, and use words correctly. One of the best ways to achieve these goals is to get feedback from others. Consider working with a speech coach for a few weeks.

18 Ten Tips to Speak Persuasively

People in charge are people who make things happen. They get bankers to extend credit, customers to sign on the dotted line, and employees to exert the effort necessary for success. They change attitudes and behaviors. In short, they have developed the art and skill of persuasion. To achieve these outcomes you don't need to be a silver-tongued orator or possess the charisma of an evangelist. But you will want to follow some basic principles of persuasion.

1. Maintain your credibility.
If people don't believe you, no sales tips or techniques will make you persuasive. Store up credibility for when you need it by being known as someone who cares for others, who makes reasonable requests, and whose word can be trusted. Never knowingly deceive your customers, suppliers, employees, or stockholders. When you make a mistake, say so. When you're wrong, admit it.

2. Picture your communication goal.
What's your motivation to speak? What result do you want? What do you hope the other person will look like, feel like, and do when you've made your points? In other words, how do you hope to change the person? Visualize the encounter in your mind's eye. See the listener, hear your voice, experience the interaction before it actually happens. Someone once said that speaking without thinking is like shooting without taking aim.

3. Speak with conviction.
When you speak with conviction, you use your heart as much as your voice. If you don't believe in what you're saying, don't expect anyone else to believe you. In the words of Alan Cimberg, sales motivator, "Your customer will never get any more excited about your product than you are."

4. Talk about them, not you.
People what to know what's in it for them. Your message should appeal to their concerns, their needs, their problems. Don't expect to persuade unless they see that what you're asking them to do is ultimately in their best interest. Build your message on this simple law of human nature.

5. Put yourself in their shoes.

What are your listeners feeling? What are their fears? What are their feelings about you? What extenuating circumstances are affecting them? What expectations do they have of you and of your topic? Start thinking more about their concerns and less about your own. You'll immediately increase your empathy and thereby your persuasiveness. For example, a request to your sales force for an increase in sales should be tied to the resulting bonuses they can use to take a vacation, buy a car, or pay for college tuition.

6. Involve your listeners.

Ask questions requiring them to answer. Ask rhetorical questions requiring them to think. Create hypothetical situations and ask your listeners to imagine themselves in that situation. Use their names.

7. Use hard and soft data as needed.

Hard data (statistics, numbers, measurable outcomes) appeal to logic. Soft data (feelings, opinions, perceptions) appeal to the emotions. Humans are driven by both. Emphasize the one most appropriate to this situation and this listener.

8. Anticipate and overcome any opposition.

No matter how persuasive your arguments may be, there's often a reasonable and plausible counterargument. Even if there isn't a logical objection to your idea, most people can manufacture one. If you anticipate an objection, state it yourself as a valid concern. Then, while the objector looks on as a spectator of the objection— rather than as an owner of it—show how your proposal eliminates it as a problem.

9. Be prepared for unexpected objections.

When you face an unexpected objection, follow these five steps:

- Listen to it thoroughly without getting defensive. (31)
- Restate it to be sure you understand it and to weaken it.
- Validate it as an appropriate concern.
- Test to make sure it's not a smokescreen by saying, "If I can prove that's not a problem, will you support my proposal?"
- Finally, show how your position addresses that concern.

10. Ask for the sale.

Don't beat around the bush or wait for people to guess what you want. Ask for it! Before you began, you had a mental image of what your audience would do after listening to you. Tell them what that is.

19 Twelve Ways to Send Powerful Nonverbal Messages

Many people believe that when they speak, their words are the primary transporters of their thoughts. That's just not the case. Become aware of nonverbal messages to harness your communication power.

> Verbal communication accounts for only about 7% of the meaning others will extract from your speech. More important is the 38% accounted for by vocalics (intonation, inflection, pitch, emphasis, speed, volume, dialect, enunciation, vocabulary, and fluency) that clothe your words. *Far* more important is the 55% accounted for by body language (eyes, face, hair, size, posture, motion, gestures, clothing, cosmetics, accessories, touch, personal space, use of time, and surroundings) that either confirms or contradicts what you're saying.

1. View yourself on videotape.
Tape the next speech you give. Bring in a communication consultant to view it with you and to offer tips on how to make better use of body language and how to modulate your voice for greater impact.

2. Enrich your vocal variety.
Many executives speak in a boring monotone. Strive to put more feeling in your voice to reveal the enthusiasm and conviction behind your ideas.

> Try this exercise. List the following emotions on a sheet of paper: anger, anxiety, arrogance, confidence, confusion, contentment, dejection, determination, enthusiasm, frustration, insecurity, joy, kindness, uncertainty, worry. Give the list to a friend. Say one of the sentences on this page to the friend while forcing yourself to feel one of the emotions. Repeat the exercise until your friend can consistently guess correctly the emotion you feel.

3. Make direct eye contact.
Look people in the eyes (or bridge of the nose) when you speak to them and when they speak to you. Accompany all handshakes with smiling eyes.

4. Open your face.
At any given moment you show the world one of three faces:

- The *closed face* is when your eyebrows are lowered. As a result, your voice drops and becomes gruff. Try saying, "I'm enjoying this book" while in a closed face. Would anyone believe you? Don't allow the work pressure you're under to lower your eyebrows. You'll either frighten or depress your subordinates.
- The *neutral face* is the look most people achieve by relaxing the muscles on their face.
- The *open face* is achieved by raising the eyebrows above their natural position. The voice that accompanies an open face sounds enthusiastic and optimistic. Repeat "I'm enjoying this book" while in an open face. Hear the difference? Remember when you meet others to lift your eyebrows for an instant improvement in both your features and your voice.

5. Choose a smart hair style.
Decide with an image consultant on a complimentary hair style that is neither outdated nor too trendy.

6. Keep your shape.
Eat sensibly and exercise regularly. People who look fit are more credible than those who let themselves get out of shape.

7. Watch your posture.
An erect posture is a sign of respect for others and a statement of the confidence you have in yourself. Lift your collarbone one inch for an immediate improvement.

8. Avoid the cupped handshake.
Most executives know that their handshake should be firm yet not overpowering. However, few of them make an effort to truly connect with the hands they shake by making palm-to-palm contact. The cupped handshake distances you from the person you are greeting.

9. Be careful of gestures.

If you travel internationally, take the time to learn which of our everyday gestures may insult the people you're visiting.

> One of the most offensive gestures in *any* country is to point your index finger at someone. Point at dogs, not people. When you wish to direct your physical attention to someone, do so with palm up, tilted slightly inward, and all four fingers aimed at the person you refer to.

10. Maintain personal space that is comfortable for others.

While speaking face to face, standing too far away from the other person may be interpreted as a sign of disinterest. Standing too close may be seen as a sign of aggressiveness. For most Americans about three feet is a comfortable distance. Read body language cues from people to see if they appear to want more or less personal space.

11. Monitor your use of time.

Are you often late for meetings? Do your meetings typically run over? Do you keep people waiting for appointments? Do your presentations almost always take longer than the time allotted? What does such behavior say about you to those who are inconvenienced by your thoughtlessness?

12. Monitor the impact of your surroundings.

Walk into your office today as though you were a visitor. What impression do you get from the furniture, from the pictures and posters on the walls, from the amount of clutter, and from the overall feel of the office? What first impressions would you form? Think about what you might change. Do the same thing for other important areas in your building and any car that you use to transport others.

20 Nine Ways to Write Easy-to-Deliver Manuscript Speeches

Sometimes you're so familiar with a speech that you present it with little or no help from notes. Other times you know the material reasonably well but benefit from having an outline of your ideas to work from. However, some situations call for a manuscript speech—when you're not intimately acquainted with the material or when you must deliver the ideas in a precise fashion. A manuscript speech is fully written in advance and delivered exactly as expressed on the paper in front of you. When you don't adhere to the tips in this list, a verbatim presentation can be mind-numbing for your audience.

1. Write the way you speak, not the way you write.

Most people write more formally than they speak. If you make the mistake of writing a speech the way you write, the words won't sound like yours. As you write your speech, read each paragraph aloud to yourself. Revise it as necessary until you feel comfortable. Once your whole speech is written, read it to a colleague for a check of its friendliness. (15, 16)

2. Write with a "you" attitude.

Write with the listener in mind. Use more second person pronouns (you, your) than first person (I, me, my, mine). Many of the first person pronouns of speeches should be wiped out altogether. "The point I want to make is that our profit picture is bleak" is much weaker than "Our profit picture is bleak."

3. Use active verbs.

"Our marketing department designed a forceful campaign" is more memorable than "A forceful campaign was designed by our marketing department."

4. Keep sentences short and simple.

Complex sentence construction is difficult enough to read. It gets much worse when the information is heard. Keep your average sentence length to within eight to twelve words and try never to exceed twenty. Avoid sentences with multiple or lengthy adverbial clauses.

5. Keep paragraphs short.

Make paragraphs three to five sentences long. This will help the listener grasp the logic supporting your conclusions. You'll also have an easier time keeping your place in your notes.

6. Use contractions.

Writing the way you speak means that you should write down the same contractions you'd use delivering this same information in a staff meeting. If you wouldn't say "would not" in a conversation, don't saddle your audience with it. One exception to this rule is when the audience expects formal language.

7. Type the manuscript so that it's easy to read.
Double-space within paragraphs, triple-space between. Use large type (14 pt. or larger). Leave pages unstapled so you can simply shift sheets to the side of the lectern after you've finished reading them. Use two columns to enable your eyes to scan lines of type more easily.

8. Write marginal notes to cue your delivery.
Notes in the margin can remind you where to pause, to emphasize a word or phrase, to insert a slide, and to perform other stage directions.

9. Practice. Practice. Practice.
Know the speech so well that you can deliver it with your eyes up much of the time and with the same feeling that John F. Kennedy and Martin Luther King, Jr. put into the great speeches they delivered.

21 Seven Strategies for Working with a Ghost Writer

You won't always have time to write the speech you need to deliver or the statement you want to publish. Furthermore, your writing skills may not be nearly as good as those you can hire. Contracting for a speech writer is a delicate matter, however. You want a person who can write the way you think. The following tips will help you match thoughts and words.

1. Read samples of what the person has written.
Don't hire a dancer until you see a dance, don't hire a singer without listening to a song, and don't hire a writer without reading prose. Get samples of several candidates' work. Which one would be most effective with the writing challenge you pose?

2. Give candidates a writing sample test.
On the telephone explain a communication challenge you face. Ask them to bring 200 words to the interview that meet that challenge. Evaluate candidates on how well the finished product sounds like you and on how penetrating their questions were on the telephone.

3. Help your ghost writer study you.

The best surrogate writers manage to retain the good aspects of your style. Give your writer a package of what you've written and any audios or videos on which you appear.

4. Make sure the writer knows what you'd say if you had the time to write it.

Meet with the writer before every assignment to define the purpose of your speech or article, rattle off the main points you want to make, and state the values and beliefs that are at the foundation of your thinking.

5. Read everything before it gets published or before you deliver it.

Never be surprised. Never put yourself in a position where you have to apologize or retract your comments.

6. Have your speech writer coach you in delivery.

The writer knows what words to emphasize, where to vary your intonation, and when to pause for effect. Without face-to-face coaching the speech may become little more than a lifeless essay.

7. Give ghost-written speeches your personal imprint.

Incorporate a favorite saying, anecdote, or pearl of wisdom. This personal touch will give the piece your unmistakable imprint.

22 | Sixteen Tips for Delivering Compelling Speeches

Someone once said that three things matter in a speech—what is said, who says it, and how it's said—and that of these three the first matters the least. In other words, your presentation success will stand more on the audience's perception of you and their reaction to your delivery than on the content of your message.

1. Construct a clear speech purpose.

State your purpose in terms of how you plan to change the audience (rather than in terms of how you plan to inform them). Complete this sentence: "Upon listening to my speech, the audience will . . ."

2. Analyze the audience.

Don't whisper to the deaf or wink at the blind. Find out who your listeners are. Learn their current experiences, history, values, mood, needs, aspirations, prior knowledge, prejudices, political beliefs, demographics, socioeconomics, and expectations of you and of the topic. Prepare to push their hot buttons.

3. Research the topic thoroughly.
Collect more information and supporting material than you can use in the speech. This will increase your confidence, arm you to answer questions, and empower you to take the presentation in whatever direction appears to be best at the time.

4. Cluster your ideas into three to five main points.
It will be easier for your audience to follow, understand, and accept your ideas.

5. Create and use a set of reassuring notes.
If you're speaking from an outline, use trigger phrases for each point, not full sentences, so that your eyes will be up most of the time and you won't sound unnatural when you look down.

6. Use memorable audiovisuals.
People may forget what they hear, but they will remember what they see. Make certain your slides, charts, handouts, models, and board writing are attractive and easily seen.

7. Rehearse.
Before any new presentation, practice two or three times until you feel comfortable with it—in the room where you'll give it, if possible. The best time for the final rehearsal is the night before the real thing.

8. Avoid oral distractions.
As you rehearse, listen for unnecessary utterances ("aah," "uhm," "you know," "OK"), repetitive phrases, poor uses of language, mispronunciations, and throat clearing.

9. Arrange the room for maximum advantage.
Seat everyone comfortably where they can see you and your audiovisuals easily. Ensure fresh air, moderate temperature, and bright lighting. Favor larger over smaller rooms. Open the drapes for a more spacious feeling.

10. Manage your stage fright.
A little performance anxiety is a good thing; it energizes you. If it becomes excessive just before you perform, get it out through your

mouth by shouting, through your hands with a vise grip on a marker or on the edge of the lectern, or through your legs by walking, running, or climbing stairs. Of course, nothing beats being super-prepared as an antidote for stage fright.

11. Get off to a great start.
Georgie Jessel once said, "If you don't strike oil in three minutes, stop boring." Prepare an attention-getting, interest-arousing, rapport-building, and purpose-revealing opening. Avoid opening with an apology: "I'm not an expert on . . . ," "If I'd had more time to prepare . . . ," "I hope you will . . . ," or "I'll be as brief as I can . . ."

12. Connect with the audience.
Relax, smile, tell humorous stories about yourself (avoid jokes), don't hide behind a lectern, dress like the audience (perhaps a bit better), avoid pretenses, empathize with the audience, fix your eyes on audience members as you speak.

13. Inject vocal variety.
Use vocal contrasts in inflection, pitch, volume, emphasis, and speed to hold your audience's attention and to demonstrate your enthusiasm for your ideas.

14. Use your body for positive effect.
Move throughout the audience; air out your armpits; be animated. Show your excitement. Avoid distractions such as twirling your hair, jingling change in your pocket, putting both hands in your pockets, tapping the lectern, turning away from the audience, swaying, leaning on the lectern, playing with a pen or marker, or doing anything repetitively. (19)

15. Maintain control and credibility.
Handle disruptions firmly, yet tactfully. Answer questions honestly, always repeating them for large audiences. Respond to challenges with data, not emotion. Prepare for the toughest audience objections and dismantle them confidently, yet diplomatically.

16. Finish on time.
Most presenters take longer than promised. Finish on time, or better yet a little early, and your audience will love you.

23 Seven Tips for Giving Off-the-Cuff Speeches

Isn't it amazing how some executives seem to be able to say exactly the right thing whenever they're called upon to speak? You look at these people, maybe with a little envy, wondering how they're able to pull off this seemingly difficult trick. It isn't a trick. They probably have considerable experience at collecting their thoughts quickly and have learned a few instant organizing strategies along the way.

1. Focus on three angles of a single key point.
Write down a single word or phrase on a sheet of paper that captures the essence of what the audience needs to know—for example, how to increase sales. Then write three actions, techniques, reasons, explanations, or qualities in support of the point: (1) make more cold calls; (2) ask for customer referrals; (3) improve customer service. Jot these on the back of one of your business cards and flesh them in when you speak. You'll look organized and sound great.

2. Build on these six key questions: Who, What, When, Where, Why, and How.
Begin with what your audience needs to hear—for example, the re-engineering of the company. Then tell them *what* re-engineering is, *who's* heading up the project, *why* it's being undertaken, *when* it will begin, *where* it will occur, and *how* it will be carried out. You may reorder the questions to get a particular effect.

3. Use a current event to draw a moral and make your point.
Begin with what your audience needs to hear—for example, revisions in their health care coverage. Then show how current events in the industry, technological, economic, political, and social landscapes connect to what you propose in the revisions.

4. Build on an analogy.
Begin with what your audience needs to hear—for example, the future of our business. Say "Our business is like [you fill in the blank] because [draw the comparison]." Analogies are powerful communication tools that create memorable impact on your listeners.

5. Relate a personal story and link it to the key point you want to make.

Begin with what your audience needs to hear—for example, the requirement to improve customer service. Then tell a story of exceptional treatment you recently received as a customer and how it won your loyalty. You might also tell a story of receiving awful treatment and how that lost your loyalty. Personal stories are remembered long after statistics and urgings are forgotten.

6. Stay on top of trends.

You'll never be at a loss for words if you have a storehouse of information. Know your company, your industry, your technology, and current economic and political forces so well that you're always prepared to speak intelligently. (35)

7. Memorize four or five favorite quotes.

Memorize a handful of memorable sayings about leadership, communication, productivity, motivation, or teamwork. Choose quotes of famous people for heightened credibility. Audiences are impressed by those who can connect the words of respected experts to their own. (14, 30, 41, 55, 72, 89, 99, 117, 130)

---

24 Eleven Tips for Using an Interpreter

An ad for a popular international credit card concluded with the tag line: "Don't leave home without it." When it comes to conducting business overseas or with foreign executives in your country, there may be one other thing you shouldn't leave without: an interpreter. When executives don't speak a common language or speak it but not with confidence and fluency, an interpreter is essential. But an interpreter isn't a passive conduit of information; he or she may significantly alter the content and the scope of the dialogue. Make sure your interpreter adds to, rather than detracts from, the impact of your messages.

1. Screen candidates carefully.

Not every bilingual person can effectively interpret. Seek references from colleagues, contact your state office of economic development, check with the foreign language department of your local university, or call Berlitz International. When screening candidates, find out if they have professional accreditation. Ask them to describe the types of meetings they have interpreted; don't offer them a learning experience in a context they've never encountered before.

2. Find out if your interpreter uses a verbatim or figurative style.
Some interpreters say precisely what you say. Other interpreters modify words and expressions to best fit your overall intended meaning and the culture of the listener. Discuss this important distinction with your interpreter. You'll probably want your interpreter to modify your language to fit the situation, without changing your intent.

3. If the transaction is technical, hire an interpreter with the same technical background.
An interpreter may be fluent in the languages you need, but not understand a term used in the industry you represent. So you may not want to hire a social scientist to translate at a meeting of petroleum engineers.

4. Brief the interpreter.
Before the assignment tell the interpreter your goals for the sessions. Answer his or her questions. Make sure the interpreter knows the outcomes you hope to take away from the meetings.

5. Use your interpreter as a cultural coach.
As well as linguistic skills, interpreters often have knowledge of various cultures. Ask your interpreter for advice on customs you should honor and taboos you don't want to violate. (10)

6. Avoid using idioms or slang.
Idioms are expressions unique to one culture. Examples of American idioms include: "the ball's in your court," "par for the course," "roll it out," "sit on it," and "in the home stretch." When such expressions are interpreted literally, they make no sense to people of other cultures. Do your best to speak to your interpreter in standard English.

7. Speak slowly and distinctly.
The interpreter shouldn't have to wonder about what you've just said. Make a special effort to distinctly enunciate the final syllables of your words.

8. Use nonverbal language effectively.
When you speak through your interpreter, look at the foreign executive, not the interpreter, and imagine he or she understands everything you say. This makes your honesty apparent and enables the executive to see how you feel as you speak. Continue in this posture as your interpreter translates. When it's your counterpart's turn, again look at that person to read nonverbal language. As you listen to the interpreter, look at the interpreter to increase your understanding of the message; this is the one time to look away from the foreign executive.

9. When negotiations are crucial or adversarial, bring your own interpreter.
Don't rely on the interpreter provided by the other party. An interpreter on your payroll has a vested interest in representing your views with as much clarity and fidelity as possible. Also, multiple interpreters provide an accuracy check.

10. Expect a translated meeting to take longer than single-language meetings.
With an interpreter, everything is said twice. Set aside enough time. (Another reason to reserve some extra time is that you may be encountering a culture where starting times for meetings are rarely as planned.)

11. If you use an interpreter for a speech, let him or her study the text beforehand.
Interpreting from text requires more preparation because of the necessary precision in language—precision that may not be necessary during extemporaneous conversations. Sharing your notes in advance enables interpreters to ask questions, to help you avoid cultural faux pas, and to write notes on their copies of your speech.

25 Eighteen Ways to Handle Media Interviews with Aplomb

You may be great at satisfying six employees clamoring for the truth about rumors of layoffs. But how well would you handle a single news reporter needling you about the same subject with a microphone one inch from your lips and a TV camera in your face? Even the most seasoned corporate executives would be stressed by the encounter. You may never be able to come off like a network anchor, but the following tips will reduce much of the anxiety created by investigative interviews, and make you and your company look good.

1. Grant requests for friendly interviews.

When a media representative calls for help with a nonthreatening story, go out of your way to cooperate. This is a chance for free publicity, positive public relations, and building rapport with the reporter and his or her employer. In the same way, when you think you have a story or some information of benefit to the media, volunteer it.

2. Ask for the thrust of the interview or even for sample questions beforehand.

If the interview is intended to enlighten listeners or viewers and is nonadversarial, the interviewer will try to grant your request. If the interviewer won't reveal the scope of the interview or share sample questions, you might assume the interview *will* be confrontational.

3. Before the interview ask if you can help the interviewer develop the "hook."

Interviewers want to make their stories attractive by giving them an intriguing angle or "hook." Create a partnership to develop that angle. An interviewer isn't likely to ask a partner difficult or obscure questions.

4. Look for the best chance to say what you want to say.

You can probably think of several points you hope the questions will enable you to make. Memorize those points and state them when questions give you even the slightest opportunity to do so. Don't wait for the perfect question.

5. Never make off-the-record statements.

Don't trust the media. Trust yourself. Even an interviewer acting in good faith may later forget and include your statement in the story.

6. Count to five before answering tough, threatening questions.

Take your time. Speak with assurance but in slow, measured phrases. Don't frown or lower your eyebrows. You're in a public forum. Make sure your brain is in gear and your emotions are in neutral before you speak.

7. Answer the premise, not the specifics, of a difficult question.
Answering a question as stated may make you look bad no matter how you respond. Answering the *premise* of a question allows you to give it a more helpful twist.

> You're asked if your company will be laying off employees. To answer that question directly might compromise efforts to avoid the layoffs. Your response is, "Economic conditions have encouraged us to explore a number of cost-saving alternatives. We haven't ruled out any of them."

8. Never lie, deceive, or distort.
All attempts to get out of a tough situation with a lie will return to haunt you and may make a tough situation even tougher. If you unknowingly provide false information, set the record straight as quickly as possible.

9. Don't criticize anyone.
Interviewers sometimes reveal dissension and conflict to evoke interest in their stories. Don't be seduced into creating it for them. Whenever your answer to a question tempts you to blame another company or another person, bite your tongue.

10. Speak in plain English.
Industry or company jargon and pompous language will only confuse the audience and make you seem like an officious bureaucrat. Don't use words like *officious*.

11. Personalize the answer.
If the interviewer is trying to make you out to be cold, aloof, and insensitive, communicate verbally and nonverbally that you're just the opposite. Look directly into the camera. Smile and talk as though you were talking to a friend in your living room. Use personal examples and stories.

12. If you can't divulge information, explain why.
"No comment" raises doubts in the hearts and minds of your audience. Say, "I'm sorry that I can't say more at this time," and then explain why you can't.

13. If you're expecting many requests for interviews, get formal training.

Study yourself on video with the help of a coach. Role-play responses to the toughest questions the coach can dish out until you feel unstoppable.

14. Refer interviewers to your official company spokesperson for selected issues.

For whatever reason you may decide that a public relations specialist on your staff should handle all or certain requests for media interviews. However you set this up, take care that you not override the plan at your whim or you'll undercut the credibility and the effectiveness of your spokesperson.

15. Prepare written statements.

When the issue is highly volatile with legal implications, prepare a written statement. Read it to the media in an engaging and warm style. End by saying, "Thank you. That concludes my remarks." When you get pressed for further comments, say something like, "When more information comes to light, I'll make it available to you."

16. Anytime you execute a high-risk venture, think about what you'll tell the media if you fall flat on your face.

Picture the worst case scenario. What will you say to the press? Does imagining that scene cause you to rethink the execution of the venture in any way?

17. If a reporter wants to conduct an investigative interview, take precautions.

Show your willingness to be interviewed but not to relinquish total control. Get a written guarantee that the interview will be shown without editing. Cuts and splices can characterize your comments in ways that you didn't intend, unfairly putting you in a negative light. Have your attorney present.

18. Tape-record your interviews with the media.

Play it back right away to hear how you did and to learn what not to say next time. The tape also provides proof of what you said, should there be a dispute.

26 Ten Tips for Improving Communication with Your Board

Imagine going through life never having anyone to bounce ideas off of or anyone to give you a reality check. Chances are your life wouldn't be as rewarding or as secure as it could be. A board of directors plays precisely that role for top management. They're a sounding board for ideas and strategies, and they confront you with the truth that subordinates and even peers may withhold. Unfortunately, some top executives and their boards act like members of a dysfunctional family, unable to enjoy or benefit from everyone's talents and abilities. The tips in this list on board communication should help both you and your organization prosper.

1. Select board members carefully.
Choose board members who have the ability, time, energy, and interest to serve. Resist temptations to choose directors solely for their prestige or to "rubber stamp" top management decisions. (84)

2. Negotiate roles and expectations with the chairman and board members.
The CEO of an organization serves at the pleasure of the board of directors. Successful CEOs fulfill the expectations of the board for their leadership of the organization. If you're the CEO, *find out* what your board expects. One way to do this is to make a list of the performance standards you believe the board ought to hold you to. Get the board to review the list, revise it as appropriate, and approve it. Encourage the board to develop similar lists of expectations for the board chairman and for each member.

3. Ask your board to assess your performance regularly.
One function of the board of directors is to evaluate the performance of the CEO. If that person is you, hold your board accountable for holding you accountable. Ask them for a performance review every year, or more frequently if possible. The basis for your review should be the expectations generated according to #2 in this list. Without this feedback you'll be operating in the dark, and you might not learn of any displeasure until it's too late.

4. Don't hide bad news from your board.
The board would rather hear bad news from you than from a plaintiff's lawyer, the state attorney general, an investigative reporter, or a disloyal subordinate. Members will respect your honesty.

5. Base meetings on formal, written agendas.
Written agendas serve multiple functions. They provide goals and a sequential outline for the meeting. They provide a documented history of the meeting for corporate records. They make it tough for board members to introduce surprise personal issues. (26)

6. Provide relevant information for agenda items.
Board members aren't as familiar with the company or its problems as you are. They'll need some background to update them on most agenda items. Digested reports and abbreviated presentations are better than reams of printouts. Graphs and charts are better than tables of numbers. Give them the overall picture and have more detailed information available if they ask for it. Get this information to them at least one week prior to the meeting.

7. Take good minutes.
Board minutes are a legal document and should be recorded accurately and stored carefully. Get them out quickly after the meeting to encourage members who committed to do something before the next meeting to fulfill those commitments. Minutes shouldn't carry any more detail than the law requires. You don't want to make attendance at meetings seem pointless and you don't want to give readers a lot to quibble with.

8. Don't become defensive when board members offer advice.
People in charge have strong egos and believe they know what's best for the organization. But why have a board if you aren't willing to listen to advice? Even if you hope to avoid a particular piece of advice, it may be wise to hold off your objection until the entire board rules on it. Let someone else be the obstacle if possible.

9. Create alliances at your own risk.
Boards tend to be political animals. Different members espouse different agendas with alliances shifting as the issues shift. As you align yourself with one subgroup, you could alienate other subgroups who may gain control someday.

10. Don't let the executive committee become too powerful.
Most boards have executive committees made up of officers who conduct business that can't be efficiently handled by the full board. They're in closest touch with the CEO, help formulate the agenda, and may have voting rights beyond the general membership. See that your executive committee doesn't get so strong that regular board members feel valueless, become alienated, or lose enthusiasm for their roles.

27 Twelve Ways to Make Valuable Contributions to Meetings You Attend

You won't always be leading meetings. Even so, you and every other person attending play a vital role in the meetings' success. Here are a few tips on how to communicate effectively in business meetings.

1. Come prepared for the discussion.
Read the agenda before the meeting and think about your position on each item. Perform whatever research will enhance your input. As appropriate, call the leader or other members of the group to test your ideas before the meeting.

2. Arrive on time.
You'll accomplish four goals by getting there before the meeting begins.

- You'll send a message of commitment.
- You won't miss anything and can make fully informed contributions.
- You can network or conduct business with other early arrivals.
- You can choose a smart seat.

3. Choose a smart seat.
When you arrive, don't send a message of indifference by sitting far away from those already there. Sit in easy vision of the person running the meeting, so your contributions will be fully noted and considered. Sit next to someone you wish to get to know better. Don't sit across from the person you expect to challenge your ideas.

4. Listen to others.
Don't allow yourself to daydream and don't show rudeness by doing work while others speak. When someone is discussing something that interests you, don't jump in with your ideas until the current speaker has stopped talking. (31)

5. Build on others' comments.
Add to the present discussion. Compliment the ideas that have gone before yours. Don't change the focus to meet your own needs; such selfishness won't go unnoticed.

6. Stick to the agenda.
Keep your attention on the agenda item being discussed. When others stray from the current focus, pull the group back on track. Be careful, however, not to usurp the authority of the meeting leader.

7. Speak up, but not too much.
When you have something to add to the goals of the meeting, share it. Don't sit on your great ideas. However, don't monopolize the discussion or elaborate excessively. If you suspect you might be saying too much, look at people's eyes when you speak. If they return your gaze, you're doing okay. If they look down, either the quantity or the quality of your comments is probably not appreciated.

8. Remain upbeat.
When the discussion is dominated by gloom and doom, counter naysayers. Direct the group to what it *can* do whenever members are agonizing over what it can't do. (18, 19)

9. Prepare to solve problems, not place blame.
When group failures are being discussed, focus the discussion on fixing the future rather than rehashing the past. Once the causes for the failure have been identified, move the group quickly to the commitments people will make to ensure that history is not repeated. See that results, not people, are criticized.

10. Challenge bad ideas.
When someone says something you disagree with or you know won't work, say so. But be sure you attack the idea, not the person. It is better to say, "I have a problem with that idea" than "I have a problem with your idea." (51)

11. Help the discussion leader.
Running a meeting is a difficult task, especially when massive egos are involved. Assist the leader whenever you can to keep the meeting on track. Ask what you can do to help before the meeting so that your well-intentioned assistance during it won't be taken as a threat. And whatever you do, don't use someone else's group as an opportunity to grandstand and upstage that person.

12. Perform post-meeting follow-up as promised.
Take seriously any pledges you make to completing a task for the group prior to the next meeting. Deliver on your promises. One way to ensure this is to do it within twenty-four hours of the meeting where it was pledged.

28 Ten Tactics for Resolving Disagreements with Others

For many executives conflict is a daily event. You object to your business manager's actions for solving a cash flow shortage. A subordinate expresses anger over your decision to reorganize the company. You clash with a colleague over personal values. Whatever the cause of a conflict you may be experiencing right now, the steps in this list will help you resolve the issue.

1. Listen.
Hear others out fully before responding. This will help calm the person down, put you in a good light, and give you the information you need for an intelligent response. When it's your turn to speak, you'll be listened to because you will have emptied him or her of emotions, attitudes, and opinions, thereby making room for your emotions, attitudes, and opinions. (31)

2. Ask questions or paraphrase.
Make certain you understand what was said to you. Ask clarifying questions such as, "Are you saying that . . . ?" or "Tell me if this is what you're saying: . . ." (33)

3. Remain calm.
No matter how misinformed, irrational, or hurtful the other person is, keep your cool. Here are some guidelines:

- Accept the other person's right to disagree. Recognize that you may have said some pretty stupid things yourself.

- Don't tolerate verbal abuse.
- Recognize where the person's feelings stem from—either pain or fear. Think what you might do to ease the pain or calm the fear.

4. Know why you're arguing.

Why are you getting into this disagreement? What do you hope to accomplish? Are you striving toward a necessary solution for your organization? Are you standing up for an important principle? Or are you merely protecting yourself from something? Confront people only in the name of a good cause.

5. Be firm.

When you speak, state your views unequivocally, yet without taking hardened positions from which you might later have to back down. Be assertive (insisting on your right to be heard) without being aggressive (insisting that you're right). (18)

6. Be constructive.

Propose a counterplan for anything you argue against. Don't knock down others' ideas without having something better to put in their place.

7. Remain descriptive, not judgmental.

Limit your account of the situation to what you know, as opposed to what you surmise or suspect. Give plenty of examples to support your assertions. Base your argument on facts; use documented statistics; quote respected people; cite universal principles. Don't attribute motives or malice. Don't accuse the person of devious intent. Avoid personal affronts or insults. Remain powerfully polite. Identify the behavior you wish to have changed or the situation that must be corrected.

8. Accept responsibility.

Admit to the contributions you made to this dilemma in order to encourage the other person to do the same and to move the two of you forward to a solution. Apologize when appropriate.

9. Concentrate on a solution.

Be sure you both focus on fixing the future, rather than rehashing the past unnecessarily and reopening old wounds. Don't prevail by destroying your opponent. Ask, "What can we do to keep this from happening again?"

10. Focus on needs, not positions.

Develop a win-win mentality. Aim to meet both your needs and those of the other person, rather than defend a one-sided position. Once the two of you have stated your needs clearly, ask for the other person's ideas on how to meet both needs at the same time. When you use this technique to resolve conflict with a subordinate, your needs represent the company and must be met even if the employee's can't be.

A key supervisor asks for vacation during the busiest month in your business cycle. You count on that manager above all others to get you through that month. Rather than outright denying the request (i.e., taking up a position), you say, "Lucy, I'd love to let you take your vacation then, but you know that's our busy season, and I'm counting on you to get us through it. Now if you can convince me that in your absence those responsibilities will be handled, have a great vacation."

---

29 Twenty-Two Smart Ways to Communicate Using Information Technology

Cellular phones, fax machines, portable PCs, modems, and voice mail have changed the way we relate to one another and the way we conduct business. These new technologies give us capabilities for communication, document preparation, and numerical calculations that can give us an advantage over competitors if we use them more thoughtfully than they do.

FOR FAX MACHINES:

1. Don't tie up others' machines.

Nobody likes junk faxes. They tie up your machine, use up your paper, and force you to skim them before throwing them away. Faxing a twenty-page document that could just as easily go through the mail is thoughtless.

2. Don't misuse fax machines.

Personal notes belong in sealed envelopes. Invitations to important events should be engraved on good paper stock. When sharp copy quality on the receiving end is essential, don't fax except from computer to computer.

3. Use voice mail to record personal reminders.
Your voice mail doubles as a personal electronic memory. Call yourself and leave reminders about appointments, projects, or anything else.

4. Use voice mail to improve your speaking skills.
If you can, listen to your messages before you send them. Listen for ah's and uhm's, mispronunciations, and a nonconvincing tone of voice. Record a better message before pushing the send button.

5. Record voice messages slowly and distinctly.
How many times have you been frustrated and angry because the caller rushed or slurred a message, forcing you to replay it two or three times? If you haven't called someone before, spell your name and repeat your telephone number.

6. Use cellular phones with tact and etiquette.
If you're involved in a face-to-face conversation and your phone rings, give preference to the ongoing conversation. Unless the call is an emergency, return the call later. Turn your ringer off in meetings. When calling someone on his or her cellular phone, be brief.

7. Use call waiting judiciously.

- When you're on the telephone and get a call-waiting signal, limit the interruption to ten seconds. Say this to the interrupter, "Hello,———; I'm with another caller; may I call you right back?" Write the interrupter's name and number in front of you, so you don't forget to return the call.
- When someone calls you while you're expecting another call, and you plan to take the other call, say so at the beginning of the conversation.
- If you hear the other person's call waiting clicking, be thoughtful by encouraging him or her to answer the call.

8. Ask the people you call if they have time to talk.

In today's busy world, few people are just sitting around waiting for your call. Chances are they're very busy when they answer their phones. Ask them, "Is this a good time for you to take my call?" You needn't ask when you've gone through a secretary and the person has decided to take your call. However, if you need more than just a few minutes, you might explain why and offer to reschedule.

FOR TELECONFERENCES:

9. Use speaker phones judiciously.

Don't call or take calls on a speaker phone except to include a group in the conversation. If others are with you listening over a speaker phone, introduce the caller immediately to each person. Have each person speak up when you give his or her name so the caller can attach voices to names.

10. Before a video or teleconferencing meeting distribute an agenda.

All meetings should follow an agenda, even those conducted over telecommunication lines. Without an agenda you'll waste valuable time getting people "on the same page" and keeping them there.

FOR ELECTRONIC MAIL:

11. Get an Internet address.

Where do you live on the information superhighway? Print your e-mail address on your business cards along with your fax number. Include your e-mail address in messages. But don't let the capacities of the Internet distract you or your employees from business responsibilities.

12. Don't overload e-mail in-boxes.

With a single keystroke you have the potential to send a message to everyone in your company or on your network. But should you? Many e-mail recipients resent junk mail.

13. Communicate your emotions clearly.

It's hard to transmit emotions over e-mail because you have no tone of voice or body language to work with. Before you send any message, read your words literally. Are you as clear as you can be?

14. Think before you "flame."

"Flaming" is the term used for an emotional outburst on e-mail. Often flaming takes the form of confrontational and aggressive, if not profane, discourse. If you wouldn't say it face to face, over the telephone, or on paper, don't say it in e-mail.

FOR PERSONAL COMPUTERS:

15. Take full advantage of your computer software.

Most people know how to use less than 25% of the capabilities of their word processing or spreadsheet programs. A few hours spent in front of your computer with a good book about your software could multiply your capabilities with it.

16. Use computer diskettes properly.

Keep diskettes away from excessive heat or cold. Label them carefully so you and others can find what you need on them. Don't forward them to anyone without first verifying compatibility.

17. Give your laptop a rest now and then.

Little else frightens squeamish flyers more than to see your laptop screen glow after the flight attendant has asked for computers to be turned off. Someone whose fingers are constantly tapping on a keyboard annoys his or her neighbors in any quiet setting. It's rude to type away on any keyboard during a meeting or phone call.

18. Keep the number of a help desk in your wallet.

Know whom to call if your hard disk crashes, when you need help with your software, if your fax malfunctions, or if you lose an e-mail message.

FOR PUTTING IT ALL TOGETHER:

19. Work across modalities.

A voice mail message announcing an incoming fax creates anticipation and prepares the receiver. An e-mail message announcing a fax followed by voice mail underscores the importance of your most vital messages.

20. Don't forget the power of handwritten notes.

A handwritten note will never go out of style. In fact, the technology glut can heighten the impact of more traditional modes of communication. Handwritten notes are particularly powerful as reminders and thank you's.

21. Don't forget the power of face-to-face communication.
When your message is sensitive or contains an emotional component, no communication channel is superior to being there. There's a distinct danger today that high-tech business will breed a generation of "low-touch" managers.

22. Turn off everything that beeps when you don't need it.
Some people enjoy being beeped or called on a cellular phone in the presence of others. If you're beyond the status value of an electronic beep coming from your pocket, turn off your equipment when you don't need it—better yet, don't even carry it. Shut off wristwatch alarms; there are few ruder ways to interrupt a meeting.

30 Twelve Quotes Worth Quoting About Spreading the Word

1. The ability to speak is a shortcut to distinction. It puts a man in the limelight, raises him head and shoulders above the crowd, and the man who can speak acceptably is usually given credit for an ability all out of proportion to what he really possesses. —*Lowell Thomas*

2. It is so plain to me that eloquence, like swimming, is an art which all men might learn, though so few do. —*Ralph Waldo Emerson*

3. If you would be pungent, be brief; for it is with words as with sunbeams—the more they are condensed, the deeper they burn. —*Robert Southey*

4. Nine-tenths of the serious controversies which result in life result from misunderstanding. —*Louis D. Brandeis*

5. An executive can't ignore his communication any more than a driver can forget to oil his engine. —*Chester Burger*

6. If people around you will not hear you, fall down before them and beg their forgiveness, for in truth you are to blame. —*Fyodor Dostoyevsky*

7. Make thyself a craftsman in speech, for thereby thou shalt gain the upper hand. *—Ancient Egyptian tomb inscription*

8. Newspaper editors are men who separate the wheat from the chaff, and then print the chaff. *—Adlai Stevenson*

9. My father gave me these hints on speech making: "Be sincere . . . be brief . . . be seated." *—James Roosevelt*

10. The most valuable of all talents is that of never using two words when one will do. *—Thomas Jefferson*

11. Communicate unto the other guy that which you would want him to communicate unto you if your positions were reversed. *—Aaron Goldman*

12. Half of the world is composed of people who have something to say and can't, and the other half who have nothing to say and keep on saying it. *—Robert Frost*

3
GET THE WORD

If you follow the prescriptions in this chapter, you'll never lose touch with the people who are out there fighting the battles for you. You'll learn how to become a dry sponge for their ideas, their concerns, and their impressions of your leadership style. This chapter is your ticket to earning the respect of your employees, finding out what's going on with their work, and building their self-confidence.

31 Twelve Ways to Improve Your Listening

Once you get to be in charge, your ears become even more essential to your success. They reveal what's going on around you. They enable you to understand other people's motives and needs. They increase your learning, thereby making you more competent and more powerful. They win the respect and build the self-esteem of followers who appreciate your attention. They defuse anger by giving others a chance to vent. They help you find out what type of leader your people need you to be.

1. Commit to improve your listening.
If you aren't already a good listener, you're not likely to reform without a total commitment. Most "deaf ears" have to get good and angry about what they're losing by not listening well before they muster the motivation to change.

2. Think about the speaker in advance.
When you know someone will be speaking to you, start thinking about that person and the topic he or she is likely to discuss with you before the encounter.

3. Limit your talking.
Shut up! You can't talk and listen at the same time.

4. Stop worrying about what you're going to say next.
Don't begin planning your answer while the other person is still speaking. You'll have plenty of time to form a response once the speaker is finished.

5. Stop coming to quick conclusions about people and things.
Many people go through life searching for the same "holy grail": to find information that confirms what they already know to be true. We listen only to the people we consider worth listening to, and when we decide to listen we often hear what we *expect* people to say regardless of the message sent. In other words, as soon as you decide what's right (or wrong) or who's right (or wrong), you stop listening for evidence that might contradict your decision. (85)

6. Become less self-centered.
When someone else begins to speak, it's our nature to tune into "WII-FM"—"What's In It For Me?" And it's rare that we conclude that the other person is saying something as important as what *we* have to say. Transform this thinking 180 degrees. When the other person is speaking, tell yourself, "There's something for me to learn here." There always is.

7. Get into a listening posture.
Face speakers; move towards them if you are more than five feet away; see that both of you are standing or both of you are seated; if you're seated, sit forward in your chair without being physically aggressive; smile; nod your head now and then; maintain eye contact. (19)

8. Hold your fire.
When other speakers say things that excite, please, or trouble you, hang onto your emotion until they complete their thought. If you interrupt them, you risk offending, angering, or disappointing them. As a result, the rest of the message is likely to be distorted, and the person may be less likely to share ideas with you in the future.

9. Focus on the speaker's words.
Since most of us can listen at a rate that's four times faster than the average oral delivery (480 words per minute versus 120 words per minute), we tend to focus on something other than what the person is saying. You might allow yourself to get caught up in some unusual

aspect of the speaker's style of delivery; your stereotype of the speaker might cause you to hear what you expect to hear; you might become distracted by external noises in the environment; or you might be seduced into daydreaming. Don't let this happen. Think only about the speaker's message.

10. Monitor nonverbal messages.
Without being distracted from the words, note the speaker's tone of voice and body language. Does the nonverbal language reinforce or conflict with the verbal? (19)

11. Ask questions.
One great way to remain fixed on a speaker is to ask questions of clarification about the message. Ask something like, "Are you saying that . . . ?" or "How does that relate to what you said before about . . . ?" (33)

12. Tell the speaker what you heard.
Communication is never one way only. What you do after the speaker has stopped talking completes the conversation. Give the speaker immediate feedback by saying whether you understand what he or she said. In most cases, the speaker will also want to know if you agree. Fulfill this obligation as well. It's rude and confusing to leave your speaker wondering how a message got through to you.

32 Fifteen People to Listen To

Sometime over the next thirty days make at least one opportunity to give these important people a good listening-to. They may be ready to talk with no prompting. Otherwise, we suggest a number of questions for each to get the ball rolling. Add your own to probe further and to explore other issues important to you.

1. Your spouse.
How was your day? What can I do to be a better helpmate to you? What can we do to be a better team?

2. Your children.
What's new since the last time we talked? What are some of the great things happening to you right now? Are you struggling with any problems? What can I do to help you with those problems?

3. Your parents.
What's one thing I can do to make your life a little easier? How's Mom (Dad) doing?

4. Your friends.
What do you see me doing that doesn't serve me well? If you would have me change one thing in my life, what would that be? How can I be a better friend to you?

5. Your boss.
What might I have done to make that work the best you ever saw? What's one thing I can do to serve you more effectively? What challenges can I help you with?

6. Your employees.
What frustrations are you experiencing? What are the greatest challenges you face right now? What are some of your most recent successes? What do you really like about your work? What's one thing I can do to help you be more effective?

7. Your colleagues.
What do I do that helps you succeed? What do I do that frustrates you? What can I do to be a better team player?

8. Your customers.
What's one thing we can do to improve your experiences with us? What do you need that no one's providing? What's your wildest dream product or most wished-for service? What will it take to keep you as a customer for life? (94)

9. Your suppliers.
What can you do for us that you're not doing now? How can we make it easier for you to serve us more fully?

10. Your mentor, personal management coach, or consultant.
Am I doing anything to shoot myself in the foot? What am I doing that you think is highly effective? What can I do to give my employees a stronger sense of ownership of our organization's goals? What should I be doing to increase the accountability my employees feel for their performance? What personal development goals should I set for myself? How can you help me attain them?

11. Your financial advisor.
Do my investment strategies make sense in the light of my financial goals and retirement objectives? If you would have me change one of my attitudes toward investments, what would that be? How can you help me increase the value of my portfolio? (128)

12. Your physician.
How often should I come in for a complete physical? What one thing should I be doing to take better care of myself?

13. An estranged person at home or at work.
What have I done to contribute to the breakdown of our relationship? May I tell you how I believe you contributed to the rift? What can I do to create the future relationship we both need? Will you commit yourself to change as well?

14. Your inner self.
Is this something that I really want to do? Am I setting a positive example for those around me? Am I pleased with myself?

15. Your "higher power."
Does this action match my deep-seated values and beliefs? How am I making the world a better place? Am I serving others or only myself? God, how can I best serve you? What will you have me do with my life?

33 Ten Ways to Ask Powerful Questions

Just because you're in charge doesn't mean you always know the right thing to say at the right time. Actually, the most effective leaders are those who don't necessarily always say the right things, but rather always *ask* the right things. Asking the right questions is an art that separates mediocrity from greatness. The right question at the right time turns confusion into clarity, conflict into consensus, and frustration into satisfaction.

1. Recognize the power of questions.
Stop thinking in terms of what you have to say and start thinking in terms of what you have to *ask*. Questions focus thought like a lens condenses sunlight. They bridge conflicting views. They strengthen relationships. They deflect anger and hostility. They show your

caring and concern. Stop thinking in terms of exclamation points and start thinking in terms of question marks. (32)

2. Seek to understand before you seek to be understood.

Listen. Probe. Seek clarity. You build consensus, teams, and unity by determining the needs and values of your people. Questions provide this information. (31)

3. Monitor your nonverbal cues when asking questions.

When you speak, your tone of voice, facial expression, and posture can communicate condescension, regardless of how neutral the words might be. Ask questions in a genuinely inquisitive tone of voice, with an anticipatory look on your face, and in a nonthreatening posture. (19)

4. Whenever discussion meanders, ask a question to get back on track.

What can I do to help you? What are we trying to accomplish? Is this what we're here to discuss? What are we hoping to get out of this meeting? Questions like these help get the discussion back on track—or bring it to a natural close. (38)

5. Whenever you're at a loss for words, ask a question.

How would you like me to respond to that? Would you please repeat that? How do you think I should feel after hearing that? Such questions buy time to think of an appropriate response.

6. Whenever you're under attack, ask a question.

Why do you believe my idea won't work? What have I said to make you feel that way? What evidence would convince you that's not true? Each of these questions can turn an awkward moment into an advantageous one.

7. Whenever a relationship is in trouble, ask a question.

What can we do to solve this problem? How do you think we can work together better in the future? What do you suggest we do to make the situation better for both of us? Where do we go from here? These questions build bridges.

8. When a customer complains, ask a question.

Please tell me: Exactly what happened? Where did we go wrong? What will it take to get you back as a customer? What can we do to make it right? These questions show your concern and commitment and have the potential for turning a raving antagonist into a die-hard fan. (91)

9. **When you want people to think about what they're doing, ask a rhetorical question.**
Rhetorical questions evoke introspection and contemplation. Why do you work as hard as you do? What does quality really mean? Have you ever wondered why customers choose to buy from us and not our competitors?

10. **Whenever you want to build rapport with employees, ask a question.**
What's your advice on this problem? How does the situation look from your perspective? What do you think I'm overlooking? What ideas do you have for strengthening our team? When you ask people for their opinion, you show how much you value them. (39, 40)

34 Fourteen Strategies for Getting a Reality Check

Leadership can be lonesome, and the higher up you sit the more lonesome it can be. At the top you tend to get little day-to-day reaction from others on how well you're doing your job. Sure, you can look at the bottom line of your organization to measure your effectiveness, but that doesn't give you the immediate feedback you need.

1. **Examine your working relations with subordinates.**

   - Do you have contentious relations with many of your subordinates? Do you complain that subordinates don't set their priorities or do their work correctly? Either of these situations suggests that you've failed to share your vision with them or that you haven't made your performance expectations explicit. (43, 74)
   - Do many subordinates have a hard time understanding you? If so, before you give directions, ask yourself: "How can I send this message in such a way that it can't possibly be misunderstood?" Be careful, however, not to allow such determined communication to come across as patronizing. (15–18)

- Are your subordinates honest with you? If not, you may intimidate them.
- Are they brutally honest with you? If so, you may have angered them into getting even.
- Are you surrounded by groveling boot-lickers? If so, find out what you've been doing to encourage their sycophancy.

2. Consider your working relations with superiors.
Do they trust your judgment, give you all the authority you need, and back you up? Or do they constantly investigate your operation, make decisions for you, and fail to support you in tough times? Consider a yes to the second question as a vote of no confidence. Find out why it was cast.

3. Consider your working relations with peers.
Do other people at your level—perhaps in other companies—seek your advice and counsel? Do peers in your own company cooperate with you? If not, they may see you as too competitive, as a back stabber, or simply as unfriendly.

4. Study the kinds of friends you have.
What kind of people enjoy being around you? If your friends are thoughtful, considerate, and helpful, there's a good chance that the same is true for you.

5. Scope out other work climates.
Whenever you have the opportunity to visit another company, department, or team, observe the employees. Listen to them talk; note the quality of their interactions with superiors; watch them work. Compare their energy, commitment, and attitudes to those of your people. The differences you see indicate your ability to hire good people and earn their dedication.

6. Ask for feedback from someone whose judgment you value.
To do it in a way that will encourage honesty, ask this question: "What is one thing I could do differently to get better results with . . . ?"

7. Ask others to tell you what they hear about you.

- Peers are often on the receiving end of blunt opinions about your leadership. Ask them what they hear, but don't pressure them to reveal their sources.

• If you ask a subordinate to tell you what other subordinates think about you, consider the likelihood that the reaction he or she attributes to others may in fact be his or her own.

8. Conduct customer surveys.

Whenever customer survey data rolls in, acknowledge both the direct and indirect role your leadership plays in the results.

9. Conduct employee surveys.

Opinion surveys can be an effective and reliable source of upward feedback. On the next one administered in your company, include questions about your leadership. Get back to employees immediately with the tabulated results. Get back to them soon thereafter with the actions you plan to take in response to the results.

10. Bring in a consultant to interview employees.

Ask the consultant for recommendations on what the interviews indicate you should begin doing for better results. Ensure employee confidentiality of their comments to maximize their honesty.

11. Read the press.

A periodical might publish evaluations of your leadership or organization. It could be a company newsletter, a trade journal, or a newspaper. Analyze relevant write-ups for what they say—and what they don't say.

12. Use this book as a guide to important behaviors.

These chapters detail the qualities the world expects from people in charge.

From this book's table of contents select the 25 leadership behaviors you believe are most essential to your success (e.g., "Managing your time effectively"). Give the list to your employees and ask that they identify the three behaviors that you display most consistently and the three you display least consistently. Tabulate the results. Ask humbly for explanations and perhaps examples of feedback you don't understand. (For even greater impact, ask employees to choose the 25 leadership behaviors they'll evaluate in you.)

13. Read good management books.
Stay current with leadership literature. Each time you finish a good book, commit yourself to practicing one behavior that it has told you is crucial to your success. Before you take action, however, check with a trusted colleague to confirm that you're planning a worthwhile change. (2, 36, 123)

14. Enroll in an executive leadership seminar.
Get away from the office for an extended learning experience. The seminar should be designed to make you reflect on how your leadership performance relates to its subject. Some of the best seminars survey your bosses, peers, and employees before the seminar, enabling you to concentrate on the leadership concepts they say will be most useful to you.

35 Eleven Tips for Keeping Up with Trends

Someone once said that there are three kinds of people in the world: Those who make things happen, those who watch things happen, and those who don't know anything's happening. You can't afford to fall into this last category. You must have more than a heightened awareness of what's going on around you and you must anticipate trends.

1. Set aside one hour each day to absorb new information.
On a typical day you're likely to read letters from suppliers and customers, balance sheets, memos and reports, and a variety of other written communication. You read this material to maintain control of your business. Monitor emerging trends by reading material that describes the world *beyond* your four walls.

2. Select an information source that fits your needs and schedule.
Some executives feel comfortable skimming newspapers and magazines. Others are more at home absorbing information from on-line news services transmitted over their PC. Choose the format most comfortable for you.

3. Subscribe to newsletters in your field.
Entrepreneurs have already taken the trouble of synthesizing data into trend analyses and describing these trends in newsletters. Check with friends in your industry to find out what they read and recommend.

4. Read the *Wall Street Journal*.
Much of what's new in business today was featured first in *WSJ*.

5. Scan the front covers of national news magazines.
News magazine covers feature the major stories of the nation. Visit a bookstore or newsstand weekly to view the front covers of the most popular news and business magazines; look for trends and themes.

6. Join a local group of top managers from various industries.
Some local chambers of commerce establish executive roundtables for peers from noncompetitive industries to explore ideas and trends. You can also establish networks of peers around the country and maintain them via quarterly meetings, electronic mail, and teleconferencing.

7. Join or start an executive book club.
Reading and discussing business best-sellers will keep you on the cutting edge of knowledge. You can create a reading club for coworkers or for associates in other local businesses. Set the goal of reading at least one best-seller a month and devoting at least one hour to discussing its implications. Once your club gets off the ground, you'll be amazed that you ever got along without it.

8. Attend regional and national meetings of your professional trade association.
Such meetings offer several valuable learning opportunities:

- motivational or keynote speakers who are on the forefront of new ideas
- a panoply of sessions that expose you to innovators in your field
- resource areas where you find the most up-to-date publications
- perhaps most important of all, a forum for spending time informally with your counterparts in other organizations so you can discuss the impact of current trends on your field (7)

9. Pay for the consulting time of a local or national guru.
Experts reach their level by devoting much of their time to studying their field, noting how it's changing, and analyzing the forces creating the change. Consultants can be well worth their fees if you use them wisely to take you further out on the learning curve. (83)

10. Attend at least one seminar a year that will challenge your thinking.
Top managers are strategic thinkers. They ask the what-if and why-not questions. Seek seminars that will teach you how to pose (and answer) these questions for your business.

11. Consult with your attorney and accountant.
Lawyers and accountants are in excellent positions to spot trends that will affect you and your business. Their perspective is broader than yours since they see the problems confronting *many* clients. You're already paying for legal and financial advice. Ask them what they see going on that represents future dangers or opportunities for your business. (115, 116)

36 Eighteen Management Classics You Should Read

To be labeled a "classic," a book must transcend time, be cited by many other authors, and present ideas that have had far-reaching impact. Start working your way through this list of management classics. Intersperse them with current business best-sellers. Your reward will be greater insight into what it takes to succeed as someone in charge, and a heftier bag of proven techniques to get more out of yourself and the people around you.

1. Peter Drucker's *The Effective Executive* (Harper and Row, 1966).
The "dean" of management writers dissects and analyzes the qualities of effective and efficient managers.

2. Henry Mintzberg's *The Nature of Managerial Work* (Harper and Row, 1973).
Based on observations of real managers doing real work, Mintzberg discusses the frenetic, often chaotic, nature of managerial roles and responsibilities.

3. Tom Wolfe's *The Right Stuff* (Bantam, 1980).
This case study of the recruitment, selection, and training of the first NASA astronauts provides an illuminating analysis of teamwork, talent, and performance. It also provides insights regarding the impact of egos and personal agendas on team performance.

4. **Thomas Peters and Robert Waterman's *In Search of Excellence* (Harper and Row, 1982).**
This book's eight criteria for excellent companies spawned a movement towards excellence and is as applicable today as when it first appeared.

5. **Douglas McGregor's *The Human Side of Enterprise* (McGraw-Hill, 1960).**
One of the classics of the human relations movement. Discusses the importance of values and needs as determinants of productivity and morale.

6. **William Ouchi's *Theory Z: How American Business Can Meet the Japanese Challenge* (Addison-Wesley, 1981).**
Compares American and Japanese management styles and proposes Theory Z as a hybrid of the two to solve contemporary management problems.

7. **Herbert Simon's *Administrative Behavior* (Free Press, 1957).**
Not easy reading, but a must in every management library. The Nobel laureate in economics introduces the concept of "satisficing"—meaning that managers are always negotiating for the best solution given the constraints of the situation.

8. **Carl Rogers's *On Becoming a Person* (Houghton Mifflin, 1961).**
Often cited as a classic in the field of human resource development. Though not a management book per se, every executive should read it for its potential to raise introspective questions.

9. **Frederick Herzberg's "One More Time: How Do You Motivate Employees?" (*Harvard Business Review*, Jan.–Feb., 1968, pp. 53–62).**
This article fueled a continuing debate on the role of money as a motivator. Herzberg believes that motivation derives from the nature of the work itself (intrinsic), not from rewards and fringe benefits (extrinsic).

10. **Michael Porter's *Competitive Advantage: Techniques for Analyzing Industries and Competitors* (Free Press, 1980).**
A seminal work on the nature of competitive advantage and competitive strategy.

11. **Terence Deal and Allan Kennedy's** *Corporate Cultures: The Rites and Rituals of Corporate Life* (Addison-Wesley, 1982).
This book made *corporate culture* a buzzword. Presents strategies for analyzing corporate cultures and highlights prototypical cultures.

12. **Warren Bennis and Burt Nanus's** *Leadership: Strategies for Taking Charge* (Harper and Row, 1985).
Insightful analysis of the qualities and characteristics of effective leaders. Demystifies and debunks much of what is associated with the concept of leadership.

13. **Roger Von Oech's** *A Whack on the Side of the Head* (Warner Books, 1984).
This fun book is a creativity seminar unto itself. After you read this book you'll see decision making in a new light.

14. **Roger Fisher and William Ury's** *Getting to Yes* (Penguin Press, 1981).
The most frequently cited book on how to incorporate "win-win" into negotiations.

15. **W. Edwards Deming's** *Out of the Crisis* (MIT Press, 1986).
A gospel for those interested in implementing total quality management and statistical process control.

16. **Anthony Jay's** *Management and Machiavelli* (Holt, Rinehart and Winston, 1967).
Power, influence, and authority are the essence of management. This treatise uses Machiavelli as a case study in analyzing the uses and abuse of power.

17. **Kenneth Blanchard and Spencer Johnson's** *The One Minute Manager* (Morrow, 1981).
This million seller provides an easy to understand and easy to implement model of behavior modification. Takes complex ideas and discusses them simply and entertainingly.

18. **Dale Carnegie's** *How to Win Friends and Influence People* (1936).
Over 30 million copies sold and still in print. Carnegie's timeless message was how to communicate effectively with other people, motivate them to achieve, and discover the leader inside yourself.

37 Fourteen Rules for Handling a Gripe Session

One or two disgruntled employees indicate just that—one or two disgruntled employees. A *group* of disgruntled employees indicates a management problem. How should you respond? By providing a forum where those employees can vent their frustrations and reveal the dimensions of the problem to you. But follow these steps very carefully—deviations might lead to disaster.

1. Prepare to take the heat.
The purpose of the gripe session is to entice discontented employees to empty their arrows and spears into you. You want these blades in front of you where you can see them, rather than in your back. A true leader can absorb criticism when it achieves the purpose of improving the organization.

2. Don't get defensive.
In order for the gripe session to have a positive outcome, you must see it as an opportunity to improve and not as an occasion to defend your honor and judgment. A gripe session represents catharsis, not crisis.

3. Convene a *small* group.
Gripe sessions should be conducted with about ten to fifteen employees. With fewer people, participants may feel too intimidated to say much. With more, you risk spontaneous combustion or allowing quiet employees to sit there without saying anything.

4. Ask for their concerns.
Say something like, "We're here because I'm at a disadvantage. I've heard concerns about the new telephone system, but I don't have as clear a statement from you as I need to have about those concerns. The only way I can respond intelligently is to know your precise needs and expectations, so please share them with me."

> A consultant advised one manager to initiate a gripe session with several dissatisfied employees. The manager responded, "Are you crazy? All they'll do is complain!" To which the consultant retorted, "I hope so—that's just what a gripe session is for."

5. Promise a response, not repercussions.

Guarantee participants that their input to the meeting will be seen as positive, no matter how critical they are, so long as that criticism is given in the spirit of making things better. See that your subordinate managers also fulfill this pledge!

6. Pose a clear question.

State the question you want them to answer. For example, "What problems are being created for you and your colleagues by the new telephone system?"

7. If no one says anything . . .

You may have to get the ball rolling. One way to do this is to propose to the group a list of concerns you believe they have and ask them to begin the session by voting for those concerns they feel are most valid. ("These are the potential difficulties that have been pointed out to me about the new telephone system. Which three of these will affect *you* the most?") This icebreaker will get them talking.

8. Record their answers.

A flip chart has several advantages over other data collection methods. Taking such notes demonstrates that you're listening and that you value what's being said. All participants can see the group's points. Most importantly, the permanent log it provides suggests that you plan to do something with the information you receive.

9. Assess priority opinions.

Once the entire list is generated, get the group to vote for the ones that are most troubling, so that you know where to focus your response.

10. Say nothing.

Your participation at the gripe session is limited to the asking of clarification questions ("Are you saying that . . . ?"). If you were to respond at this time, some of your reactions would almost certainly be defensive and possibly punitive. Saying nothing is crucial. Many a gripe session has been blown by a leader who revealed anger.

11. Invoke a 48-hour promise.

Once everything has been said, shun the typical and often insincere "we'll get back to you" pledge. Instead say, "I'll be in this room 48 hours from now with a response to the issues you have raised." The

48-hour promise proves you're serious. It gives you the time you may need to cool down and see things from the perspective of employees. Better yet, it has you getting back to them so quickly that they won't expect the miraculous cures they'd hope for if you took 48 days.

12. Thank the employees.
Your employees have gone out on a limb in being honest with you. Tell them how pleased you are that they've been so forthcoming and constructive with their feelings, attitudes, and opinions.

13. Answer the concerns.
When you return to the group 48 hours later, address their list of concerns, nondefensively, one by one.

- First, acknowledge that each of the points made were valid in the sense that the employees honestly felt them.
- Second, identify those issues on the list that have risen out of miscommunication, and clear up the misunderstanding as you see it.
- Third, identify the issues that you believe are invalid, and say why you view them this way.
- Finally, identify the issues that you believe warrant attention, either immediately or in the future, and commit the organization to resolving them in specific ways. Involve the gripe session participants as much as possible in the search for solutions, perhaps by asking some to join a focus group to resolve certain issues.
- If a particular issue is beyond your control, say so.

14. Remain accountable.
Show through your actions that valid concerns won't be ignored. Reconvene the group in three months to check on progress and see what else needs to be done.

38 Fourteen Rules for Chairing a Meeting

Many employees complain about the meetings they attend, and the problems can often be traced to poor leadership. The two biggest mistakes meeting leaders make are: (1) they dominate the meetings, trying to manipulate the group into the outcomes they seek; or (2) they relinquish control of the meeting, not fulfilling their obligation to mold the group into a well-oiled decision-making machine. You can harness the full resources of the groups you lead when you take these actions.

1. When you're determined to get what you want, make the decision yourself.

Employees get frustrated and feel their time is wasted when they're brought together in the guise of contributing to a decision that has already been made. Not all decisions should be made by a group. When you know what you want, be honest enough to admit it. You can consult with others individually to explain your idea to them and to elicit their reaction to the idea. If you pull the group together to accomplish the same thing, don't allow them to mistakenly believe that you're asking them to help you *make* the decision.

2. Consider letting someone else run your meetings.

Your presence at meetings may intimidate certain employees into holding back their great ideas. Your leadership of those meetings may be so heavy-handed, or at least perceived that way, that you may have more influence over the outcomes than you want. When you do run your own meetings, spend more time listening than speaking as long as the group is making good progress.

3. Circulate an agenda prior to the meeting.

Help participants hit the ground running with an agenda that specifies date, place, starting and ending times, attendees, purpose, topics, and perhaps the time to be devoted to each discussion.

4. Specify outcomes.

At the beginning of the meeting, make certain everyone understands the significance and the meaning of each agenda item, and what will satisfy each one. ("With regard to item number three, *Hiring a Vice President of Sales*, we're looking for a list of fifteen to twenty capabilities for the search committee to use in interviewing the first group of candidates.")

5. State your expectations for member behavior.

When you start a group meeting or take over one's leadership, establish expectations for attendance, punctuality, participation, treatment of each other, and all aspects of member contribution. At the same time, learn what expectations the members have for how you'll run the meetings. Strike a mutual performance contract.

6. Make these "process" interventions.

- When you can see that two members don't understand each other, point this out to them and clear up the miscommunication.
- When conflict, disagreement, or personal antagonisms block progress, confront the issue directly, tactfully, and quickly.
- When discussion strays from the agenda, lead the group back to the topic.
- When criticisms are made of people rather than of ideas, identify this and insist on improvement.

7. Defeat "groupthink."

Many groups implement ideas that look wonderful on paper, but prove later to have been ill-conceived. "Groupthink" typically happens when group members think too much alike, agree with each other too easily, or just refuse to rock the boat. Don't allow your group to arrive at consensus hastily. Assess the assumptions upon which the conclusion was made. Lead members through a critical evaluation of decisions before they are implemented. Counteract groupthink in these ways:

- Appoint a devil's advocate.
- Have a "second chance" meeting to revisit major decisions before you implement them.
- Bring in outsiders to be part of the decision-making process or to critique the outcome.
- Insist that each member think of at least one idea why the decision might not achieve the desired results.

8. Help ideas grow.

When the group is working toward a solution or making a decision, insist that, when appropriate, their ideas build on each other before moving the group in a totally new direction. ("Sandy, I'd like to ask you to hang onto your idea for a moment. Larry had made a point before that I'm not sure we explored fully.")

9. Draw noncontributing members into the discussion.

It's a waste of a valuable resource when someone who could have a lot to add to a meeting just sits there. Try these ideas:

- Use the person's name in an example to get the person's attention and to encourage a comment.
- Look directly at the person during the meeting.
- Ask for that person's opinion on what's being discussed.
- Go around the room to get everyone's comments on a particular point.
- In between meetings talk to the person about your desire for greater contributions.

10. Focus the group on *process*.
About halfway through every meeting ask the group to stop thinking about the decision it's making, and focus on the process it's using to make it. Ask people questions like these:

- Do you believe we're making good progress?
- Are you happy with your contribution so far?
- Do you think people are listening to each other?
- Are we making the best use of the group?
- Am I contributing too much or too little as the leader?
- Do you recommend doing anything differently for the rest of the meeting?

11. Give refreshment breaks.
Every ninety minutes, or sooner if attention and energy levels fall off, call for a short break. Healthy snacks and beverages are appreciated and can help rebuild energy.

12. Summarize.
At the end of every meeting you run, review the decisions made and assertively repeat whatever responsibilities for follow-up actions people have assumed or you've assigned. Hold members accountable.

13. Express your appreciation.
At the end of every meeting thank people for their attendance, punctuality, and contributions to the team's success. Praise your team publicly and extol them to others.

14. Put life back into your staff meetings.
Regularly scheduled meetings held for the purpose of communication and coordination of your team can get "old" and nonproductive very quickly. Here are a few ways to keep them interesting and valuable:

- Rather than chair every meeting yourself, rotate leadership among members.
- Ask each person to report on the biggest current challenge faced by her department.
- Ask everyone to reveal one thing other team members could do to serve them better.
- Have each member describe the hottest project currently underway in his or her area.
- Ask everyone to share one piece of information others need to know right now.
- Ask each member to propose one thing the team could be doing more of to become more mutually supportive.
- Bring in an outside expert to brief the team on a matter of importance.
- Meet less often.

39 Thirteen Ways to Get Employees to Keep You Informed

You learn about a service problem from a customer. You hear about a potentially volatile disciplinary situation from the employee being disciplined. A failing product line first comes to your attention as an excuse for a disappointing quarterly report. In each of these situations, a subordinate manager should have told you beforehand. After telling your subordinates how much you need better upward communication, you reflect on your own behavior. Do you encourage managers to give you bad news as well as good? How many of the strategies on this list do you practice?

1. Remain accessible.
If you're often out of town, out of the office, or just hard to call or meet with, employees may get discouraged and give up on keeping you informed.

2. Engage in MBWA (Managing By Wandering Around).
One of the many advantages of spending at least a few minutes each day with the troops is that they have the opportunity to take you aside to reveal some new development in their work. (45)

3. Enable people to see you privately.
Your people need to have the opportunity to meet with you in confidence, especially when their news might embarrass you or them.

4. Be a good listener.
Some managers only *think* their employees aren't keeping them informed. They're so often in a state of mental distraction that they don't absorb much of the information sent their way. (31)

5. Train your people to communicate well.
Send them to seminars where they learn how to send accurate, timely, and comprehensive messages. (15–18)

6. Pass good news up the line.
When employees know that you're likely to boast about their accomplishments to others, they'll report more of them to you.

7. Impress upon your people that *all* news is good news.
Make sure they know exactly what you need to hear and how you can use that information, whether good or bad, to improve organizational effectiveness.

8. Don't "kill" the bearer of bad tidings.
Avoid getting upset with the person who brings you bad news. Direct your response toward what can be done to keep the problem from happening again, rather than on punishing the person responsible.

9. Don't show pain when you get bad news.
If employees see that bad news causes you anguish and they respect you, they'll want to protect you from suffering. (19)

10. Thank people for bad news.
And well you should. Before you learned about the problem, it was out there cutting down on your effectiveness and you were helpless to solve it. Only after you learn about it can you defeat it.

11. Make sure employees know the importance of their jobs.
If employees have a narrow view of their jobs, they may not realize the importance of advising others about changes in it—both positive and negative. Show people how their successes and failures are connected to yours.

12. Don't get annoyed when people overinform you.

Some bosses get nasty when employees tell them something they already know. They practically attack employees who overinform them ("I *know* that!"). If you worked for such a boss, wouldn't you tell that boss news selectively and hesitantly?

13. Don't get annoyed when people ask you questions.

Some bosses get impatient with employees who ask questions— especially when the bosses think they should already know the answers. Once burned by such intolerance, employees become less open.

40 Fourteen Ways to Get Great Ideas from Employees

In some companies employees send a flood of ideas to upper management. These ideas enable work to be done less expensively, more efficiently, and more profitably. In other companies the bottoms of suggestion boxes are coated with dust. What's the difference? It's not in the quality of the employees, but in the quality of the leadership they receive. Some managers know how to encourage employees to share their ideas.

1. Share your vision with employees.

Employee ideas increase in value when they're on the same wavelength as you. They're empowered to help you when they know the dream you hope to realize. You have a vision for your organization; you can see tomorrow today. Let them in on that tomorrow so they can help you get there. (23, 73, 74)

2. Ask them for ideas.

It may seem silly, but one of the biggest reasons employees don't pass their ideas up the line is that no one asks them to. Beg your people for recommendations if you have to. Make your desire for employee suggestions well known in your written and your spoken pronouncements. Don't let up. After a while they'll believe you.

3. Don't be so quick with your opinions.

One of the reasons you got to the top is your keen mind. You're quick to understand relationships, to figure out causes, and to discover opportunities. Stifle that adroitness a bit when you're brainstorming with employees. The ones who aren't as snappy as you with their ideas may be intimidated into silence.

4. Install an employee suggestion system.

An employee suggestion system can take many forms. Successful ones tend to have these characteristics in common:

- wide publicity
- top management support
- easy submission process
- no danger of retribution
- immediate feedback to employees on all suggestions received
- swift action on valuable ideas
- both recognition and tangible rewards given to those whose ideas are used

5. Hold "better-faster-different" meetings.

Executives who are serious about cultivating creative thinking in their company provide a means for it to happen. One such mechanism is the "better-faster-different" meeting. As the name suggests, employees are asked to recommend ways to perform work better to improve quality, faster to save money and please customers, and differently to distinguish the company from the competition.

6. Hold "save money, make money" meetings.

This meeting is simple to run, and its outcomes can be very powerful. Convene a group of about a dozen employees with two flip charts in the front of the room—one of them headed "make money," the other headed "save money"—and turn employees loose.

7. Thank them.

Take time personally to thank employees who made the effort, and may have taken a risk, to suggest an improvement. Do this even before you say what you plan to do with their ideas.

8. Get back to them quickly.

Employees should never have to say, "I wonder what they ever did with that idea I submitted six months ago." Convene a group to help you evaluate and decide what to do about each employee suggestion. Respond quickly, even if to tell the submitter that you need a little extra time to decide what to do.

9. Reward employees.

Recognize and tangibly celebrate the good ideas you get. Consider starting a reward program that shares a stated percentage of expenses saved or profit generated. (50)

10. Reject ideas gently and tactfully.

Top Japanese companies have reported one of the highest acceptance rates of employee suggestions in the world—as much as 75%. Even if your rate was that high—and it's probably closer to 25%—you'd have a significant number of unusable ideas on your desk. Take care how you reject them so as not to embarrass or condemn those who submitted them. Say something like this: "Thank you for your idea on——; the only thing that keeps us from using it is——. If you can think of a way to get around this constraint, please take another crack at it."

11. Move employees closer to the customer.

The people who are in most direct contact with customers often come up with the most good ideas for serving them better and cheaper. Keep all your employees as close to the customer as possible to take advantage of this tendency. For those employees who rarely encounter customers this means making sure they know exactly how their work ultimately benefits the customer and perhaps even giving them occasional opportunities to meet customers face to face. (96)

12. Invite them to cross disciplinary lines.

The best innovators in any field often prove to be those who aren't absorbed in that field on a daily basis. Enable employees to spend some time working in areas peripheral to theirs; listen to their ideas on how those areas can be improved.

13. Delegate more responsibility.

Delegate meaningful new jobs to employees who show the inclination to make suggestions. The more meaningful work that people do, the more significant their good ideas will be. And when work is new to employees, they're more likely to have fresh thoughts about it. (46)

14. Give your employees confident and secure leaders.

Many employees withhold good ideas when they discover that their immediate supervisor is threatened by them. Do three things to boost the confidence of managers beneath you:

- see that they continually update their knowledge in the field;
- expose them to solid leadership training;
- maintain an ongoing and positive coaching relationship with them. (44)

41 Twelve Quotes Worth Quoting About Getting the Word

1. Instead of listening to what is being said to them, many managers are already listening to what they are going to say. —*Anonymous*

2. I keep six honest serving men
   They taught me all I knew:
   Their names are What and Why and When
   And How and Where and Who. —*Rudyard Kipling*

3. You don't hear things that are bad about your company unless you ask. It is easy to hear good tidings, but you have to scratch to get the bad news. —*Thomas J. Watson, Jr.*

4. There is no quicker way for two executives to get out of touch with each other than to retire to the seclusion of their offices and write each other notes. —*R. Alec Mackensie*

5. Most of the successful people I've known are ones who do more listening than talking . . . You don't have to blow out the other fellow's light to let your own shine. —*Bernard M. Baruch*

6. The one that listens is the one that understands. —*Jabo proverb*

7. It is all right to hold a conversation, but you should let go of it now and then. —*Richard Armour*

8. The best way to persuade people is with your ears—by listening to them. —*Dean Rusk*

9. It is the disease of not listening, the malady of not marking, that I am troubled withal. —*William Shakespeare*

10. A closed mouth gathers no feet. —*Anonymous*

11. Learn to receive blows, and forgive those who insult you. —*Mishna, The Fathers According to R. Nathan*

12. The key to success is to get out into the store and listen to what the associates have to say. It's terribly important for everyone to get involved. Our best ideas come from clerks and stockboys. —*Sam Walton*

4
LEAD YOUR TEAM

Employees look to people in charge not just for ideas, but for leadership. The lists of this chapter show you how to become a source of inspiration to your employees. Follow this chapter's advice and you'll embody the kind of leadership excellence that excites people to rally 'round the corporate flag.

42 Sixteen Phrases of Great Leadership

Someone once said we are what we speak. If this is true, it follows that one way to become a great leader is to start using the words of great leaders. Each sentence in this list indicates leadership behavior that inspires followers to feel ownership of the goals you want them to achieve.

1. "Here's one way to do it."
Take your teaching responsibility seriously. Share your knowledge and experience with your people, but don't force them to do it your way.

2. "That looks great!"
When employees meet your expectations, thank them.

3. "That job will have to be redone."
When employees fail to meet your expectations, identify the failed deed without condemning its doer.

4. "What'll it take to keep this from happening again?"
When something has gone wrong, this is an assertive way to get commitment to doing it right the next time. It's often better to let employees tell you how they plan to fix things than to give them your solution. Their remedies may make more sense, they'll be more committed to them, and they'll learn how to solve problems when you're not around.

5. "We'll get 'em next time."

Show your employees how to cope with failure. Represent failure to them in two ways: as a learning experience that strengthens them for the future and as an increase in their resolve to win. Encourage them to take calculated risks and to make well-intentioned mistakes.

6. "What do you need from me?"

Find out what their expectations are for your leadership. Learn what you can do to serve them better and thereby empower them to meet your expectations.

7. "How am I doing?"

Get feedback on your leadership performance. In case employees are reluctant to be honest, ask the question this way: "What's *one* thing I could have done on that project that would have made your efforts even more successful?"

8. "Watch me."

Lead by example. Most people are eager to follow a positive role model. All people are disheartened by a negative one.

9. "I'd like to ask you to help me on this."

When people are happy with your leadership and you have to ask them to do something especially difficult, or even distasteful, asking it as a personal favor may get the best results.

10. "What's *your* idea?"

Employees are the best resource you have to discover ways to do things quicker, cheaper, and better. And when you use their ideas, the resulting rise in their self-esteem spurs them on to search for even more ways to help. (40)

11. "Tell me about yourself."

Whenever you take on a new leadership assignment, enter with your ears turned on. Interview each of your new associates. Find out everything you can about their backgrounds, desires, fears, ideas, ambitions, suggestions, prejudices, opinions, attitudes, concerns, dreams, needs, and abilities. Only once you've met people in this way can you create a vision that will excite them.

12. "I was wrong."

Most managers incorrectly assume that to admit error or to apologize for their actions will be taken by employees as a sign of weakness. Quite the opposite is true. People respect leaders who are big enough to acknowledge their mistakes and even their wrongdoing.

13. "Look at the silly thing I just did!"

Bring humor to the workplace. Make fun of yourself on occasion; lighten up; smile a lot; laugh at adversity, even as you are a model of seriousness of purpose. (3)

14. "It's exciting to excel and it's misery to be mediocre."

Make it clear that you expect the finest possible performance from each of your employees while doing your best to make work fun. Give your employees every opportunity to find joy in their jobs.

15. "We're in this together."

Successful leaders convince subordinates that the interests of subordinates and their own are the same. But it's not enough just to say this. Back up this statement with your actions if you want to earn respect as a teammate.

16. "Let's be the best company [team] in this industry [company]."

Set high goals for your people and show your optimism that they can attain them. Consider the potentially motivating force in placing groups of people—but perhaps not individuals—in competition with each other.

---

43 Thirty-Six Great Expectations to Have of Subordinate Managers

Stating your expectations to subordinate managers has three direct benefits. The communication empowers subordinate managers to succeed. You create a solid foundation on which to build performance evaluations. And you develop criteria to use when you hire new managers. Here's a sample set of expectations you might have for subordinate managers.

SUPPORT YOUR SUBORDINATES IN THESE WAYS:

1. State your performance expectations clearly and in writing.

2. Teach them.

Pass on to them your accumulated knowledge and experience. Show them how to solve problems rather than giving them solutions.

The majority of American managers and first-line supervisors operate in the dark. They work for "puzzles" who appear to want one thing one day and something completely different the next. Are *you* that inconsistent? Probably not. Your expectations of subordinate managers don't change that much from day to day. The problem occurs when managers never know how you expect them to behave in various situations. Sometimes they guess right, and sometimes they guess wrong. Why not end the guesswork? Tell them exactly how you expect them to support subordinates, peers, and you, and how you expect them to add value to customers, the organization, and to themselves.

3. Thank them for their efforts and praise them when they excel.

4. Criticize their performance constructively when it falls short.

5. Spend thirty minutes a day in MBWA (Managing By Wandering Around).

6. Continually ask them for ideas on doing the work better, faster, and differently.

7. Take time to listen to them.

8. Delegate increasingly more challenging responsibilities to them.

9. Develop them. See that they are properly trained. Encourage them to improve themselves. Enhance your subordinates' ability to take over in your absence.

10. Stand behind them; support their well-intentioned efforts.

11. Get feedback from them on how well you're serving them as their leader.

12. Hold them strictly accountable for their performance.

13. Accept the responsibility for their performance and the outcomes of their efforts.

SUPPORT YOUR PEERS IN THESE WAYS:

14. Cooperate with them; serve them; look for ways to make them a success.

15. Resolve your disagreements with them quickly, directly, and tactfully.

16. Find out what they need from you; be a reliable source of it.

17. Be a team player.

SUPPORT ME IN THESE WAYS:

18. Keep me informed on your progress.
See that all the news I hear about your area, good and bad, comes from you.

19. Solve most problems before they get to my desk.

20. Don't come to me for unnecessary guidance.
Instead of merely offering me alternatives, tell me which one you recommend.

21. Find out what I value; make my priorities your priorities.

22. Brief me in a clear, direct, and concise manner.
Anticipate my questions and the information I'll need.

23. Tell me when you think I've made a mistake.
Correct me with tact, especially in front of others.

24. Once you state your disagreement with me on an issue but don't succeed in changing my mind, support me fully.

ADD VALUE TO YOUR CUSTOMERS IN THESE WAYS:

25. Exceed the expectations of your customers.
Treasure your customers and dazzle them.

26. When you fail to satisfy a customer need, make it right quickly, happily, and generously.

ADD VALUE TO THE ORGANIZATION IN THESE WAYS:

27. Be a self-starter.
Don't wait to be asked or to be told before acting. Volunteer for difficult and unwanted assignments.

28. Organize your work; attack your priorities systematically.

29. Find ways to save money.

30. Find ways to make money.

31. Represent this organization well in the virtue of your conduct.

32. Represent this organization well in the quality of your communication skills.

ADD VALUE TO YOURSELF IN THESE WAYS:

33. **Accept criticism in stride.**
Always be a tough self-critic.

34. **Accept praise graciously.**
Don't feign false modesty or negate praise by saying, "That's what you pay me for."

35. **Continue to grow in your field.**
Take charge of your professional development.

36. **Maintain a healthy balance between life and work.**
Don't let work destroy your home life.

---

44 Eleven Ways to Support Subordinate Managers

Your subordinate managers will thrive when you follow the leadership advice in this chapter and the next. They'll be empowered to act on their own to fulfill the corporate vision you've created. However, they'll need something more from you. Subordinate managers require your blessing, your backing, and your protection. Only when they know they can count on you to be there can they get on with the business of making you look good.

1. **Promote ceremoniously.**
A surprising number of managers are promoted to supervise employees who are never told about the promotion or about exactly what it means. Those managers then struggle to capture the legitimacy they need to succeed. Don't do this to your managers. Announce promotions, first to those directly affected and then to the entire organization. Personally introduce new managers to the employees they'll supervise.

2. **Delegate liberally.**
Don't manage too close to the vest. Give employees the information, the authority, and the decision-making power they need to carry out

their assignments. Ask your subordinate managers if they believe you've delegated enough to them. (46)

3. Get out of the way.
Once you've turned a responsibility over to a subordinate, keep your fingers out of it unless there's a problem or the subordinate asks for your help. Let people learn and grow through their mistakes.

4. Ask for their expectations and feedback.
Perhaps the best way for you to support your subordinate managers is to give them the type of day-to-day leadership they require. Find out what that leadership behavior is and find out how well you're providing it. (34)

5. Don't undermine them.
Remain available to *all* employees, but refer subordinate complaints to appropriate managers for resolution. Once you make the referral, get out of the loop. Never give employees the impression they can come to you to get around their supervisors.

6. Stand behind their actions.
When subordinate managers act in good faith, support their decisions. You may have to criticize their poor judgment on occasion, but don't do it in front of an audience unless you're planning to fire the person. When it's apparent to others that a manager has erred, and you feel a responsibility to acknowledge the error, express your confidence in that manager in the same breath.

7. Tell them how they're doing.
Give your managers day-to-day feedback on how well they're meeting your expectations. Even the highest level managers will appreciate that you take notice of their accomplishments. Never make the mistake of thinking that executives have risen above the need for praise. Conduct formal performance reviews at least twice a year. Coach them over the rough spots. (65–67)

8. Showcase them.
Make sure they get due credit throughout the organization for their contributions. Publicize their achievements. Hold them up to your boss and to the world.

9. Promote their careers.

Find opportunities for your corporate heroes to advance. Promote from within. Recommend them for new and more challenging assignments, even if it means you lose their service. The dedication this practice generates in incumbent managers will more than offset your loss when one of your rising stars ascends to a new galaxy. (62)

10. Resolve their disagreements.

Nothing is more frustrating than to have no place to turn when you can't resolve a dispute with a colleague, especially if that colleague is more powerful than you. When subordinate managers are enmeshed in conflict with each other, it's up to you to step in to resolve the issue in the best overall interests of the organization. (52)

11. Move them from "me" to "we."

Now and then you'll encounter managers so determined to succeed that they put the welfare of themselves, their team, or their department above that of the larger organization. Other managers and employees suffer, as does the organization. It's your job to squelch this kind of behavior by focusing your management team on the welfare of all.

45 | Twelve Guidelines for Managing By Wandering Around (MBWA)

The prescription for MBWA is simple. Get out of your office to visit employees where they work. As you practice this method, follow these prescriptions for maximum impact.

1. Do it to everyone.

You may remain in such close contact with your direct reports that MBWA is redundant. The real power of the technique lies in the time you spend with those in lower levels of your area of responsibility. Get around to see those who work for your direct reports and any others whose work is important to you.

2. Do it as often as you can.

MBWA sends positive messages to employees. It reveals your interest in them and in their work and it says you don't consider yourself too good to spend time with them. MBWA also enables you to stay in touch with what's going on in your organization. Put aside at least

At one time people in charge prided themselves on their open door policy. Subordinate managers, and even front-line employees, were encouraged to bring their concerns to the direct attention of top management. This policy sounded like a great idea except for one thing—it didn't work very well. Those who darkened the threshold of upper management were the most vocal and most strident employees. Others never came. The interactions it spawned were almost always negative ones. Why else would you trouble your boss or other high ranking officer? A much better policy was suggested by consultants Tom Peters and Nancy Austin. They described it as "managing by wandering around," or MBWA.

thirty minutes a week to spend with employees. Aim for once a quarter to see those you must travel long distances to visit.

3. Go by yourself.
MBWA is more meaningful when you wander alone. It encourages more honest dialogue and speaks loudly of your personal commitment to the idea.

4. Don't circumvent subordinate managers.
Some employees may take advantage of your presence to complain about their supervisor (your subordinate) or a decision that a supervisor made. Counsel them to discuss the issue fully with the supervisor. When they claim they already have, say something like, "I'm sure your supervisor had a good reason for that decision; perhaps you should ask again for an explanation." If you have cause to question the supervisor's judgment, don't indicate so to the employee, but follow up privately with the supervisor.

5. Ask questions.
MBWA is a great opportunity to observe those moments of truth when your representatives serve the all-important customer. Say something like, "So tell me, how do we handle situations where . . . ?" Take care to sound inquisitive rather than intrusive.

6. Watch and listen.
Take in everything. Listen to the words and tone of employees as they speak to you and to each other. You'll learn a lot about their

motivation and their levels of satisfaction. Watch how they handle equipment and supplies, and how they treat customers and each other. In the words of Yogi Berra, "You can observe a lot just by watching."

7. Share your dreams with them.
As Sergeant Preston of the Yukon used to say, "The view only changes for the lead dog." MBWA is a solid opportunity to make sure that when you lead the sled in a new direction the employees behind you won't trip over themselves trying to follow. Tell them about the tomorrow you see. Reveal the dreams that you want them to help you fulfill.

8. Try out their work.
Plop down in front of the computer; get behind the wheel; pick up the telephone; ring up a sale. Experience what they endure. Sample their job just enough to show your interest in it and to understand how it goes.

9. Bring good news.
Wander around armed with information about recent corporate successes. Give them the good news. Increase their confidence and brighten their outlook. So often employees are fed only gloom and doom. Neutralize pessimism with your own optimism, without being a Pollyanna.

10. Have fun.
This is a chance to lighten up, joke around, and show your softer side without being disrespectful or clowning around. Show employees that work should be fun and that you enjoy it too.

11. Catch them in the act of doing something right.
Look for victories rather than failures. When you find one, applaud it. When you run into corporate heroes, thank them on the spot, being careful not to embarrass them in front of peers or to leave out other deserving employees.

12. Don't be critical.
When you witness a performance gone wrong, don't criticize the performer. Correct on the spot anything that must be redone, but wait to speak to the wrongdoer's supervisor to bring about corrective action.

46 Thirteen Steps to Delegate Effectively

Few executives delegate the right amount; even fewer delegate too much; most don't delegate nearly enough. Why? Most people in charge know they should delegate but are reluctant to take the time to teach someone a new task. Others feel too much ownership over what they do to give any of it away. Some don't trust employees or are afraid of losing control. Yet the arguments in favor of delegating are compelling: you can reduce your burden; get rid of the busy work; feel more secure when you have to leave the office; challenge and develop your employees more thoroughly; and maybe even have some of the jobs you now do done a little better. Delegation is an investment that if spent wisely—according to the sequenced steps below—will yield endless benefits.

1. Inventory employee talents.
Assess the strengths and weaknesses of all your direct reports. What do they do well? What do they *like* to do? Where have they shined for you in the past? Create a list of desires and outstanding qualities for each person.

2. Match employee talents to your responsibilities.
Which of your current activities requires a talent or an interest of one of your direct reports? Exactly what parts of those activities might you delegate to the appropriately talented and interested employees? Can the jobs of the proposed recipients be logically extended to encompass the new responsibility?

3. Be certain you *want* to delegate a particular responsibility.
Don't give away all the fun parts of your job. Don't abdicate responsibilities that only you should fulfill.

4. Check out your tentative decision.
Get approval from your boss for major shifts in responsibilities. Coordinate your plans with peers who might be affected. Discuss them with key subordinates, including recipients of the delegation, who might have better ideas. Confer with customers on whom you'll be counting to accept the changes.

5. Anticipate repercussions.
What accommodating changes need to be made in the organization to support the transfer of responsibility? How will you avoid any potentially negative fallout and minimize risk?

6. Communicate your expectations clearly.

Describe the delegation fully and state your precise requirements for how it is to be carried out. Anticipate these questions: What exactly are you expecting? What should the completed project look like? What special features should it include? What should it exclude? (43)

7. Provide for latitude and creativity.

Allow employees some freedom and discretion in how the job is performed. Control the outcome, not the creativity for obtaining it. Expect employees to have a few additional, and perhaps even better, ideas for completing the project than you had.

8. Show benefits.

Explain the advantages of accepting this new assignment from the employee's perspective. Will it lead to wider exposure, access to higher managers, or reduction in less desirable duties? Ask for a reaction; listen to it; respond to resistance and fears with under-standing. Express your optimism and confidence in the employee's ability to succeed. Pledge your assistance. Secure a firm commitment to accept the delegation.

9. Support the delegation.

Provide the necessary resources. Train and instruct employees thor-oughly in new assignments. Coach them throughout the process. Furnish the information, time, money, authority, personal contacts, and related support that employees will need to succeed. Reassign work that may be crowded out by the new activities.

10. Remain accessible.

Act as a safety net when employees fall off the wire. Remain avail-able for counsel, advice, and wound-licking, but don't hover over them as they perform.

11. Delegate both the menial and the significant.

Develop employees' skills by trusting them with challenging assign-ments.

12. Evaluate the results.

Choose a set of mutually agreeable dates on which you will meet to formally review progress on the delegation. Do this at least monthly until the transition is complete. Make adjustments in the assignment as indicated by the evaluations. Make it clear to the employee when you schedule the dates that you're prepared to reverse the delegation if it doesn't work well.

13. Reward successful performance.
Praise both effort and accomplishments. Thank people who help you. Tangible rewards for success send a powerful message to those who might be asked to help out in the future. (48–50)

47 Ten Actions that Excite Employees

When you meet people who are thrilled about their work, do you ever wish those people worked for you? It can be arranged. Here are ten ways to make it happen.

1. Praise your employees.
Most people want to please the person they work for, but most bosses don't make the effort to say how pleased they are with great performances. Be in the minority. Commend, compliment, congratulate, and celebrate their achievements. Uplift them with your attention. (48)

2. Let them get wide recognition.
When your people excel, hold them up to the world. Help them gain a reputation as winners. Take more than your share of blame for their defeats and less than your share of the credit for their victories.

3. Give them exciting work to do.
Try to assign people to jobs they enjoy. Find out what they get the biggest kick out of doing, and let them do it.

4. Give them exciting people to work beside.
Hire interesting people who will challenge one another with exciting ideas.

5. Foster a climate of innovation.
Tell employees you want to hear their wild and crazy ideas. Create an entrepreneurial fund to bankroll creative ventures. Feed their enthusiasm by helping them to build up their ideas before becoming critical of them. (40)

6. Be excited yourself.
Show people how much you love your work. Get especially excited when they succeed. Be their wildest cheerleader and biggest fan.

7. Convince them that they make a difference.

Most people want to feel that they're making a positive contribution to a worthy pursuit. Show them the importance of their work. Help them see the tangible benefits that result from their efforts. Point out the differences they're making in the lives of others.

8. Help them grow.

Work is exciting when it helps you grow. Delegate increasingly challenging responsibilities to your employees. Let them rotate to assignments where they can learn new skills. Send them to top-quality seminars.

9. Install self-managed teams.

Self-directed work teams can be highly motivating. Employees who once waited for managers to tell them what to do turn into self-starters, stimulated by the responsibility of making their team a success. (78)

10. Let them compete.

Someone once said that competition brings out the best in products and the worst in people, but that needn't be the case. It's true that interpersonal rivalries often result when employees are pitted against each other. However, when work teams are matched in a race for supremacy, the spirit of competition can yield better results and increase the thrill of victory.

---

48 Nine Guidelines to Make Praise Motivating

Catch employees in the act of victory and praise their efforts. Such recognition is a deserved and desired reward for past accomplishments and is a powerful *motivator* for continued performance in the future. This list is a collection of ideas that will show you how to overcome common barriers to saying thanks, how to find company heroes, and how to say the right things to them.

1. Overcome your reasons for not praising enough.

Which of these explains why you may be a praise miser?

- *I expect the best.* When you hire good people and pay them well, you expect outstanding performance. But don't forget to get excited when you get it. Even your consistently top performers will be pleased to know you appreciate their efforts.

- *I'm a high achiever myself.* You got where you are because of your extraordinary competence. Do you have difficulty recognizing employee accomplishments not up to your personal standards?
- *I'm not a warm person.* When you thank someone, you reach out in a personal way to them. Some managers have a tough time with intimacy, even in this mild form.
- *I don't believe in praising people for doing their job.* Should you go out of your way to thank people for simply doing what they're paid to do? Of course! Praise is a *motivator.* Your praise can encourage an average employee to become an exceptional one.
- *I have no time to catch people in the act of doing something right.* Even the busiest of smart executives find the time to give praise because they know that in the long run it will increase productivity and make their jobs easier.
- *I'm a failure preventer, not a success insurer.* If you're a success insurer you go to work in the morning thinking, "What can I do to put my people over the top today? How can I get them excited about their jobs?" If you're a failure preventer you go to work in the morning thinking, "How can I make sure they do their work? How can I keep them out of trouble?" Failure preventers usually don't say thank you, and when they do it sounds like this: "Way to go—you didn't screw up all day!"

2. Be sincere.
Don't praise merely because this book or someone tells you to. If you don't truly believe in the value of praise, you won't have a smile on your face and a smile in your voice when you deliver it. Don't pass it out indiscriminately like candy. Praise behavior that both you and the recipient feel warrants your positive response.

3. Do it in the right place.
There's a misleading bit of advice that says, "Criticize in private, praise in public." Be careful with public praise. It might alienate other employees or embarrass the recipient. One universally safe form of public praise is when it is directed at an entire team, even in the presence of other teams, who are more likely to be spurred on than resentful.

4. Praise the deed, not the doer.

You want your employees to be pumped up—but not by you. They should be pumped up by their work. So, instead of telling employees how great *they* are, tell them how great *their work* is. You'll also have fewer "praise junkies" on your hands.

5. Don't negate your praise.

> After thanking a previously disorganized employee for adopting a comprehensive calendar/planning system, a manager ended with, "It's about time." What else can that employee conclude but that the manager will never be happy and that the employee might as well stop trying?

6. Put a name on your calendar.

Each week identify an employee whom you'll go out of the way to catch in the act of victory. Take advantage of the most likely opportunities you'll have to learn of something great that person does. Look for instances of exceptional customer service, speed, efficiency, great results, problem solving, cost savings, new business generation, creativity, initiative, and teamwork.

7. Create a "catcher" system to identify corporate heroes.

> Each month assign a different group of managers to catch employees other than their direct reports in the act of praiseworthy events. Issue small prizes they can give to recipients—something like a $2 cafeteria certificate. At the same time have them briefly write up the event, detailing what the employee did. One copy of the "summons" goes on a company bulletin board for a month, the other is dropped in a barrel. Draw names out of the barrel quarterly for attractive prizes. Possible prizes include cash, special parking privileges, escape weekends, vacation days, and tickets to cultural or sporting events—ask employees what they'll value! Appoint a group to empty the barrel each year and choose the six most noteworthy accomplishments. Honor these people at a highly publicized dinner with their supervisors, their families, and the CEO.

8. Initiate an employee-of-the-month program.
Employee of the month works best when:

- employees have a say, and even a hand, in how it's administered
- there are numerous employees to choose from—otherwise, there are too many repeat winners, and nonwinners feel stigmatized
- when the CEO plays an active role in the program, thanking the winner personally and perhaps posing for publicity photos
- families are included in the process, perhaps through a congratulatory letter sent home

Review your program each year for possible improvements in the coming year.

9. Initiate a team-of-the-month program.
Your company will be one of the very few that elevates work teams in this way.

49 Thirteen Ways to Make Sure Your Incentives "Incent"

Every time a dolphin at Sea World performs a trick, its trainer gives it a reward. If only rewarding human behavior were that simple. Employees are motivated to perform not only by extrinsic rewards that you can provide, but also intrinsic ones. You won't always know why a particular employee performs well or how much of what reward to give to encourage repeat performances. Many management consultants have spent careers trying to solve the incentive puzzle. If you follow some simple advice about incentives, you can save the money you might have spent for a consultant.

1. Find out what's important to your people.
Ask employees either formally via opinion surveys or informally in conversations about their favorite extrinsic incentives. How do they feel about advancement, job security, bonuses, merit pay systems, improvements in benefits, gifts, and the like? Also learn their feelings toward intrinsic rewards. What are their preferences among achievement, creativity, knowledge, independence, leadership, recognition, service, and the like?

2. Light fires *inside* them.
Assign employees to jobs and orchestrate the job environment so that they can receive the greatest number of their important intrinsic rewards as they perform the work. This is the most powerful of motivational strategies. Unfortunately you may not always have the option or the flexibility to enrich jobs in this way.

3. Make sure your salaries are competitive.
Money can be the most powerful *demotivator* in the workplace. It's the first thing people complain about when they don't feel they're getting a fair return for their labors. Low pay becomes particularly alienating when employees are being asked to make personal sacrifices to keep the company in the black. Ensure that your salaries are comparable with similar companies in your region.

4. Never tell someone making less than you that money isn't important.
Don't try to motivate poorly paid employees by downplaying the importance of money, especially if you make several times more. This is the worst sort of condescension.

WHENEVER YOU DESIGN A PAY-FOR-PERFORMANCE SYSTEM:

5. Be certain money is important to those you hope to motivate.
Earning more of it must be a goal. While this is true of most employees, some are satisfied with what they make. They aren't likely to be turned on by a chance to make more.

6. Be certain you have a fair measure of performance.
Sales, piecework, and athletic accomplishments can be quantified, but not everyone's output can be gauged as reliably. How do you objectively compare the effectiveness of two managers? Is the relative success of their subordinates a valid yardstick, and how do you assess that success?

7. Don't use a performance measure that sacrifices the long term.
When you *can* quantify performance, be careful that employees don't become so consumed with making the measure look good that long-term value suffers. For example, a night crew paid according to how much product goes out the back door might turn out gobs of product at the cost of equipment abuse, product quality, or customer service. Commissions and bonuses should be carefully designed so

that the long-term interests of the customer and the company are served, and not just the pockets of employees.

8. Don't tie the hands of your managers.

Supervisors must have the freedom to vary the compensation of employees according to the quality of their performance. Don't make it difficult for them to use the system. Don't let it get bogged down in office politics.

9. Add feedback to merit pay.

Pay for performance works only when employees realize that compensation increases in *direct* response to their effort. They must be convinced that they got a raise because of their hard work and know what that hard work was. Then they'll be encouraged to repeat the effort in order to repeat the reward. Give them daily feedback. Record their worthy performances in writing and document them on formal performance review forms. When you're generous, tell them why.

10. Put performance under the employee's control.

Employees won't be encouraged to work towards performance goals if achieving those goals depends on factors beyond their control. You'll only frustrate people if you dangle carrots in front of them that are kept out of range by unpredictable or unmanageable circumstances.

11. Be generous with merit pay increases.

Reward your thoroughbreds in a fashion that will sustain their motivation and keep them in your stable.

Assume you budget an amount equal to 7% of your payroll for year-end pay raises. Your guidance to subordinate managers is to give 5% across the board to counter the effects of inflation, with the remaining 2% divided among meritorious employees at the managers' discretion. Two $36,000 employees who work side by side are widely known to be the least and the most contributing members of the organization. Under your system the shirker's 6% adds up to a new monthly paycheck of $3,150. The star performer rewarded with 10%—the highest raise given out in the company—now earns $3,300. The comparative size of the two new salaries is not likely to look fair to the star performer following a year of contributing so much more than the shirker.

12. Don't forget teams.
Most pay-for-performance plans recognize the accomplishments of individuals only. Reward teams. Every hero on your payroll has a behind-the-scenes staff supporting his or her performance. Rewarding the hero and ignoring the support staff fails to encourage team spirit and team excellence.

13. Don't expect miracles.
Pay for performance can only go so far, for reasons like these:

- Some employees resist differential pay, believing that raises should be uniform, according to seniority or some other egalitarian standard.
- Some employees don't trust managers to be fair.
- Some employees aren't capable of more or better work.
- The equipment employees rely on may not support significantly increased levels of output.
- Even the most lucrative of financial incentives may not entice alienated workers to put forth more effort.

A hundred and one other reasons may prevent money from spurring on higher levels of performance. Find out what barriers may exist in your organization before offering such incentives.

50 | Seventeen Inexpensive Ways to Reward Employees

If the rallying cry for business in the 1990s was "do more with less," then the rallying cry for the first decade of the 21st century will be "do even more with even less." As competition increases, managers work with tighter budgets, shorter deadlines, and smaller staffs. Yet managers will still be required to achieve ever challenging goals in order to not only survive but thrive. Motivating employees under these competitive and stressful conditions will test your talent and skill. Part of passing this test will be to give employees attractive rewards that won't cost much.

1. A simple sincere thank you.
We all want to feel needed and appreciated. Gratitude endures long after checks are cashed.

2. A handwritten note expressing thanks for a job well done.
Don't wait for the scheduled performance appraisal to put in writing
your feelings about what an employee has done well. You can also
do this through e-mail, but the personal touch of the handwritten
note makes the sentiment all the more appreciated.

3. Showing off a complimentary letter from a customer.
When a customer writes a letter complimenting a product or service
give it to the employees directly responsible. Share the good news
with those who made it happen. Place a copy of the letter in their
personnel files.

4. Springing for breakfast or lunch.
Don't wait for the annual picnic or holiday bash to buy a meal for
your people. Walk into someone's office and say something like,
"For that great job you did on the Miller account, I'd like to take you
to lunch. When are you available?"

**5. Periodically rotating a company perk among deserving em-
ployees.**
A choice spot in the company parking lot, free coffee or soft drinks
for a month, or similar perks are welcome rewards.

6. A plaque commemorating an employee's contributions.
Following an important accomplishment many people appreciate
receiving a tangible reminder to show to family, friends, and visitors. Employee-of-the-month plaques prominently displayed for
customers, suppliers, and coworkers are powerful incentives. If you
can't see your name in lights, seeing it on a wall is the next best
thing. A plaque will rekindle pride years after a bonus has been
spent.

7. A smiling face.
When you walk around the office with a smile on your face, employees will assume that they had something to do with it. Smiles
also tend to be contagious.

8. Asking about the health and well-being of an employee's family.
Someone once said that people don't care how much you know until
they know how much you care. A boss who cares enough to find out
about family is a boss who cares. A boss who remembers what an

employee said a few days later is the boss for whom employees will put forth extra effort. (122)

9. Showing concern about the health of employees.
When any of your employees is seriously ill, send flowers, go to the hospital, or call the caregiver at home to offer your support. Word of your concern will spread throughout the office.

10. Empathizing with the frustration an employee experiences in a new job.
When you learn that an employee is having a tough time with a new project, offer your help if appropriate or at least say something like this: "I know that this assignment is a real challenge. I don't expect it to be easy for you. I want you to know that I really appreciate your willingness to take it on."

11. Soliciting an employee's advice for solving a problem.
We all need to feel that we're contributing. You "double dip" when you solicit an employee's advice. You make the employee feel important and you may end up with a solution that never occurred to you.

12. Taking a member of the support staff on a sales call.
People in support roles may spend their entire careers without meeting those people who ultimately pay their salaries—customers. What this trip will cost is puny compared to the motivation it will purchase.

13. A surprise pizza bash.
One day announce that you're ordering lunch to be brought in the next day. It's a great way to thank a large group for their efforts and to spend a little time with them.

14. Discounted merchandise or services from suppliers.
Suppliers may be more than happy to provide discounted merchandise or services to your employees in order to keep your business.

15. A party following the successful completion of an especially difficult project.
Celebrate with your employees after they've gone the extra mile. Have fun, sing songs, and personally thank them for making the project a success. Memories of these happy times will help employees get through workdays that aren't parties.

16. Inexpensive but thoughtful gifts for important contributions to the team.
A coffee mug, box of chocolates, helium balloon, or plant are inexpensive. Every time the employee drinks from the cup, eats a piece of chocolate, smiles at the balloon, or waters the plant, he or she will remember your thoughtful gesture.

17. Public recognition in front of peers.
The sound of praise is always sweet. It's even sweeter when your peers look on approvingly as you hear it. Just take care when you praise publicly that no deserving recipients are being left out, that employee jealousies won't be fired up by the ceremony, and that you don't embarrass the recipient.

51 Sixteen Tips for Constructive Criticism

Ask a group of employees what they think of the feedback they receive from their bosses and the response is likely to be, "What feedback?" The biggest complaint most people have is not that they're criticized too much or too harshly, but that they don't hear anything at all. Why are so few leaders willing to confront subordinates for shoddy performance? Two answers to this question are that few people want to encounter the anger that criticism often generates, and that many people realize they do a poor job of correcting others. This list will help you on both counts. You'll gain confidence in your ability to criticize effectively and you'll minimize the recipient's defensiveness.

1. Don't expect to eliminate defensiveness entirely.
Indeed, *expect* the first reaction to criticism to be negative. Look instead to the second response. If you apply the suggestions on this list, the knee-jerk defensiveness to your words will cool down to compliance.

2. Get the facts straight.
Benjamin Disraeli once said it's much easier to be critical than to be correct. Make sure you're correct. Check and double-check. Never make the mistake of criticizing an undeserving employee. You'll lose points with all employees and you'll forfeit the whole ball game with the innocent victim. In the same way, don't let even one person escape correction while others are held accountable.

3. Examine your heart.

How do you feel about this situation? Are you angry? Do you feel betrayed? Are you out to get even? If you answer yes to any of these questions, you're almost certain to come across as punitive. Calm down and rethink your approach before proceeding. When your goal is instead to improve performance or head off a destructive situation, your criticism has a greater chance of being accepted.

4. Choose the best timing.

There are three basic choices of when to deliver criticism:

- Right away. The action will still be fresh in the employee's mind, but you risk shooting from the hip, rather than considering the long-term impact of your words.
- Sometime later. You get the chance to calm down, but you may calm down so much that you'll decide to say nothing or will downplay the importance of what happened.
- Just before the next opportunity the employee has to screw up again. This enables you to turn the criticism into a teaching opportunity (e.g., "During the question and answer period of your presentation this afternoon, I suggest you repeat each question so everyone hears it. I'm not sure that was the case last month."). The problem with waiting so long, in addition to missing the earlier chances, is that in the interval the employee may have encountered another situation where your feedback would have been helpful.

5. Choose the best place.

You'll never make a more serious mistake as a leader than criticizing someone in front of others, especially when those others are peers. Play it safe; do it in private offices with closed doors.

6. Disagree tactfully in public.

When you must register dissent with someone in public, do it according to one of the following models for lead-off sentences.

- "I'm not sure I agree with that."
- "My experience says just the opposite."
- "I can see how your perspective on the problem would lead you to that conclusion."
- "If we did it that way, how would we deal with . . . ?"

7. Condemn the deed, not the doer.

Hate the sin, not the sinner. Reject the performance, not the performer. Describe what happened, not what the person did. You may have success in attacking others' behavior; you won't get away with attacking them.

8. Use "you" sparingly.

If *you* or *your* is the first word out of your mouth, the criticism will automatically malign the person rather than the act. ("Your sales were off in February.") If possible, don't use *you* at all. Before you reprimand the next time, practice it first without *you*. As an alternative the pronoun *I* or even *we* can get your first sentence off to a good start. ("I see that February was a poor month for sales. What happened?")

9. Say what you see.

When possible the first words out of your mouth should describe what you saw, heard, or know happened. If a limousine driver failed to pick up someone at the airport, don't say, "You didn't show up at the airport." Instead say, "Ms. Gonzales wasn't met at her arrival gate."

10. Say what's wrong with the performance.

Sometimes the employee won't understand why the behavior you're attacking is a problem. For example, if you just witnessed a new employee delivering nonresponsive customer service, you may need to add a statement of impact to the criticism. ("That customer didn't hear an answer to her question about the warranty. When that happens, customers are less likely to buy from us.")

11. Defuse with humor and creativity.

Sometimes, because of who the employee is or because of the nature of the infraction, the situation calls for either more heavy-handed criticism or a gentler approach than you'd achieve with the advice above. To be more heavy handed, simply violate many of the suggestions on this list! The lighter touch requires a bit more creativity. Here are three options:

- Use humor, while taking care not to trivialize performance or appear sarcastic. "I just took an ear beating from Ms. Gonzales because she had to catch a taxi from the airport. Before she mauls me in person, what can I tell her?"

- One idea that works great for normally reliable employees goes something like this: "It's not like you to miss an airport pickup."
- You can also deliver "conditional" criticism. "If your punctuality in picking people up were as good as your driving, there wouldn't be a better limo driver in the state."

12. Ask questions.
Somewhere early in your criticism give the employee the chance to explain anything you don't know about the situation. The more upset you are, the earlier you should ask the question. Sometimes the employee reveals an extenuating circumstance that stops you before you put your foot in your mouth. For example, how would you feel about chewing out the delinquent limousine driver in item #9 after learning she had stopped at the scene of an accident to pull an infant out of a burning car?

13. Get a commitment to corrective action.
Tell the employee what you think it will take to improve performance. Better yet, get the employee to suggest a remedy by asking, "What's it going to take to keep this from happening again?" (For certain employees you want to soften this to, "What can I do to help you avoid that result in the future?") When you hear something you like, get the employee's commitment to it. Insist upon hearing, "Yes, I will." Saying, "I'll try," "Maybe I could," or "I'll do my best" is not a commitment.

14. Give a positive stroke at the end.
The often-heard recommendation of saying something nice just before you criticize can be manipulative. Certainly, if you feel positive about other things the employee is doing, say so. The danger in saying something nice *before* you deliver the bad news to soften the blow of criticism is that the recipient will feel set up by you. ("You're a great limousine driver, *but* . . .") A positive stroke *following* the criticism and a commitment to corrective action may be better timed. Describe how you value, appreciate, or admire the person. Praise some particularly outstanding feature of his or her performance. ("I'm glad you're willing to cooperate with this. I hear nothing but praise for your driving.") Take care, however, not to negate or downplay the criticism.

15. Don't change the subject.

When you've achieved your goals with criticism, ask for any questions or suggestions and then leave. Give your words a chance to sink in. If you change the subject to something more pleasant or to an ongoing project, the impact of the encounter will be diminished.

16. Follow up.

Look for an opportunity to praise the employee doing it right the next time. If the problem persists, recycle the employee through this list with more urgency and seriousness.

52 Eleven Steps for Refereeing Disagreements

Somewhere in the description of your responsibilities should be a reminder to play the role of Solomon. People in charge sometimes inherit controversies that subordinate managers can't resolve. When they take the form of disputes between two individuals, how do you respond? Follow as many of the steps below as you can apply to the situation.

TO KEEP CONFLICT FROM ERUPTING IN THE FIRST PLACE:

1. Establish a strategic plan.

A strategic plan for a team or an organization is a clearly understood and universally accepted set of goals and actions that provide a common direction. Without a unifying strategic plan your managers will take different and often conflicting paths. (74)

2. Establish unequivocal office policies.

Be clear and specific on your requirements regarding lines of reporting, areas of responsibility, job titles, delegation of authority, privileges, performance standards, treatment of subordinates, treatment of customers, treatment of peers, ethics and honesty, collaboration and cooperation, deadlines, and other issues having the potential to cause friction.

ONCE CONFLICT ERUPTS BETWEEN TWO SUBORDINATES:

3. Speak separately to combatants.

Before you handle disagreements in your office, spend some private time with each person. Understand the quarrel from each person's perspective. Reserve the right to bring anything discussed to light at a later point if and when you decide that's best. Accepting information in confidence might compromise your ability to facilitate the disagreement.

4. Bring them together.
When you invite conflicting parties to your office, set the ground rules that conversation will be controlled, civil, and nonaccusatory. State that you have no desire to find fault—only to bring about a resolution that will satisfy the three of you.

5. Remain neutral.
Don't take sides. The antagonists need to have confidence in you and trust that you will remain impartial. Be a facilitator, not a judge.

6. Get the facts out.
Let one person speak first without interruption. Have the second one paraphrase, to the first person's satisfaction, what was said. Next, hear the second person's side of the story in the same way. Continue until the parties either discover that the argument stems from a communication breakdown or agree what the conflict is all about. If you don't feel comfortable insisting that they play the paraphrasing game, you can serve as the paraphraser before each person is permitted to respond to what the other person just said.

7. Keep the spotlight on a solution.
Move them past rehashing the past and placing blame. Get them to focus on fixing the future—all that really matters—by insisting that no one bring up anything that happened more than a half hour ago.

8. Keep the spotlight on needs, not positions.
Ask each person to describe the needs they wish to have met, rather than taking up a hardened position vis-à-vis each other.

9. Choose a solution.
Ask them for a resolution the three of you can live with. The best outcome will be one that meets both of their needs—plus yours—as much as possible. If you like what they come up with, declare the deadlock broken. If they can't come to an agreement, impose or negotiate a settlement of your own.

10. Thank them.
Express your appreciation for their problem-solving attitude. Provide face saving if one of the antagonists might be perceived as the loser. Show that person how important his or her cooperation is to you.

11. Follow up.
Monitor success of the resolution. Check progress at another meeting in two weeks and again two weeks later. React as necessary.

53 | Eleven Ways to Inspire Ethical Conduct

Being in charge today requires meeting challenges that yesterday's executives never had to confront. Years ago, issues of ethical behavior and corporate social responsibility were moot. Organizations were managed solely for the economic well-being of stockholders. Questions of morality and ethical conduct were reserved for Sunday sermons, not Monday board meetings. Today your employees, customers, stockholders, community, and government expect you not only to run a profitable business but to also be a good citizen. They expect you to create a corporate culture based on a morally upright ethical stance.

1. Always provide value to the customer.
Delivering what you promise makes sense both economically and ethically. Economically, the marketplace rewards companies that fulfill customer needs at a fair price. Ethically, delivering what you promise communicates a message to your employees and customers that you take pride in workmanship, honesty, and dependability. (90)

2. Inspire ethical behavior by incurring costs.
Exhorting others to be ethical is a less powerful message than showing them your willingness to pay a price for ethics. Whenever you lose money by exchanging new merchandise for damaged merchandise, spend time making a personal call to a dissatisfied customer, or terminate business with a supplier suspected of unethical behavior, you walk the talk. (53)

3. Keep an open door.
Remain accessible to your employees. They know when rules are broken and who's breaking them. Communicate through word and deed that you want to be the first person to find out about corrupt behavior.

4. Make heroes out of those who serve as the corporate conscience.
Employees who detect unethical or illegal behavior shouldn't have to wrestle with their consciences, contact a lawyer, or be ostracized.

They should find a receptive audience in your office followed by a sincere and heartfelt "Thank you for bringing this to my attention." Once an employee takes the risk of revealing infractions to you, investigate them quickly while affording every possible protection to the whistle blower.

5. Require your suppliers to be upstanding corporate citizens.
It's difficult to maintain the moral high ground if you do business in the gutter. (82)

6. Develop a formal code of ethics.
If you believe that ethics are important, make them a part of your corporate culture. Demand that this code serve as the corporate commandments guiding the behavior of all employees. (110)

7. Punish any and all violators of the code.
If you wink at the code or give the impression that the plaque on which it's carved is little more than public relations for visitors, you've wasted your time writing it.

8. Conduct training programs on corporate ethics and resolving ethical dilemmas.
Most employees won't have to be sold on the importance of ethics. But they will have questions about what to do when they encounter an ethical challenge. Coach them in the tactics they should use for resolving dilemmas. (64)

9. Incorporate discussions of ethics into all recruitment and selection activities.
Don't hire dishonest people and expect to teach them honesty. Stress your unyielding expectations for upright behavior before applicants sign on. (61)

10. Design incentive systems that promote organizational growth and customer satisfaction along with personal benefit.
Rewards can profoundly distort even the best code of ethics. Examine your commission and bonus systems to remove any encouragements they may contain to commit unethical acts. (49)

11. Make sure pressures on the job don't get out of hand.
You're paid to run a tight ship and to expect excellence. Unfortunately, a high-pressure work environment sometimes pushes

employees to the point where they rationalize unprincipled actions. When your people are stressed out, take care that they're not being encouraged to cut ethical corners.

54 Twenty-Four Ways to "Walk Your Talk"

Someone once said that people don't listen to you speak—they watch your feet. In other words, one of the most powerful leadership tools at your disposal is your behavior. While employees may not always believe what you say, they'll believe what you do. And what they see you doing often ends up being what they do. What do your employees see in your behavior? How many of these positive and influential actions are a part of your leadership repertoire?

1. Honesty.
Is your word your bond? Can employees trust that as soon as you know something important for them they'll hear it from you? Has your behavior made it clear that you won't mislead them or feed them half truths?

2. Self-confidence.
Do your people see a self-assured leader or do they see you second-guessing yourself? Are you willing to take risks, or do you constantly play it safe?

3. Sacrifice.
Whenever employees are asked to incur some loss or give up a prized benefit, do you lead the way by taking at least as heavy a hit? Are you willing to give up something to them in order to get something in return?

4. Thoughtfulness.
Are you compassionate with employees in difficulty? Do you treat people with kindness? Do you help others retain their dignity and self-respect?

5. Consideration.
Are you as concerned for the needs of others as you are for your own? Are you considerate of other people's time or does your schedule always come first?

6. Accountability.
Are you willing to pay the price for your mistakes? Are you as concerned about good results as you expect your employees to be?

7. Dedication.
Do *you* have the whatever-it-takes attitude you preach to others?

8. Loyalty.
Is the welfare of your employees at the top of your list? Do you earn their loyalty by giving them yours?

9. Selflessness.
Are you less concerned about your fame and fortune than you are about the reputation and bottom line of your company? Do you share the spotlight with your direct reports, pushing them out in front when the cameras whir?

10. Punctuality.
Do you work long hours? Do you get to meetings on time? Do you meet performance deadlines? Do you get back to employees at least as quickly as you promise?

11. Enthusiasm.
Are you upbeat, optimistic, and energetic? Do you maintain a positive attitude even in the worst of times?

12. Resilience.
Do you bounce back quickly from defeat? Do you see failure as a learning experience? Do you routinely look for opportunity in adversity?

13. Reliability.
Can you be counted on to fulfill your promises and your obligations? Are you there when people need you? Do you stick with a task (and with people) from beginning to end?

14. Creativity.
Are you constantly looking for a better way? Are you recognized as an innovator in your field?

15. Maturity.
Do you behave professionally? Do you communicate a seriousness of purpose? Is your deportment admired?

16. Humor.

Do you crack people up, but not at the expense of others? Can you laugh at yourself? Can you help others see the lighter side of the most dire situations?

17. Adaptability.

Do you like to try new things? Are you open to change? Are you willing to revise your decisions when someone points out something you hadn't thought of?

18. Teamwork.

Do you entrust your team with responsibility and stay out of their way? Are you a good team player on the teams of which you are a member?

19. Knowledge.

Have you stayed up-to-date on the latest knowledge in your field? Do you make it easy for employees to go to seminars and otherwise advance their education? Do you go to seminars? Do you read? Do you listen to tapes? Have you used a personal coach? (35)

20. Decisiveness.

Are you able to make decisions once you get enough information to make a good one, rather than delay decisions until you have "perfect" knowledge? Do you make a point not to be unduly swayed by the last person you spoke to? (1)

21. Openness to criticism.

Do you ask employees to tell you when they think you're off the mark? Do you respond positively when they tell you?

22. Organization skills.

Do you manage your time well? Do you organize your work so that you are working on the highest priority item at any given moment? (8)

23. Long-term thinker.

Do you ask employees for ideas that have long-term payback? Do you anticipate the future impact of the decisions you make and the actions you take?

24. Appearance.

Do you take care of yourself physically, groom yourself carefully, and dress yourself meticulously? (4, 5)

55 Twelve Quotes Worth Quoting About Leadership

1. Leadership is liberating people to do what is required of them in the most effective and the most human way possible. —*Max DePree*

2. We have too many high sounding words, and too few actions that correspond with them. —*Abigail Adams*

3. Of the best leaders, when their task is accomplished, their work done, the people all remark, "We have done it ourselves." —*Lao-Tzu*

4. A good leader takes a little more than his share of the blame, a little less than his share of the credit. —*Arnold Glasow*

5. The final test of a leader is that he leaves behind him in other men the conviction and the will to carry on. —*Walter Lippmann*

6. There are no bad soldiers, only bad officers. —*Napoleon*

7. Some citizens are so good that nothing a leader can do will make them better. Others are so incorrigible that nothing can be done to improve them. But the great bulk of the people go with the moral tide of the moment. The leader must help create that tide. —*19th-century Japanese philosopher*

8. The horse never knows I'm there until he needs me. —*Willie Shoemaker*

9. Twixt kings and tyrants there's this difference known:
Kings seek their subjects' good, tyrants their own. —*Robert Herrick*

10. The best executive is the one who has sense enough to pick good men to do what he wants done and self-restraint enough to keep from meddling with them while they do it. —*Theodore Roosevelt*

11. I consider my ability to arouse enthusiasm among the men the greatest asset I possess. The way to develop the best that is in a man is by appreciation and encouragement. —*Charles Schwab*

12. Whoever wishes to be great among you must be your servant, and whoever wishes to be first among you must be slave of all. —*Jesus Christ*

5 BUILD YOUR TEAM

Work teams have ups and downs, opportunities and constraints, and stars and shirkers. The advice in this chapter shows you how to seize the advantages present in your teams and how to overcome the handicaps that plague them. You'll emerge from reading these lists with fresh ideas for getting your entire organization to pull in the same direction.

56 Thirteen Tactics for Increasing Teamwork

One definition of *organization* is a group of people acting together to achieve a common purpose. Unfortunately, in our culture the sanctity of one is often valued over the good of many. Your employees live in a country established through the "pioneer spirit," where individual rights are cherished and where teams aren't elected into sports halls of fame. You'll want to apply as many of these tactics as possible to overcome the handicaps placed on your company by society.

1. Create a teamwork culture.
In everything you say and do be clear that employees are expected to be team players. Create a teamwork culture in your organization in one or more of these ways:

- Use the word *teamwork* liberally in your written and spoken communications.
- Rename staff meetings "team meetings."
- Substitute the word *team* for other designations for groups of employees, such as "department" and "staff."
- Hang posters and other teamwork graffiti on walls.
- Send a "welcome to the team" letter to the home of new hires.
- Show an inspirational team-oriented video at new employee orientation.

• Pair all new employees with an enthusiastic, team-oriented mentor.

2. Start at the top.

Ensure that your senior executive staff functions as a close-knit team. Get them to exchange feedback on how well they meet each other's expectations, and as a result extract commitments for what they'll do to work together more effectively. Organize a team-building retreat. Tolerate nothing less than a unified staff. (59)

3. Hire team players.

Recruit job candidates with a history of successful team play, who enjoy working with others, who thrive in a team setting, and who come to the job hoping to contribute to a collective effort. Ask prospects whether they feel their on-the-job performance should be judged more on their own individual merits or on how well they play on a team. Make them pick one and reject those who favor individual merit. (57)

4. Insist on exceptional internal customer service.

Demand that your service departments prize their internal customers as much as their external ones. Reward department heads whose units serve others exceptionally and impose consequences on the heads of departments that don't fulfill the expectations of internal customers. (93)

5. Use teams to interview and select job candidates.

There are few responsibilities of greater importance than hiring. When you trust that responsibility to a team of employees, you send an unmistakable message of your faith in them. (61)

6. Define teamwork.

Broadcast a clear set of expectations for all employees throughout the organization for the precise team-player behavior you require. Put them in writing and discuss them with each employee to make certain they are understood and embraced. Examples might be:

• Cooperate with coworkers.
• Pitch in to help them when they get behind.
• Show newer employees the ropes, and set a good example for them.

- Say "we," not "they," when describing our unit to customers.
- Tell me what customers are saying about our products and services.
- Volunteer for new and more challenging assignments.
- Participate actively and constructively in team meetings.
- Suggest ways of doing things better, faster, and differently.

7. Make employees feel like part of the team.

Increase the ownership that employees feel for the goals of your company and for the success of their team through these or other means:

- sharing your vision for teamwork with them
- profit sharing
- asking for, using, and rewarding their ideas
- placing them closer to the customer
- setting up friendly, yet spirited, competitions
- seeing that they get better leadership and coaching

8. Create teams.

Form focus groups, quality circles, task forces, and cross-functional teams to solve company-wide problems and exploit new opportunities. Endow them with clear goals and broad powers and implement their best recommendations.

9. Experiment with self-directed teams.

Form empowered work groups. Give them responsibility for achieving specific goals; make your expectations for their outcomes clear; offer incentives for success; provide them with ongoing feedback on their performance; then get out of their way. (78)

10. Serve customers through teams.

Assign groups, rather than individual employees, to assist customers and service accounts. Train them to swing into action as a team whenever a customer need is identified. (90, 92)

11. Celebrate team victories.

Recognize and reward individuals for team play. Give linemen and supportive second-stringers the same attention as the leading ground-gainers. Respond to team successes with team rewards like these:

- pizza lunches
- escape weekends
- tickets to sporting, cultural, or fun events
- paid vacation days
- gift certificates
- free dance, swim, ski, golf, or cooking lessons
- memberships or subscriptions
- maid service
- seminars of choice
- college scholarships
- ribbons, plaques, or trophies
- photographs of the team in a booklet
- golf scramble
- shares of company stock
- appreciation dinners
- dress down days (50)

12. Get tough on those who thwart the teamwork initiative.
Impose consequences on those who won't cooperate. Make an example of employees who set their own welfare above that of their team. (51)

13. Grant special dispensation.
Save a small amount of room for, and be careful not to punish, those creative mavericks who contribute best as independent operators. Isolate these Lone Rangers from others so as not to endanger the health of cohesive teams.

57 Eight Strategies for Hiring Team Players

One of surest ways to create a cohesive team is to hire one. If you make the mistake of hiring a bunch of Lone Rangers, you'll have them each riding off into the sunset on their own. Maybe you can't hire a team intact, but you can hire the type of people who work well with others.

1. Look for evidence of a stable work history.
Team play requires a measure of loyalty and stability not typically found in job jumpers.

2. Check references.

Ask past employers to score candidates from 1 (lowest) to 5 (highest) in response to one or more of these statements.

- "Looks beyond the success of his or her own area and advances the good of the overall organization."
- "Cooperates with other employees."
- "Pitches in to help fellow employees in need."
- "Gives coworkers what they need in order to succeed."
- "Shows newer employees the ropes."
- "Volunteers for new and more challenging assignments."

3. Get referrals from your best team players.

Your best employees should have a good idea of the kind of employees you need. Also, they'll feel some responsibility for helping you find good people.

4. Look for positive team experiences in their background.

Favor candidates who have done well in organizations such as sports, clubs, and Scouts, as well as corporate team settings. They succeeded in those venues by collaborating with others.

5. Ask for their evaluation preference.

Question candidates about how they feel about sinking or swimming based upon team success. Ask if they prefer being evaluated on their individual accomplishments or the triumphs of their work team. Be wary of those who balk at team evaluation.

6. Hire enthusiastic people.

Look for cheerful, smiling, courteous, optimistic, and enthusiastic people who want to serve others. They'll make great coworkers.

7. Listen for "we" and "our" vs. "they" and "their."

Which plural pronouns do applicants use when you get them to talk about their previous jobs? If they felt so detached from earlier employers to say "they" and "their," are they likely to put forth the effort to get any more connected to your organization?

8. Introduce them to the people they will work with.

When candidates hit it off with their prospective coworkers, you have a powerful endorsement. Ask the employees they meet what they like best and least about each candidate. Consider this information in your selection decision.

58 Twenty-Seven Actions that Instill Pride in Your Workforce

When people ask your employees where they work, do they announce the name of your company quickly and cheerfully? Employees who don't take pride in *where* they work often don't take pride *in* their work. Employees who don't take pride in what they do often don't do a very good job of it. What can be done to increase pride? Just about everything in this book. If your employees lack pride, ask yourself which of the items on this list, in its absence, appears to be the cause.

1. Show *your* pride.

2. Spend time managing by wandering around.
Show employees how much you care about their work. (45)

3. Create an inspiring vision for your company.
Communicate a set of governing values and beliefs that will excite people. (74)

4. Walk your talk.
Ensure that both your conduct and that of your management team are characterized by the highest levels of ethics. (54)

5. Applaud and celebrate your teams' victories. (50)

6. Give employees leaders they can look up to.

7. Give people the best equipment to work with.

8. Hire competent people for them to work with.

9. Put them in self-directed teams.
They'll take pride in what they do without close supervision. (78)

10. Set up competitions among teams.

11. Let them meet and serve customers directly.

12. Produce the best products and deliver the best service in the industry. (90–93)

13. Orient employees into a "movement," not just a job.

14. When you orient employees, welcome their families as well.

15. Sponsor family-oriented events.

16. Sponsor company sports teams.

17. Give them the best training programs in the industry. (64)

18. Show them how their work fits into the overall company goals.

19. Show them how everyone else's work fits with theirs.

20. Let them "sign" their work.

21. Maintain a respected company wellness/safety program.

22. Create an attractive, eye-catching corporate logo.

23. Decorate your buildings attractively.

24. Keep company successes in the news.

25. Encourage employees to get involved in their community. They'll feel good, and they'll represent the company well.

26. Conduct tours through your operation for dignitaries and foreign visitors.

27. Use employees as models in advertising campaigns.

59 Seven Ways to Build Your Senior Management Team

In the words of an old African proverb, "When the elephants fight, the grass suffers." Is a lack of cohesion, coordination, and collaboration at the top causing your employees to feel trampled? If so, your senior management staff—and your entire organization—may benefit from team building. Here are some proven techniques, one of which might do the trick for you.

1. Conduct a conference retreat.
Take your staff and their spouses off for three or four days in the mountains or on the beach. Let them learn together in the mornings and play together in the afternoons. Divide each morning between great seminars and business updates.

2. Perform a team assessment.
With the help of a consultant put together a survey of ten to twenty descriptions of highly effective teams. At a half-day seminar get each

team member to score how closely each description characterizes your team. Then take the following steps:

- Discuss the results and identify the three or four factors on which your team is weak.
- Identify the reasons for the weaknesses.
- Next, decide what can be done to strengthen the three or four factors.
- Finally, commit to actions that will strengthen the team and assign specific team member responsibilities for what will be done.
- Back on the job, review the commitments and responsibilities weekly to hold the team accountable.
- Six months later, devote a few hours to scoring the survey again and discussing the new results.

3. Administer group decision games.

A number of relatively inexpensive decision-making simulations are available. One, entitled "Marooned," finds the group on a deserted island setting priorities for actions to ensure its survival. At the end of the game, a discussion of the team's decision-making process and the behavior of individual members can reveal a great deal about how the group functions on a daily basis. These games plus discussion can often be completed in less than three hours.

4. Administer group project games.

These games place teams in competition against each other. In "The Tower" each team receives an identical sack filled with building supplies such as poster board, straws, paper cups, shirt hangers, and scissors. The teams are given one hour to build a tower reflecting a theme relevant to the overall organization. The towers are judged on beauty, height, strength, use of all materials provided, and relevance to the theme. The discussion after the tower building can reveal a great deal about teamwork and individual member behavior. The entire activity takes less than three hours.

5. Go on a group survival mission.

A number of organizations specialize in hosting teams for a weekend outdoors in a simulated hostile environment. In one exercise the team is given a certain period of time to negotiate several miles of rough terrain. Part of the rationale behind these games is that after two people have helped each other scale a rocky cliff they're more likely to collaborate on the job.

6. Organize a sports team.

When your management staff becomes a softball team, interesting things happen. The "suits" come off. The person who organizes and manages the team is typically not the boss. Athletic ability may not match management ability. Everyone is a cheerleader for the team. Deeper layers of personality are revealed. Success and failure are mutually experienced and shared.

7. Conduct a team-building retreat.

Bring in a facilitator to create a nonthreatening environment for a day where team members can give each other candid feedback on how well they work together.

> In one retreat activity up to twelve team members are presented with twenty-four critical behaviors of senior managers. Members are asked to identify the three they personally practice most fully and consistently, and the three they practice with least success. Then they make the same judgments for every other member of the team. The results are discussed with each person's feedback summarized on a large sheet of flip chart paper taped to the wall. Finally, each member makes three commitments for new, renewed, or extinguished behavior in support of the team. Mentors from within the team are assigned to coach each other and give daily feedback on fulfillment of the commitments. The facilitator returns in three months to check on progress.

60 Nine Qualities to Look for in a Senior Manager or Assistant

Select your trusted lieutenants with the greatest care. These people can give you the support you need to succeed, may have to assume your duties sometime in the future, and are a daily reflection on you. You'll want to apply the same comprehensive strategies to this hiring decision as you do to all others. In addition, look for these particular qualities.

1. Willingness to accept responsibility for performance.

Ask candidates to describe their greatest failure or most disappointing result on their previous job. Ask them to list the reasons why things didn't go well. The more they blame others or make excuses for their mistakes, the less you should be interested in them.

2. Loyalty.

Encourage candidates to talk about the negative side of their relationships with previous superiors. If they can be easily encouraged to complain about their past bosses, guess whom they'll complain about next. End the interview as soon as possible.

3. Commitment to excellence.

Ask applicants what they think about the concepts of total quality management, continuous improvement, and zero defects. Probe with additional questions into how they apply these concepts to their own work. Ask them to describe projects where they were most committed to excellence. Question how they plan to achieve excellence in the job they are applying for.

4. Communication skills.

You depend on close associates to keep you informed. You count on them to communicate your vision clearly throughout the organization. You rely on them to represent you fairly, accurately, and impressively. You bank on their collaboration and coordination with each other. Finally, you need them to listen to you and understand your needs. Does the candidate in front of you appear to have the communication skills that will make all this happen?

5. Humility.

The last thing you need on your senior team is a "hot dog" who wants to grab the headlines and perform on center stage.

6. Fearlessness.

Managers with low self-confidence may not take risks or be open to change. They may feel the need to keep the lid on enterprising employees. They may not be willing to challenge your ideas. They may move so deliberately and cautiously that little gets done.

7. Tolerance for ambiguity.

You don't want to have to give your senior managers day-to-day guidance on how to perform their jobs. You want to give them your vision and then watch them run with it. Find out how much structure applicants had to work with in previous jobs and how well they did with it.

8. Openness to new ideas.
Don't hire know-it-alls. Favor candidates who show you that they are lifelong learners. Stay away from those who have a quick answer to everything.

9. Balanced life.
You certainly want assistants who are dedicated to their craft, but you should shy away from those whose only life is behind a desk. Hobbies, recreation, and family life provide the spark that keeps the flame of work burning brightly. (122)

61 Eighteen Tips for Conducting a Selection Interview

The selection interview is perhaps the most important tool at your disposal in making a hiring decision. You'll have an application to read. You'll solicit comments from past employers. You'll ask opinions of colleagues who meet candidates. You may even have the opportunity to use a job sample test, which measures the ability of candidates to perform a particular duty. Ultimately, however, you'll rely on the impressions that the candidates make when they're sitting in front of you.

1. Decide on the role the selection interview will play in your hiring strategy.
Here is a typical plan for hiring high-level managers. (Plans vary by level and industry.)

- Appoint a search committee.
- Decide on the precise duties of the position and on the behaviors you're looking for in the new person.
- Advertise the position through existing networks and ads in appropriate professional publications, or retain a search firm to generate candidates.
- Screen applicants using applications, known reputation, reference checks, and perhaps a phone call to several of them.
- Invite some applicants—as many as a dozen—to a first selection interview.

- Intensify reference checks. Invite a smaller field—as many as five—back for a second interview.
- Give future colleagues an opportunity to meet and comment on the candidates.
- Make a final choice and a job offer.

2. Decide on comparative uses of the first and second interviews.
At the first interview uncover *performance factors* that reveal whether candidates can do the job. At the second interview, you may have a little more detective work to do regarding competence. Otherwise, this is your opportunity to conclude how well candidates *fit in* with the culture of your organization, with the team they will join, and with the particular superiors they will report to.

DO THIS TO PREPARE FOR AND TO CONDUCT THE FIRST INTERVIEW:

3. Identify performance factors.
What really matters in hiring? Whether the person can do the job! Choose fifteen or twenty behaviors and competencies from among the following as being most important for success in the particular job being filled. Consider:

- *Intellectual characteristics* such as intelligence, ability to learn, analytic ability, creativity, systematic decision making, memory, curiosity, quick thinking, and rationality.
- *Personal qualities* such as innovativeness, emotional maturity, resourcefulness, adaptable to change, sense of urgency, persistence, good humor, honesty, enthusiasm, high energy, positive attitude, risk taking, and self-confidence.
- *Interpersonal skills* such as openness to criticism, admits errors, friendly, expressiveness, competitiveness, empathy, defuses anger, humility, emotional control, and patience.
- *Communication skills* such as writing, speaking, listening, reading, and signing.
- *Leadership qualities* such as vision, decisiveness, applauds others, professionalism, tolerance of individuality, conflict resolution skills, meeting leadership skills, accepts ideas of others, results oriented, ability to teach, low tolerance for mediocrity, inspirational, and earns respect.
- *Follower qualities* such as meeting participation skills,

reliability, works without supervision, enjoys serving customers, team player, loyalty, acceptance of authority, and trustworthiness.
- *Technical skills* such as precision, awareness of field, knowledge of new developments, technical competence, physically capable to do the job, and proven track record.

4. Order the performance factors according to their importance.
During the candidate search focus the greatest attention on the most critical factors.

5. Elaborate on the chosen factors.
Get more specific in the description of your chosen factors. For example, "defuses anger" might become, "Handles complaining customers with tact and assertiveness within the guidelines of company policy."

6. Turn each factor into an interview question.
Use performance factors as the basis for your interview questions. Once the interview gets rolling, ask only those questions that measure one of the performance factors.

7. Stay away from hypothetical questions.
Whenever you ask, "What would you do if . . . ?" you encourage the candidate to guess at what answer you're looking for rather than tell the truth. These are hypothetical questions calling for hypothetical responses. Since you're not hiring a hypothetical candidate, it's best to avoid them. Instead ask, "When was the last time you encountered . . . ? How did you handle it?"

8. Put the candidate at ease.
Smile broadly, shake hands, maintain eye contact, escort the candidate to a seat. Engage in a few minutes of small talk. Then tell the interviewee how you'll conduct the interview. Start by asking questions that break the ice and allow the applicant to speak on a comfortable topic (e.g., "Tell me about your educational background.") before moving to the meaty questions that get at performance factors.

9. Find out what the person did to solve tough problems.
Build on performance factors to ask about specific situations involving conflict, customer complaints, ethical dilemmas, stressful working conditions, and difficult employees. How has the applicant

shown commitment, drive, energy, and interpersonal skills? Find out what the applicant did to solve real problems.

10. Probe, probe, and probe some more.

Each interview question you ask is made more powerful by its follow-up probes. Once you get an answer to an original question, dig deeper until you feel you have a reliable basis to evaluate that performance factor.

> Here's a good example of questioning designed to explore the performance factor: "Handles complaining customers with tact and assertiveness within company policy." After the interviewee has put the candidate at ease, he or she asks, "In your past job, were you ever confronted by an angry customer? When was the most recent occasion? Tell me what happened. What did you say? What was the outcome? How might you have handled it differently? What results would you expect from that different approach?"

11. Don't break laws governing appropriate interview questions.

Check with your human resources officer, legal counsel, local state employment office, or local human relations commission. Your need to know does not supersede an applicant's rights to privacy.

12. Listen for both content and style.

Listen to the answers to your questions with your eyes and your ears. What are candidates saying and how are they saying it? Are they tense and rigid, or relaxed and composed? Are they speaking with assurance and assertiveness or doubt and insecurity?

13. Solicit questions from applicants.

If applicants do their homework, they'll be able to ask you challenging questions. If they don't, you might want to reconsider their candidacy.

DO THIS TO PREPARE FOR AND TO CONDUCT THE
SECOND INTERVIEW:

14. Identify those performance factors you haven't measured with confidence.

Even after scouring the application, talking to references, and holding the first interview you may still be in doubt about certain abilities of candidates. Plan to ask pointed questions at the second interview to remove that doubt.

15. Write your expectations.

Far less than 50% of new hires are still on board a year after being hired. Perhaps the greatest cause of early failure is that people accept jobs without a clear picture of what's expected of them, and organizations hire people without a clear picture of what employees expect in return. In other words, no performance contract is struck. Create the performance expectations you have for the person you're about to hire.

- As a starting point, review the performance factors of this job as well as the job description.
- Incorporate the values and beliefs that characterize your organizational culture.
- Think carefully about the needs you have for this employee for how, when, where, and how much. Remember the successes and failures of the previous job holder.
- Be certain your expectations are specific and fully stated. (43)

16. Ask candidates to generate their expectations.

Ask them to draft their expectations of you as a supervisor and their expectations of the organization as their place of employment. If they have trouble doing this, you may wish to give them some examples of expectations that a person in their position might hold. You may learn more about candidates by hearing them talk about their expectations than by hearing their responses to yours.

17. Create a mutual performance contract.

Discuss and clarify the two lists of expectations in these ways:

- Test the candidate's expectations for acceptability and appropriateness.
- Some of your expectations may be negotiable; on those, engage in give and take suitable to the situation.
- Get a sense of whether the candidate's values, attitudes, and beliefs are consistent with those held by existing employees. Ensure that he or she will be a compatible team member.
- Finally, establish a two-way performance contract that each of you pledges to fulfill if the candidate is ultimately offered the job.

Once you hire a candidate, continually review the performance contract with him or her to make sure your mutual expectations retain their validity as your relationship develops. More importantly, the expectations you agree to at the selection interview will be the most reliable measures with which to construct future performance reviews, both of your employee and of your support of him or her.

18. Paint a realistic picture of what it's like to work in the company.
It's in your best interest to bring on new hires with realistic expectations. Inflating those expectations with rosy scenarios will return to haunt you. Research shows that honest job previews are better for both the applicant and the employer. Don't bring someone on board with false hopes.

62 Eight Ways to Get Great Value from Mentoring

Mentoring describes a relationship between an executive (the mentor) and a less senior manager (the protégé) in which the mentor provides advice on professional development and career management. For example, a mentor might advise a protégé to attend a presentation skills seminar in order to become more persuasive. Mentors also help less experienced people learn the ropes within the organization. It's one of the oldest and most powerful training methods.

TO ENCOURAGE MENTORING IN YOUR ORGANIZATION:

1. See that all new managers are formally assigned a mentor.
Each time a new manager is hired or someone is promoted into management, survey your executive staff for a volunteer who feels comfortable mentoring that manager. Introduce the mentor to the protégé and explain your hope that the relationship will benefit both.

2. Train your executives in how to mentor.
Mentors have the responsibility to show employees the possibilities for advancement, to describe the dues they need to pay, and to tell them about advancement opportunities.

3. Review the health of mentor-protégé relationships regularly.
As often as once a year remind mentors and protégés of the importance of their relationship and urge them to take it seriously. Give either person in the pair the option to ask for a reassignment if it's not working. Rotate mentors every two years to give managers exposure to contrasting philosophies of career development.

TO BE A GOOD MENTOR YOURSELF:

4. Mentors and protégés must keep their relationship professional.
Sexual attraction is possible any time people work together. When one person has more power and authority than the other, attraction can be even stronger. Don't put yourself in a position where you have to respond to colleagues' questions about rumors or defend yourself against sexual harassment charges.

5. Don't let apparent favoritism towards one employee hurt the morale of others.
There's no getting around it—a protégé is shown favoritism. One employee will receive special benefit of your wisdom and counsel. Take care lest this exclusive treatment become a source of jealousy among other employees.

6. Don't let loyalty and friendship cloud your judgment.
A mentor is not a defense attorney. Don't cover up for employee incompetence, illegal action, or unethical behavior. Avoid the temptation to deflect criticism or discipline that your protégé's behavior has warranted.

7. Discuss how the relationship is fulfilling both parties' needs.
Periodically, talk about how well the mentoring relationship is working and what can be done to make it work even better.

8. Don't force a mentoring relationship.
Encourage your protégé to request a new mentor whenever he or she believes there's more value to gain in a new relationship. In the same way, you should recommend reassignment as soon as you feel you've done all you can to advance an employee's career. In no case should you ever continue mentoring an employee you don't feel positive about. When it's time for you and your protégé to part, do so as friends, not as guilt-ridden antagonists or acrimonious foes.

63 Five Ways to Get Great Value from Coaching

Coaching describes a process in which a manager gives employees feedback on how well they're performing particular duties and teaches them how to do better. For example, after watching an employee give a speech a coach might provide tips on how to deliver a more attention-getting opening.

1. Insist that supervisors coach their direct reports.
Coaching may happen spontaneously outside of the superior-subordinate relationship, but it's most needed *within* that relationship.

2. Train first-line supervisors through the CEO in how to coach.
Educate your managers that coaching is a combination of teaching and counseling. Employees need to be taught. Supervisors have the *knowledge* to teach, the *experience* to put the lessons into a meaningful context, and the *authority* to ensure employees use what they learn.

3. Train first-line supervisors through the CEO in how to counsel.
Supervisors counsel by asking employees how they're doing and what they need in order to do better. After listening to the answers, supervisors should give employees helpful advice on how they can improve.

4. Mentor and coach to develop; don't foster dependence.
Help people think for themselves. Don't feel that you must have all the answers. Actually, you won't necessarily help your protégé or your subordinate if you do. Ask questions. Before offering advice, ask how the other person would handle the situation being discussed. Help people see their options without choosing one for them. Offer your suggestions as a point of view, rather than as the final word. Try these phrases:

- "Another way of looking at that is . . ."
- "As I see it . . ."
- "You may want to consider an alternate explanation . . ."
- "It appears that . . ."

5. As a coach, teach both the task and the interpersonal dimensions of the job.
Work has two dimensions: The task requirements (how the job should be performed) and the interpersonal requirements (how to

work with people in performing the job). Your insights on the interpersonal dimension will be especially valuable.

64 Fifteen Assurances that Training Will Improve the Bottom Line

In the past the word *company* conjured up images of buildings, equipment, and people. Today a company is known by the *knowledge* it keeps. Employee knowledge about industries, economies, markets, customers, technology, processes, quality, behavior, leadership, and communication is the resource that will make your organization great. You inject knowledge into your organization in many ways, but the most important way is training. Before you invest thousands, hundreds of thousands, or even millions in employee training, take steps to ensure it will benefit your bottom line.

CONDUCT THESE TRAINING NEEDS ANALYSES:

1. Examine your company's vision statement, strategic plan, and corporate objectives.
The goal of training is to provide your employees with the information, knowledge, and skills they need to accomplish your business plan.

2. Study the requests and complaints you get from customers.
Customer complaints are symptoms of training needs.

3. Link your performance appraisal plan to employee development.
Examine the deficiencies identified in employee performance evaluations. Provide employees with the training that their managers say they need.

4. Ask your managers.
Get your managers to tell you in writing or in face-to-face interviews what training they and their employees need.

5. Ask your employees.
On the next opinion survey you administer, ask employees what additional skills they need to be more effective. On post-seminar evaluation forms, ask participants the same thing.

6. Link exit interviews to employee development.
Employees are never so honest as when they decide to leave an organization. Ask defectors what problems should be corrected. Address as many of the problems as possible through training.

7. Link training to career planning.
Your employees should be given career progression plans showing what experience and skill acquisition are necessary for job advancement. Training programs that are integral to these plans represent money well spent.

8. Get 360° feedback for your managers.
Don't waste the time of your management team in one-shot seminars that may or may not give them the tools they need. Before you develop your managers, survey their bosses, subordinates, peers, and possibly even customers on the critical success factors for leadership in your company. Let the managers fill out the survey as well. Show managers the results. Hold them accountable for coming up with a year-long development plan that includes whatever training the feedback says they need.

TAKE THESE STEPS TO INCREASE THE EFFECTIVENESS
OF YOUR TRAINING PROGRAMS:

9. Declare your support.
Let employees know how vital training is to you. Insist that supervisors support the development of their direct reports. Send the message that once someone has signed up for a seminar *that* is the best place for that person to be on that day. Censure managers who pull their people out of training sessions.

10. Decide what training should be done internally and externally.
In the long run the relative cost of using internal trainers versus calling on outside experts is roughly the same.

- Internal trainers bring the advantage of continuity and easier opportunity for follow-up. Their strength is in basic education and technical skill building.
- External trainers offer broader knowledge and more varied experience. Their advantages show up in the "soft" areas of leadership, team building, customer service, and interpersonal skills. You'd also call on an outsider to help you facilitate planning meetings and problem-solving sessions.

11. Train internal trainers.

Everyone in your company can benefit from one more communication seminar and trainers are no exception. They're usually content experts who may not be as strong on presentation skills. Bring in an expert on the training of trainers. Be sure your trainers are adept at using reinforcement techniques and hands-on exercises and that they understand the way adults learn.

12. Choose outside trainers wisely.

Don't pick a trainer based solely on a video or audiotape. Check with at least three references. For large jobs, trainers should be willing to give a mini-seminar as an audition. Give preference to those who have written books in the area of training you need; this means they generate knowledge in the field as well as teach it. Choose trainers who are enthusiastic about tailoring their materials to the particular needs of your employees and who can tell you how they plan to maximize the knowledge employees bring back to the job. Insist that they be willing to modify future programs in response to participant evaluation of earlier ones. (83)

13. Favor shorter, periodic training sessions over longer, marathon sessions.

For certain topics, such as presentation skills, two to five days of consecutive training is the design of choice because the learning is cumulative. Too often, however, this marathon approach is chosen because of travel considerations or other conveniences. It's often better to hold shorter sessions with time in between. The less that's taught in any given training session, the more that's likely to be remembered. The more time between training sessions, the more chance participants have to use what they've learned before learning something new.

14. Hold employees accountable for what they learn.

At the close of every training session, have employees write an action plan stating what they'll do differently back on the job. Part of the plan should be to meet with their supervisors to describe what they learned and to enlist the supervisors' support in carrying out the plan. Each plan should include a commitment to at least one action that will improve the team or organization. As an example, an employee might propose to teach a group of peers a particular technique from the seminar.

15. Evaluate the impact of training.
Are you getting value for your training dollars?

- A popular way to answer this question is to ask participants leaving a training program what they thought of it. They might be given a five-point scale to evaluate the instructor, the approach, the content, the materials, the facility, etc.
- A better approach might be to ask participants to declare what they plan to do differently as a result of the course. You can follow up a few months later with questions about how successful participants have been with their plans.
- Perhaps the best evaluation technique is to take a before-and-after measure of the skills taught in the session. This is easily done in something like a typing class where you can give participants typing tests. It can even be approximated for more subjective topics such as leadership. As an example, the survey administered in item #8 of this list could be readministered at the end of the year to see if scores rise.

65 Eleven Steps to Install a Meaningful Performance Review System

Most large companies have a formal procedure for appraising the performance of employees. It typically consists of an appraisal form completed by a superior, which then becomes the focal point of an appraisal interview between that superior and the subordinate. Most systems are intended to document performance quality so that future decisions about promotion, salary, or job assignment might be justified. There's a more worthy goal of performance review, however: to *improve the performance* of those being reviewed.

1. Base the appraisal on performance expectations.
Many performance review forms call for evaluations on single adjectives, such as *dependable*, which leave a great deal open to interpretation. Other forms are more explicit (e.g., "Can be counted on to complete projects on schedule"), but the behavior described may not be as important for the job being assessed as for other jobs. A much better result is achieved when each person's performance review document is based on the explicit expectations the company and the supervisor have for the person performing that particular job. (43)

2. Minimize the prominence and importance of numbers.

Some forms are extensively quantitative with employees receiving a total rating score. This encourages them to focus on the numbers with less attention to any recommendations for improvement. Other forms substitute labels, such as *commendable*, with the same negative impact. While you may use either numbers or labels to quantify performance, overwhelm them with the section on your form that reveals to employees exactly what they need to do to achieve excellence.

3. Reveal the form early.

Most employees never see the form that will be used to evaluate their performance until it's completed for their first appraisal. How ridiculous! They should see it *before* it's actually used so they know what's expected. Include an explanation of it in your orientation program. Better yet, show it to prospects during the employment interview.

4. Review performance often.

The typical performance review system requires scheduling formal appraisal interviews to discuss the completed forms. Better systems mandate twice yearly meetings. The best systems bring supervisors and subordinates together as often as quarterly. In any case, impress upon your managers the need to provide performance feedback—both positive and negative—and not to wait for the appraisal interview to communicate with their employees.

5. Train raters.

Serious morale problems are created when employees believe they aren't being evaluated consistently and fairly, or when they learn that higher authorities have overruled improperly executed evaluations. Require a minimum of one hour of instruction each year to ensure your managers are applying your system as intended.

6. Incorporate self-assessments.

Have employees assess themselves on the form as their supervisors do the same; have them include recommendations for the development experiences (e.g., training) they believe they need to become more effective. Let employees and supervisors reveal their assessments twenty-four hours before the appraisal interview. Most managers are surprised to learn how tough employees are on themselves and how accurately they identify their areas for improvement. This method also helps reduce defensiveness on both sides, enables the interview to run more smoothly, and increases the buy-in employees feel for the performance improvements requested by managers.

7. Generate upward feedback.

The most helpful of performance reviews work both ways. That is, they give employees a chance to assess the effectiveness of the leadership they receive. While employees should not be asked to appraise the overall competence of their manager, they're in the best position to comment on the quality of the direct supervision they receive. Managers who can accept the notion of upward feedback find it a helpful tool in improving their leadership.

One way to take the bite out of the process for reluctant managers is to use rankings rather than ratings. For example, you might ask employees to identify on a list of positive leadership behaviors the three they see their managers doing most often and the three they see least often.

---

8. Require follow-up meetings.

Each appraisal meeting should be followed in about a month by a coaching follow-up where performance progress is assessed and discussed, and where new improvement suggestions might be made.

9. Oversee the system.

Keep a close watch on performance reviews. They're too important to delegate blindly to your human resources or personnel office. Check the reviews done by your immediate subordinates and skim those done in the rest of the organization. This is a great way to learn about the performance trends and development needs throughout your workforce.

10. Consider separating reviews from evaluations.

Evaluation tends to generate defensiveness, but performance improvement requires openness and an enthusiastic willingness to change. If you insist on a performance review system that clearly evaluates and documents the level of employee performance so you can justify employment decisions, and yet you want to achieve performance improvement from it, you may have to conduct separate meetings.

11. Re-examine the system.
Ask both raters and ratees how well the system is working for them. Get new ideas from other companies who feel they have good systems. Review yours for possible revisions each year.

66 Ten Sections of an Ideal Performance Review Form

Each item on this list represents a section that you could include in a performance review form that will make it easy for you to apply the advice in list 65.

1. *Section I: Performance Expectations.*
List the quantitative and qualitative expectations of employees. As you see from list 43 on page 100, listings of performance expectations often contain anywhere between twenty and forty items. Fewer, and they may be too broad or incomplete. More, and you may be guilty of micromanagement.

An example of a quantitative expectation is: "Keep me informed *daily* of your progress." A qualitative expectation might be: "Provide me with information that *enables me to allocate resources appropriately* among departments." Notice that these two expectations can easily be combined into one. Expectations are often both quantitative and qualitative, and you shouldn't ignore either feature.

---

2. *Section II: Self-Appraisal.*
Before the performance review meeting, notify employees to do a self-assessment. In it employees will perform each of the remaining tasks on this list prior to the appraisal interview. At the interview, as you execute each step, you can compare their assessments to yours.

3. *Section III: Attainment of Expectations.*
Tell employees how well the expectations have been met to date. Attach a degree of accomplishment statement to each expectation. One way to do this is through percentages. "100%" would mean

complete accomplishment of that expectation, "75%" would mean three-quarters of the way there.

4. *Section IV: Actions Required to Meet Expectations Fully.*
Tell employees what needs to be done to attain mastery of each expectation. Assume you've written that an employee is fulfilling a particular expectation 80% of the time (or to that extent). You're now accountable for telling the employee exactly what behavior or evidence you need to see in order for you to conclude that the expectation is fully met. One way to do this is to tell the employee what you need to see *more of* and *less of* to reach a judgment of 100% fulfillment. Also describe what should be kept *the same*— positive behaviors are too rarely emphasized in the performance review meeting.

5. *Section V: Priority Expectations and Actions.*
Tell employees where to focus attention. Improvements on certain expectations may be more urgent than others and require more immediate attention. Improvements on other expectations will have greater impact on the organization and they need more intense attention. Help employees sort through the mass of feedback by providing an immediacy and intensity barometer for each expectation.

6. *Section VI: Training.*
List the seminars, workshops, or courses you believe employees should attend to help them fulfill expectations more fully.

7. *Section VII: Coaching.*
Describe the personal coaching that you plan to give to employees to help them achieve the "do mores" and the "do lesses" of Section IV. Identify coaching they should seek elsewhere, either inside or outside the organization.

8. *Section VIII: Other Developmental Activities.*
Recommend specific books, articles, magazines, audiotapes, videos, compact discs, and other learning tools. Suggest any job rotation or cross-training you believe would be helpful.

9. *Section IX: Leadership Requests.*
A few performance review forms include space for employees to evaluate the quality of leadership they receive. This feedback may

best be elicited in a section that asks employees to state three changes their supervisor might make in leading or communicating with them that would help them achieve what she expects.

10. *Section X: Follow-Up.*
Meet with employees thirty days after each performance review meeting. Use this section of the form to record each of your opinions of the progress made to date by each of you.

67 Thirteen Tips for Conducting a Performance Appraisal

Most executives look forward to conducting performance appraisals as much as visiting the dentist or opening a letter from the IRS. Some get knots in their stomachs "playing God." Others don't know how to make criticism constructive. Few executives relish defensiveness from subordinates. Many of them struggle with a performance review system that just doesn't work well. And finally, most have never received formal training on how to formally appraise performance. The advice in this list won't turn you into a raving fan of appraisals, but it will make the assignment less burdensome for you and more beneficial for your direct reports.

1. Approach the session as an opportunity to coach and counsel.
If you view performance appraisals strictly as opportunities to judge and critique an employee, neither of you will derive much from the sessions. Remember, the central purpose of the performance appraisal is to *improve performance.*

2. Set aside forty-five minutes of *uninterrupted* time.
Don't conduct the appraisal on the run, between other tasks, or as an afterthought. Accept no telephone calls or interruptions of any kind. Show your employees that their development is one of your highest priorities.

3. Tell employees to engage in a self-appraisal prior to the session.
If the appraisal form doesn't provide a section for self-assessment, direct employees to answer these questions.

- Which of my supervisor's expectations have I met most consistently? Which have I met least consistently?

- What has been my greatest victory since the last appraisal? What has been my most disappointing failure?
- What are my most outstanding skills?
- What are my priority areas for skill development?
- What specific training programs would be of greatest benefit to me?
- What coaching help do I need from my supervisor?

4. Create rapport with the employee.

Introduce the session as an opportunity for both of you to discuss the employee's development and what you can do to accelerate it. Focus your attention on plans for future improvement, rather than on documentation of past inadequacies. Minimize tension and anxiety by using an upbeat and helpful approach. Conduct the session somewhere other than in your office; consider doing it in the employee's office, in the conference room, or over lunch.

5. If forms contain scales or evaluative adjectives, make sure they mean the same to employees as they mean to you.

What do the words *superior* and *average* mean? What does the phrase *shows initiative* or *exceeds expectations* mean? On a five point scale, what does a 4 mean to you? What does it take for you to give someone a 5? Check with colleagues to ensure that, in fairness to employees, you all take these terms and numbers to mean the same thing. Describe to employees the norms you use in making your comparisons. Listen to any objections the employee may have and be prepared to negotiate common definitions.

6. Focus on behavior, not personality or inference.

If it can't be measured, it can't be changed. Talk about what the person *did* (performance) not what the person *is* (personality). Don't say something like, "You've got a good [or bad] attitude toward your customers." Say, "You've stayed in close contact with [or avoided] your customers." Be even more specific when you can, giving unequivocal and irrefutable examples of performance.

7. Discuss the performance gap.

The performance gap is the difference between what employees are doing now and what they should be doing. When you identify this gap, you and the employee will become focused on objective standards of performance.

8. Discuss the past less than you discuss the future.

The purpose of the appraisal is not just to pass judgment (good or bad) but to assist the employee in doing a better job for the future. What should the future look like? How does the employee fit into that picture? What new, renewed, or extinguished behavior should begin tomorrow? What skills, abilities, or talents should the employee develop in order to help you create a better future together?

9. Reduce the most common types of appraisal errors.

Before the appraisal, consider whether you've fallen into any of these traps:

- the error of the *halo effect*—assigning an overall favorable rating because of a single favorable attribute that impresses you
- the *leniency error*—inflating evaluations higher than they should be because you want employees to like you
- the *strictness error*—deflating evaluations because you don't want to be seen as a pushover
- the *central tendency error*—assigning everyone average evaluations because you don't think anyone "walks on water" or should be branded as a failure
- the *recency error*—basing your entire evaluation on what the employee did in the few weeks before the appraisal

10. Be honest, thorough, and careful.

These days many terminated or strongly disciplined employees are turning to the courts for relief. In the event of a lawsuit the employee's performance evaluations are likely to be subpoenaed. In such cases, these documents too often work against employers. One problem arises when poorly performing employees have been given satisfactory ratings because managers didn't have the courage or take the time to substantiate poor performance. A second problem occurs when the employee's inferior performance wasn't properly documented with examples, evidence, or written reports. Fill out performance appraisal forms completely, reliably, and validly. In cases of problem employees, have a colleague check them for any evidence of bias or prejudice.

11. Solicit questions and opinions from employees.

Employees will have questions and reactions to your appraisal of their performance. Encourage them and listen carefully. Respond honestly and nondefensively. The appraisal is an opportune time for candid dialogue. You want to know what employees are feeling and thinking as much as they need to know what you think of their performance.

12. **Divorce discussion of merit pay increases from discussion of performance.**
The best performance appraisal systems are driven by coaching and counseling. If you emphasize performance appraisals as the primary factor in determining salary increases, then discussions digress into debates over percentages, dollars, and perceptions of equity.

13. **Conclude with a clear understanding of what you discussed and what will change.**
Employees should sign off on the appraisal form indicating that they agree with the assessment and will commit to the changes you suggest. When employees disagree with your assessment or your plan for improvement, they should draft a rebuttal to be appended to the assessment and placed in their personnel file.

68 Eleven Ways to Respond to a Problem Employee

You just learned from an angry supervisor that an employee, who happens to be female, has flagrantly violated company rules. This isn't the first time that employee has challenged her supervisor, who happens to be male. Past breaches haven't been handled well by the supervisor; he needs help and is in your office to get it. Word of the infraction has spread among employees. They're watching your every move. Now what?

1. **Make sure that there's a real problem and not merely a personality conflict.**
Discuss the case face to face with the supervisor after he calms down. Make sure his emotions and possible prejudices haven't distorted the facts. If possible, speak to other employees you trust with direct knowledge of the situation.

2. **Triage the problem.**
Determine if the employee's alleged behavior is causing an immediate threat to herself, to others, or to your business. If so, you might want to temporarily relocate her or even send her home with pay

pending investigation. If not, don't be pressured by the supervisor into a premature or heavy-handed response.

3. Get the employee's side of the story.

Be prepared to hear a story quite different from what the supervisor told you. The truth is likely to be somewhere in between. Listen carefully and take notes. The employee's explanation will be a preview of her case if she decides to litigate. Such meetings can be difficult, but they give you an excellent opportunity to defuse the situation. Furthermore, your thoughtful handling of the employee will demonstrate your company's good faith and fairness.

4. Document. Document. Document.

Insist that the supervisor produce documentation describing what happened, with dates, times, witnesses, and impact. It should also reveal the history of previous warnings and disciplinary actions for related events. If appropriate, ask the employee to provide a written statement. Start a notebook on this case. Take notes as you speak to anyone about it. Draft a memorandum for the record of each meeting.

5. Research how other employees have been treated for similar behavior.

The law won't prevent you from managing firmly as long as you're consistent. Be certain that you know of any past exceptions, since your employee almost certainly will. Review the history of this employee's performance reviews. Don't be surprised to unearth years of satisfactory or even glowing evaluations written by supervisors who lacked the desire or the courage to confront poor performance. These records will be subpoenaed and used against you if the employee files suit.

6. Examine your responsibility for the problem.

For obvious willful misconduct such as insubordination, theft, fighting, sleeping, or disappearing from the job, the need for discipline is obvious. Appropriate responses to substandard performance are more difficult to discern. For example, does the employee simply need up-to-date training? Does she really know what's expected of her and that what she did was wrong? Is she properly equipped, supervised, and supported? If the employee is disabled, have you made reasonable accommodations? Has she been given clear, complete instructions and a reasonable amount of time to complete the job properly?

7. Decide on a response.

Once you have all appropriate information, decide on a response that both fits the offense and is consistent with past practice. This is not the time to begin using new or more severe disciplinary actions than you've applied to other employees.

8. Get help.

If serious disciplinary action is called for, discuss the case with a competent employment law attorney *before* you discipline the employee. The cost will be a small fraction of the expense of even an easily defended case. Don't forget that lawsuits against large companies often end up in the media. Even when such suits are dismissed, the publicity can darken your company's image and embolden other employees to take legal action.

9. Take action.

Once you and your advisors decide on a course of action, don't let it drag on. Tell the employee what she did wrong and what the discipline will be. Document the discipline carefully. Describe all the corrective training and opportunity to demonstrate improvement that will be offered to the employee. Delineate the new behavior that the employee is expected to demonstrate, establish the criteria you'll use to evaluate that behavior, and schedule a number of follow-up meetings where you'll provide feedback on the new behavior. Have the employee sign the document.

10. Maintain confidentiality.

Besides protecting the employee's privacy and reputation, confidentiality reduces the chance that fellow employees will encourage the employee to seek retribution. Discipline should always be under-

If you have to fire an employee, confidentiality is less important and may in fact backfire. The rest of your staff should know the basic reason that the employee deserved to be terminated. Otherwise, the grapevine (with the dismissed employee's help) may carry the news that she was unfairly offed.

taken with rehabilitation as its central purpose. You're more likely to get the employee back on track if you treat her firmly, yet with professionalism and dignity.

11. Reduce the chance this will happen again.
Take these steps both to reduce your chances of being charged with discrimination or other lawsuits and to increase your chances of surviving such an accusation.

- Communicate clear, written rules of conduct.
- Document the quantity and quality of work expected of employees.
- Conduct face-to-face performance review meetings with employees *at least* once a year.
- Train your supervisors in leadership and communication skills.
- Train your supervisors in employment law, emphasizing cultural diversity, uniform and consistent discipline, and conflict resolution.
- Establish and support a formal grievance procedure that encourages conflict resolution and mediation at the lowest level possible.
- Monitor your company's disciplinary actions to ensure that no class of employees is being disciplined disproportionately.
- Insist your supervisors document all exceptional employee behavior—both bad and good.
- Know employment law.
- Don't tolerate discrimination anywhere in your organization.

69 Thirteen Strategies for Turning Around a Poor Performer

Your sales manager isn't up to the quality of the rest of your team. His speaking and writing abilities are an embarrassment. His conceptual and decision-making skills are too shaky to trust him on his own. He tries hard at leadership, but the sales team doesn't respond well to his supervision. How does someone in charge end up with a poor performer? Probably in one of three ways. You may have inherited the sales manager from the past person in charge. You may have made a poor hiring or promotion decision. Or time just may have passed the manager by. Whatever the reason, you've decided to take action.

1. Don't pass the problem on to someone else.

Many executives take the easy and cowardly way out of situations like these. They "promote" or reassign underperformers to jobs where they'll do less damage. Some people think this may be the best strategy for a long-time manager who'd be devastated by a frank assessment or who isn't likely to improve much even after the best of interventions. The fact is merely passing the problem manager on to someone else is bad business. It perpetuates incompetence in the company. It unfairly burdens the new supervisor, who will soon see through your claims. It sends the message to employees that you lack courage to take decisive action. Finally, it's *most* unfair to the poor performer who won't be given the chance to reform.

2. Make sure it's a performance problem, not a system problem.

If the employee can solve the problem by working harder, longer, or smarter, then it's a performance problem. If no amount of effort or diligence would solve the problem, then it's a system problem. For example, don't hold your sales manager accountable for returned merchandise built from shoddy raw materials.

3. Count the number of performance problems you have.

If managerial shortcomings are the norm rather than the exception, examine the culture or the subsystems within your organization. If as many as one out of five managers disappoint you, take a close look at what you expect them to do, how you expect them to do it, the training they receive, the leadership they get, and their compensation levels. Company-wide performance problems are a sign of a sick system, not a sick employee.

4. Document the problem.

Collect unequivocal, irrefutable, and objective examples of the employee's skill deficiencies, performance mistakes, tardiness, missed deadlines, violation of company policies, or poor relations with employees, coworkers, or customers. Record dates, times, and events.

5. Conduct a counseling session with the manager.

Your agenda for this session is to achieve four goals:

- to demonstrate your support for the manager
- to reach agreement that a problem exists
- to uncover the causes of the problem
- to agree on a plan for solving the problem

6. Demonstrate your support.
Tell the manager that your reason for having the meeting is to help him be more effective. Don't place blame or give ultimatums. Declare a professional development partnership.

7. Pinpoint the problem.
Identify the gaps that exist between the manager's current performance and what you want it to be. Say something like, "After reading the recent sales plan, I pointed out over a dozen grammatical errors to you." State why these gaps represent a problem for the manager, for you, or for the company. Get the manager to acknowledge these gaps without hitting him or her over the head with them. Say something like, "Can you see why these kinds of errors should concern both of us?" (51)

8. Uncover the causes of the problem.
Ask for the manager's opinion on what may be producing the gaps you've identified. Listen to his ideas without prejudice before you refute them or add your own.

- Is this problem *personal?* Does it involve physical, emotional, or medical problems? Are drugs or alcohol involved? Is the employee burned out?
- Is the problem *task related?* Does it require skills the manager lacks? Is the manager expected to do too much? Has the job moved beyond the manager's current skill level?

9. Plan a remedy tailored to the causes.
A personal or emotional problem is best solved through professional counseling. A physical problem should be checked by a physician; if necessary, disability leave may be necessary. If the employee is burned out, a new job assignment, early retirement, or career counseling may be appropriate. If the problem is task related, consider one or more of these strategies:

- Get additional systematic feedback for the manager, perhaps on a paper-and-pencil survey from other superiors, subordinates, coworkers, and possibly customers.
- Hire a personal coach for the manager, or take on this role yourself.

- Send the manager off to a management institute at a local business school.
- Best of all, ask the manager to put a year-long professional development plan together for your approval.

10. Consider termination, as appropriate.
If the manager refuses to acknowledge the problems you see, offer a separation plan that's as generous as you and your superior, human resources officer, and lawyer agree to make it.

11. Implement the plan objectively and impartially.
Don't hire an expensive personal coach for one manager whom you happen to like and ignore another manager who doesn't lick your boots as well. Fairness keeps you in high esteem among all your employees, and it keeps you out of court.

12. Draft a letter of understanding.
Send a letter to the manager immediately following the meeting. Reiterate the behavior you expect to change, when you expect it to change, the plan proposed to bring about the change, and the consequences of not changing. Ask the manager to return a signed copy of the letter to you.

13. Support the plan.
Do your part in the plan. As the manager progresses, encourage him. When you see documented improvement, compliment him. Stay in close communication; give feedback daily. If he doesn't fulfill his part in the bargain, take appropriate steps toward separation.

70 Nine Methods to Handle an Insubordinate Manager

Insubordination comes in many forms. The least common pattern is the manager who challenges your authority one on one or outright refuses to comply with your directives. Somewhat more familiar is the subordinate manager who constantly disputes your ideas at staff meetings, deprecates your recommendations at board meetings, or goes against your assertions in the media. Even more commonly you'll discover managers who support you to your face and in public and then stab you in the back. Whatever form insubordination takes, if you fail to establish your authority with mutinous managers, you'll eventually become a doormat for all.

1. Hold up a mirror and take a close look.
Something in your behavior may play a role in this insubordination. What might it be? Have you refused to listen or give this manager an opportunity to disagree with you? Have you done something to lose this manager's respect? Do you give evidence of being a weak leader without conviction and direction? (34)

2. Consider the manager's motives.
Something in the manager's experiences, values, and beliefs is leading that person to challenge your authority. What is it? Is this manager overly ambitious? Frustrated? A know-it-all? Sneaky, slimy, or sleazy? Conspiring to do you in?

3. Don't mistake a valid challenge or objection for insubordination.
Rejoice when employees question your ideas or suggest approaches of their own. If you don't encourage your managers to disagree with you, there's something severely wrong with your leadership style. However, such contradictions must be open, honest, and respectful.

4. If you weren't an eyewitness, make sure you have the facts.
Don't blow your top over hearsay and innuendo. Insubordination is a serious charge. Make it only after you are sure it occurred. Someone else may be looking to get the person you're about to accuse in trouble with you.

5. Weigh the consequences of reprimanding vs. termination.
If insubordination creates an irreparable schism between you and an employee, or if an employee fails to show remorse, then he or she will have to go. However, if the employee momentarily exercised poor judgment and shows genuine remorse, you'll come out a winner by showing forgiveness.

6. When you reprimand, confront the employee privately on your turf.
Have the employee come into your office when you're seated behind your desk. First, give the employee the opportunity to explain what happened. In an assertive, affirmative, and consistent tone tell the employee that such behavior will no longer be tolerated. Describe the consequences of a repeat offense in unmistakable language.

7. Don't get into the gutter with the employee.
If the employee decides to verbally have it out with you, don't counterattack or defend your honor. Remain calm. The next word you say and the next action you take are likely to have long-term implications for your company. If you decide to fire this short fuse, simply describe the next step in that process. (28)

8. Draft a letter of understanding.
Document the reprimand in a letter to the manager. Summarize the nature of the insubordination, your expectation that it won't occur again, and an explicit statement of consequences if your expectations are violated.

9. Monitor the situation.
If no other problems arise, treat this manager as you do all others; don't hold a grudge. If the insubordination flares up again, either reassert your position or ask for his or her resignation.

---

71 Seven Tips for Working with Family Members

Many organizations today try to motivate their people with the claim, "We treat our people like family." Some executives take this philosophy one step further and actually hire family members. The result can be idyllic when family members work out well. When they don't, acrimony, bitterness, and jealousy sap energy from employees and detract from what they should be doing—serving the customer. To achieve the benefits that family members provide while controlling the negatives, follow these tips.

1. Remember, it's a business.
What happens around the dinner table on Sunday evening is one thing. What happens in the store, the factory, or the office is another. If a family member is unwilling to accept the professionalism expected in a business, that person shouldn't go on payroll. Keeping family strife away from work and working pressures away from the home will improve both the business and the home.

2. Non-family employees in family-owned businesses have a right to know their prospects.
Don't lie to employees about their promotional opportunities if those opportunities are reserved for family members. Giving false

hope is not only unethical but is likely to eventually hurt your bottom line. The disgruntled employee may leave you during your busiest season or may sabotage your efforts without your ever knowing about it.

3. When you start a business with family members, handshakes and hugs are fine but written contracts are better.

Siblings, parent and child, spouses, or any other relatives may start a business inspired by love and the best intentions. Over time, however, one person may wish to leave the business or to take it in a direction the other doesn't support. If irreconcilable conflict motivates one to leave, who buys out whom, under what conditions, and for what price? Family loyalty won't help nearly as much at this stage as a contract will.

4. If you run a family-owned business, don't allow favoritism towards family to kill employee morale.

Non-family members realize that family members will receive certain considerations. However, if special treatment is blatant, affecting sound business decisions or causing non-family members to feel unappreciated, then morale will suffer. One example would be to move a less qualified relative into a job for which a loyal employee has been preparing for years.

5. If you can, don't place family members in direct reporting relationships with one another.

Large companies often have formal policies precluding employees from reporting directly to relatives. The reason is the difficulty in making objective decisions about blood relatives. Small companies may not have this luxury.

6. Don't allow executives' relatives who aren't on the payroll to seek special treatment from employees.

It's a morale buster when family members ask employees to fulfill special requests that are above and beyond that employee's assigned duties.

7. Keep relatives who aren't employees out of the office.

Even if the relatives don't attempt to take advantage of their relationship to an executive, employees are likely to feel under scrutiny or under pressure with them around.

72 Twelve Quotes Worth Quoting About Teamwork

1. If a house be divided against itself, that house cannot stand. —*Mark 3:25*

2. One step by 100 persons is better than 100 steps by one person. —*Koichi Tsukamoto*

3. We must all hang together, or most assuredly we shall all hang separately. —*Benjamin Franklin*

4. It is better to have one person working with you than to have three people working for you. —*Dwight D. Eisenhower*

5. My most important contribution to IBM was my ability to pick strong and intelligent men and then hold the team together by persuasion, by apologies, by financial incentives, by speeches, by chatting with their wives, by thoughtfulness when they were sick . . . and by using every tool at my command to make that team think I was a decent guy. —*Thomas J. Watson*

6. They said you have to use your five best players, but I found you win with the five that fit together best. —*Red Auerbach*

7. People in engineering and manufacturing almost have to be sleeping together; these guys [at Chrysler] weren't even flirting. —*Lee Iacocca*

8. Check your ego at the door. —*Sign placed by Lionel Ritchie at the studio where music legends recorded the song "We Are the World"*

9. When a team outgrows individual performance and learns team confidence, excellence becomes a reality. —*Joe Paterno*

10. Teamwork is consciously espoused but unwittingly shunned by most people in business because they are deathly afraid . . . it will render them anonymous, invisible. —*Srully Blotnick*

11. Soloists are inspiring in opera and perhaps even in small entrepreneurial ventures, but there is no place for them in large organizations. —*Norman Augustine*

12. Confidence [in others] is a thing not to be produced by compulsion. Men cannot be forced into trust. —*Daniel Webster*

6

RENEW YOUR ORGANIZATION

The organizations of yesterday don't fare too well in the dynamic economic, social, political, and business climates of today. Your organization needs to be renewed periodically, and here you'll find tips, techniques, and guidelines about doing just that. You'll learn how to use concepts like re-engineering, teams, outsourcing, strategic planning, and total quality management to meet the challenges ahead.

73 Eleven Strategies to Position Your Company for the Future

When you're in charge, you have to do more than simply make sure things go right today. You're also responsible for making sure that what you do today creates the future you want tomorrow. Unfortunately, most top managers are so busy putting out today's fires they never have time to think about fire prevention. If you don't ponder strategies for positioning your company in the future, you may never have that future.

1. Keep on top of trends.
How are your markets changing? What's happening in research labs around the world that will drastically change what you do and how you do it? What's happening in American culture? What's happening in the world? Keep your finger on the pulse of change. (35)

2. Become a champion for change.
In the words of Lester C. Thurow, "A competitive world has two possibilities for you. You can lose. Or, if you want to win, you can change." Prepare yourself physically and psychologically for the reality of change. View it as an opportunity and an adventure, not a threat. Your outlook on change will have a profound impact on the ways your employees experience it. (2)

3. Hire, reward, and promote the best and brightest.
Your best employees will bring you into the future. Develop human resource systems that identify, train, promote, and reward those people. (49, 50, 57, 60, 61)

4. Train, counsel, reprimand, or terminate laggards.
Don't waste your time, energy, and money pulling employees kicking and screaming into the future. If they won't or can't help you move ahead, help them get jobs with your competitors. (68–70)

5. Think globally, act locally.
Information technology is shrinking the world, creating niche markets around the globe. Think about how your products and services could satisfy customers somewhere else.

6. Innovate or abdicate.
Whatever you're currently producing, you must constantly produce it better, cheaper, and quicker. If you aren't prepared to innovate, then prepare to lose market share.

7. Develop long-term commitments to customers.
Stop thinking in terms of the products or services you provide to customers. Start thinking in terms of the needs you help your customers meet. Stay focused on customer requirements. As you see the requirements changing, be the first on the scene with new solutions. (90)

8. Invest in technology, people, and training.
Stop thinking like an accountant and start thinking like a strategic manager. Money spent on technology, people, and training is not a cost. It's an investment. (57, 63, 64, 114)

9. Stress innovation and adaptation in your talks with employees.
Keep employees on the edge of their seats, not resting comfortably in easy chairs.

10. Fight the complacency of success.
Success is a barrier to change. When things aren't broken, there's no motivation to fix them. Unfortunately, that sometimes means there's no motivation to improve. As Dr. Oliver Wendell Holmes wrote, "The greatest thing in this world is not so much where we are, but in what direction we are moving." Struggle against the shackles of success. Even if you're number one in your market, don't for one

minute be satisfied by the size of the gap between you and the guy in second place.

11. Don't get tied down by sunk costs.

A sunk cost is any investment that has taken you to where you are today. Some organizations are reluctant to buy new equipment because of the money spent on last year's equipment. Others are reluctant to change training procedures because of the cost incurred in the old training. Stop worrying about what you've spent in the past. Invest your money in the future.

74 Seventeen Steps to a Strategic Plan

A strategic plan is the guiding document for your organization, explaining where you're going and how you'll get there. It's created by top management, often with assistance and input from throughout the organization. The strategic planning group should convene yearly for at least a day to revisit the previous year's plan and to establish one for the coming year. Bear in mind that in today's volatile environment many organizations find that portions of their strategic plans may not survive a year. Indeed, in the process of their implementation they undergo constant revision.

TO PREPARE FOR THE STRATEGIC PLANNING SESSION:

1. Contract with a capable facilitator.

For at least two reasons you or one of your managers may not be a good choice to lead the strategic planning session. The leader should be highly talented at facilitation and should have no vested interest in the final shape of the plan; otherwise, he or she will influence it unduly. (83)

2. Schedule a full-day retreat.

Get away from the office. Begin at 8 A.M. and reserve everyone's day until 8 P.M. If this is your first planning session, you may need another day. If you can't reserve that much time, set aside additional hours back in the office.

3. Assemble the planning team.

Choosing members is a tough job. On the one hand, you want to get input from as many people as possible. On the other hand, you want to keep the size of the group manageable. The ideal size for the session group is six to ten people.

4. Get input from employees before the planning session.
Involve managers and employees not invited to the session. Look at the items in #5 of this list. Ask selected people for their input on the items where they can be most helpful. Survey them before the meeting. At the meeting, after the group has exhausted their ideas on an item, reveal the suggestions from the people you polled.

PERFORM THESE STEPS IN SEQUENCE AT THE STRATEGIC PLANNING SESSION, UNDER THE FACILITATOR'S GUIDANCE:

5. Establish the corporate mission.
Nearly every organization has a mission statement describing what the company does and who its customers are. It answers these questions:

- Why do you exist? What business are you in? What products or services do you provide?
- What markets do you serve? Who are your customers? What are their requirements?
- How do you reduce the pain (anxiety, danger, costs, failures) and increase the pleasure (happiness, safety, profits, successes) of your customers?

Keep your mission statement short and simple.

6. Start a corporate vision statement with your aspirations.

- How does your company want to be seen?
- What dreams does it hope to realize?
- What reputation will it establish?
- Where do you intend to be positioned in your industry?
- What desired standards of excellence have you yet to achieve?

A *vision statement* goes beyond the mission to communicate to employees and the world what the organization aspires to become. Two primary benefits of a vision statement are to motivate employees and to make sure they're all guided by the same principles. These principles must reflect the values and beliefs of the organization or they'll be seen as hollow platitudes. After your strategic planning session you may combine your mission and vision statement on one document.

7. Finish the corporate vision statement with your values and beliefs.

The aspirations propose your *desired outcome*; the values and beliefs section reveals *how the organization will get there*. Here are the primary areas in which a vision statement presents values and beliefs, along with one example for each.

- Employees: "We invest in employee professional development and personal growth."
- Customers: "We exceed the expectations of our customers."
- Business: "We manage for the long term."
- Organization: "We assure an organization unencumbered by bureaucracy."
- Environment: "We develop only products that can be manufactured, used, and disposed of in an environmentally responsible way."
- Communities: "We take an active role in the communities in which we work and live."

You may be able to generate as many as three or four values or beliefs in each area.

8. Conduct an external environmental assessment.

What are the major trends (political, economic, technological, religious, social, intellectual, artistic) affecting your business? Which trends represent threats? Which represent opportunities?

9. Conduct an internal organizational assessment.

What do you do extremely well? What do you do less well? What are your distinctive strengths and competencies? What are your clear weaknesses and shortcomings? Do you have any particular advantages or handicaps in the marketplace?

10. Brainstorm short-term objectives.

Given the external and internal assessments, what will you do within the next year? Think of objectives to respond to change, take advantage of external opportunities, and improve your organization. Don't worry about getting agreement on objectives or creating too many at this stage.

11. Brainstorm long-term objectives.

What should you do beyond the next year out to position yourself better for the future?

12. Arrange the objectives in priority order.
First, look for opportunities to group or combine objectives that say essentially the same thing. Second, select those objectives that will have the most immediate and most powerful impact on organizational success. You're not likely to have the resources to work on more than five to ten objectives. Besides, the actions you choose to accomplish the top five or so will probably take care of the rest.

13. Perform a force-field analysis on each objective.
Don't skip this step! If you're not already achieving an objective, there are reasons why. Which forces, factors, or behavior are acting against it? Find out what they are so you can eliminate them. Which forces, factors, or behavior are acting in favor of the objective? Think of ways to enhance these positive forces.

14. Develop action plans for achieving each objective.
For each objective, what actions will minimize the negative forces and maximize the positive ones uncovered in the force-field analysis? Who on the team will accept responsibility for ensuring each action occurs? When and where will it be accomplished? What resources will be required?

TO GET FULL VALUE FROM THE STRATEGIC PLANNING
SESSION AFTERWARDS:

15. Create an accountability document.
List each proposed action in chronological order on a document distributed to each employee involved. At weekly staff meetings track progress on the tasks that were to have been started in the past week and review those for the coming week. Take remedial action as needed.

16. Communicate the results of the session down the line.
Make a report to all employees on the results of the session. Share the newly created mission and vision statements with them. Tell them what they can do to support the action plans.

17. Bring the facilitator back months later.
About four months after the session, meet with the facilitator to check on the overall benefits of the strategic plan and what, if anything, you should do to enhance its value.

75 Eleven Steps to Take When Implementing Change

Alvin Toffler said in his book *Future Shock*, "Man has a limited biological capacity for change. When this capacity is overwhelmed, the capacity is in future shock." If it seems as though your employees are in a constant state of future shock, you may want to re-examine the way you introduce change into your organization. Without strategies like those described below you can expect employees to fight changes, from small new assignments to major new policies.

1. Share your vision.
If employees know where you're headed and share your dreams for the organization, they'll see how proposed changes help to achieve those dreams. They may even become sources of new ideas. (74)

2. Keep employees in touch with the business environment.
If employees are closely connected to customers, to competitors, and to other environmental factors, they won't be sent into shock when you shift directions or priorities. (96)

3. Involve employees.
If possible, let employees who will be affected by the change help you identify the need for it and decide how to respond to it. If you can't do that, at least involve them in planning for the implementation of changes that you initiate.

4. Anticipate their concerns.
People avoid or resist change because they fear losing something: control, security, prestige, self-esteem, pre-eminence, closeness, relationships, freedom, comfort, money, and so on. Consider these factors: What objections do you expect people to raise? How can you respond to those objections as you announce, plan, and implement the change?

5. Explain the change.
Define the change clearly to all involved. Tell them the rationale for it. Specify their role in it. Describe both the short-term and the long-term implications of implementing it. Don't let doubts grow.

6. Let people vent.
Provide forums for disgruntled employees to air their concerns and ask questions. Hold gripe sessions throughout the organization as necessary. (37)

7. Give status to resistance.
Acknowledge the fears and worries you encounter. Don't ignore, belittle, or criticize them. Be patient with employees' initial reluctance to see the same value in the change that you see.

8. Respond.
Once you hear them out, answer employees with data and reassuring information. Correct inaccuracies that may be infesting the grapevine. Communicate your optimism about the change and your belief that the employees will make it work. If possible, tell them the change will be permanent only if it proves its worth.

9. Emphasize benefits.
Answer the WII-FM question: "What's in it for me?" Demonstrate how the change will benefit both the organization and the employees personally. When planning any change, always look for how you can include value for the employees who will carry it out.

10. Demonstrate your resolve.
Show your commitment to the change. Provide the resources people need to implement it. Do more than your share of the work in helping it succeed. Accept more than your share of whatever hardships it demands.

11. Anticipate problems.
While you model optimism, maintain a sharp eye for negative outcomes. Minimize problems by foreseeing the alterations you need to make throughout the organization to accommodate the change. Such alterations include reassigning duties, reconfiguring reporting relationships, ordering different supplies, and training employees in new skills.

76 Nine Strategies for Changing Your Corporate Culture

The management literature is filled with ideas for increasing effectiveness and efficiency. One that may have the greatest impact is to change corporate culture—the values, beliefs, norms, thinking patterns, customs, and rituals that are at the foundation of why employees do what they do. The culture of a company often determines its response to changes and its ability to reposition itself successfully. When you discover that your corporate culture stands in the way of the vitality of your organization, consult this list.

1. Prepare for the long haul.

You won't change your organization's culture overnight. Most experts agree that you should expect to work months and sometimes years. The larger and more physically dispersed your organization, the longer it will take to change. The older and more experienced your management team, the longer it will take to change—and the more necessary it will be to change.

2. Conduct a culture audit.

A culture audit will tell you exactly what parts of your organization are in need of change. For example, it might reveal phlegmatic middle management sandwiched between a top-management team and first-line supervisors who are poised for action. Contract with a consultant to conduct the audit so as to minimize bias. Expect the consultant to use questionnaires, interviews, and observations to assess people's attitudes about work, the future, proposed initiatives, the organization's capabilities, and themselves. (83, 112)

3. Create a clear picture of what you want the culture to become.

What's the gap between what the culture is now and what it needs to be? What do you want your employees to believe? How do you want your customers to be treated? What norms should be guiding your employees' behavior?

4. Communicate your decision to all employees.

Through words and deeds tell your employees where you're taking them and why they should go with you. Become the champion for the new vision.

5. Change yourself.

Demonstrate through relevant behavior modifications of your own that you take this culture-change business seriously. (123)

6. Recruit employees who fit into the new culture and help you develop it.

Recruitment is the lifeblood of your organization. Recruit people who believe in and advocate your vision. It's easy to teach skills, tough to teach values, so recruit values.

7. Train or terminate defenders of the status quo.

Your job is tough enough. Don't waste time and energy pulling naysayers along. Tell employees they're either a part of the future or an artifact of history—in which case they're likely to become history. Give resisters every opportunity to change, but if they won't, ease them out of the organization.

8. Make sure your incentives support the new culture.
Slogans have no currency until the reward (and punishment) system supports them. (49)

9. Reward the heroes of culture change.
Employees who go out of their way to change the culture or who incur personal cost to support corporate beliefs are your heroes. Celebrate their accomplishments. Hold them up as role models.

77 Nine Ways to Create In-House Venture Groups

You realize the benefits of being quick, nimble, and adaptive but find yourself selling the same products or services to the same customers in the same old way. You want to break out of tried and true patterns to create new products and services. One tool that can help you is an in-house venture group: a group of employees who act as entrepreneurs to design new business ventures suited to the future of your industry.

1. View your business as constantly changing, never static.
You'll never create new ventures if you believe you've already done everything you can do and your business is as developed as it's ever going to be.

> Don't confuse changing with expanding. Stop thinking of increasing market share (expanding) or increasing sales of existing lines (expanding) and start thinking of new lines and new customers (changing).

2. Establish a corporate culture of change, renewal, and risk taking.
People won't try new things if the fear of failure is stronger than the joy of success. Through words and deeds communicate that you intend to develop new businesses that have never existed before. Challenge your people to think about tomorrow and the next day, not just yesterday and today. Send a powerful message that your

employees have a vested interest in creating new business by reward-ing them when they do.

3. Incorporate creativity and new product development into your strategic plan.

If creating new ventures is important to your company, it's worth putting into your corporate vision. When it's one of the objectives in your strategic plan, employees understand the importance of behav-ing like in-house entrepreneurs. (74)

4. Commit resources to developing new business.

If you want new lines of business, you have to budget time, money, staffing, and information for their development. Start out by estab-lishing a goal of 10% of revenue, 10% of your time, and 10% of your employees' time.

5. Establish quantifiable goals for new products, services, and cus-tomers.

Shoot for a target that specifies a number of new business ideas every year. For example, your strategic plan could include this long-term objective: "Within three years 15% of our revenues will be gener-ated by lines of business yet to be created."

6. Tag your dinosaurs.

Assume that your existing products or services will be obsolete sooner rather than later. Once each quarter nominate the current product or service most in need of change or most likely to become extinct.

7. Attend creativity seminars with your employees.

New ways of doing business don't come from old ways of thinking. Innovators challenge existing ideas. They ask "why not" and "what if" questions. Creativity seminars show you how to think in novel ways. The investment you make in this training just might pay off in the form of new profits from new services. (64)

8. Create venture groups of cross-functional specialties.

Gather people who normally don't work together on a daily basis. Give them time, money, and resources to develop new business ideas. You don't need a staff dedicated to research and development; those vital functions can be performed by anyone on your payroll whose talents are unleashed.

9. Share ownership of the new business.

If you want employees to act like entrepreneurs, treat them as such. Cut them in on a piece of the action. See that any new product ideas resulting in new business ventures result in equitable compensation for them. You thus encourage employees to share their great ideas with you rather than with your competitors.

78 Twelve Suggestions for Installing Self-Directed Teams

Self-directed teams are the ultimate in delegation. Management tells a self-directed team what they are to achieve. Then it's up to the team to decide how to achieve those outcomes and to see that they happen. The team has no supervisor, though they're responsible to some person or group for their performance. The basic idea behind such teams is to turn employees on by making them feel more ownership for the goals of the organization. Management gains their motivation at the cost of giving up day-to-day control.

1. Be certain self-directed teams make sense for your organization.
Self-managed teams work best when:

- employees won't see them as a form of management manipulation
- employees are willing to submerge personal interests and sacrifice some individuality (difficult for intellectuals and those with strong personalities)
- management *trusts* employees to act in the best interests of the organization
- the organization doesn't have to respond immediately to changing customer demands or market conditions

2. Start small.
For the first self-directed teams in your company, select the department where the concept is most likely to work and nominate those employees who are most likely to thrive under the new system. Get one success under your belt and learn some of the pitfalls before you spread the idea.

3. Train everyone involved.
Instruct the teams and their leaders in the self-directed concept. Explain how they need to behave for the team to succeed. Continue training long after the teams have begun to operate.

4. Give the teams a clear purpose.
Declare your rationale for asking employees to work in this way. Emphasize the benefits to both the organization and to them. Show them how they'll be making a bigger contribution and why they'll enjoy their work more.

5. State clear expectations.
Give the teams clear requirements for what they are to accomplish and the degree of quality they are to attain. Establish mutually agreed-upon measures of success.

6. Establish the role of team leaders.
One of the distinctive features of the self-directed team is the role of team leaders. They may be responsible for coordinating work schedules, ordering supplies, and communicating on behalf of the team to upper management, but not much more. Team members share the responsibility for deciding who does what, making production decisions, and seeing that the work gets done.

7. Establish the role of coaches.
A team's coach may be its management link to the larger organization. Coaches ensure their teams have the resources they need. They remain accessible to teams and to individual members. They work closely with teams to evaluate their outcomes and they conduct performance appraisals on individual members. (Ideally, team members should evaluate each other's performance, but many employees are understandably reluctant to do so.) Ask each of your self-directed teams for a list of whatever support they need from their coach in order to succeed. (63)

8. Support coaches.
Their contribution can easily become forgotten in the excitement of newly formed self-directed teams. Coaches who previously served as line supervisors may question their value to the organization in their new role. Support them with counseling, training, and encouragement. Include them in team recognition and rewards. (63)

9. Give teams lots of feedback.
See that coaches give their teams a steady stream of feedback on their performance. Provide whatever help teams need to improve their operation. Make sure they get an avalanche of positive rein-

forcement from coaches, from upper management, from customers, and from you. (48, 51)

10. Trust the teams to make important decisions.
Let the teams make hiring decisions, select training suppliers, arrange vacation schedules, and handle a range of decisions typically reserved for management.

11. Reward the team.
When teams succeed, reward the whole team and their coach, not just the stars.

The sales manager of the western region of a large sales organization turned her sales force into a self-directed team. She gave them the organization's vision for the future, she set a sales target, and she asked what resources they needed to meet the target. Then she turned them loose to decide how they'd organize themselves. Unfortunately, the sales manager continued the tradition of commissions based on individual sales records. The team was soon torn apart by jealousies and internal squabbling over account assignments. Only when the commission structure was revised to reward everyone equally based on the success of the team did the self-directed process take hold.

---

12. Decide if it works.
After six months and again after one year, conduct a formal evaluation of the results of self-directed teams. If the bottom line is improved and if the teams are working well, simply fine tune them. If they're not succeeding, make whatever changes you believe are needed or return to more traditional work groups.

---

79 Seven Tips for Managing the Outsourced Employee

Outsourcing is drastically transforming how we conduct business. More and more staff functions in companies (e.g., accounting, finance, human resources, purchasing) are being performed by employees acting as independent consultants or by smaller firms acting as subcontractors. The advantages to outsourcing are efficiency and lowered costs. The disadvantage is that management must deal with employees not under their administrative control. This list provides advice for getting the most out of outsourced employees.

1. Develop a relationship with a single employment agency.
There are many temporary employment agencies in the market. Find one that understands the kind of employees you need, the kind of work they'll do, and what it's like to work in your company. The agency should screen out inappropriate applicants rather than waste your time trying to make them fit.

2. Make sure the contractor has no conflicts of interest.
Is your outsourced employee working for a competitor? What guarantees do you have that your company files remain confidential and secure? Probe these issues before you outsource any company activity.

3. Work with a written contract.

- What exactly will the employee be accountable for?
- How much will the employee be paid?
- How long will the project last?
- How much support will the employee receive from certain departments?
- Under what conditions will the contract be terminated?

4. Establish unequivocal lines of control and accountability.
Do outsourced employees work for you or the firm that placed them? If employees fail to meet expectations, who will intervene— you or supervisors in the outsourcing firm? Negotiate the lines of responsibilities.

5. Indoctrinate the employee in your corporate culture.
Employees should understand your organization's norms, values, and beliefs. What makes your company special? How do you want internal customers (employees) and external customers to be treated? Outsourced employees are visitors to your culture and need to learn its customs. (74)

6. Brief permanent employees.
Insist that your people treat outsourced employees with respect, professionalism, and sensitivity. They may not be immediate family, but they're at least as important as first cousins visiting from another state.

7. Invite outsourced employees to company social functions.
Immerse the employees in the corporate culture as much as you can.
Make them feel like extended family.

80 Sixteen Steps to Install a Successful TQM Process

Total quality management (TQM) is designed to improve quality,
increase productivity, and add value to all work activities in any
organization. TQM is a CEO's best friend because it simultaneously
increases customer satisfaction, improves financial performance,
and enhances employee contributions and pride. When a commitment to quality drives strategic operational decisions, a lasting
cultural change is created and sustained. Studies show a four to
five-fold return on the funds invested in well-run TQM programs.

1. Add quality to your strategic plan.
Quality is never an accident. It's created by the quality process that
you install. Many organizations have financial plans, staffing plans,
and capital plans. In the same way, you achieve high quality by
having a total quality management plan. (74)

2. Install a quality system.
Installing a quality system is hard work. There are no short cuts. The
system must involve the whole organization and address the output
of every employee. Success is measured by:

  • training employees to accept responsibility for preventing defects
  • fully satisfying the needs of both internal and external customers
  • continuous improvement

3. Become a quality leader.
Change starts at the top. Get personally involved. Become a TQM
role model. Put your quality values in writing and ensure that your
actions are aligned with the goals of the organization. Work con-
tinuously to improve the quality program. Change work processes
as needed.

4. Define quality.
Most employees will be eager to support quality—especially if they
know what it's all about. Help everyone in your company understand quality in the same way.

A definition of quality applicable to any work is *conforming to valid requirements* of the intended user. "Valid" means that the requirement must be both achievable and essential to the customer. Establish these valid requirements in consultation with your customers. Ask what they demand from you in order to achieve their mission (in the case of corporate clients) or meet their needs (in the case of individual consumers).

---

5. Measure quality.

Quality is quantifiable (e.g., seven defects cost $15 each to correct). The ability to measure quality lets you know whether you're improving and how much poor quality is costing you.

6. Establish quality goals.

You can't improve everything at once. Target the most important processes, services, or products to improve. Define the valid requirements and measures. Then display these measures for everyone to see. Tell everyone what you're pursuing and invite them to join you.

7. Prevent defects.

Why is it we always have time to do things over, but never time to do things right? By establishing valid requirements you focus on preventing defects, and the person doing the work becomes responsible for controlling quality. This results in higher quality and productivity while reducing your cost for finding and fixing defects.

8. Demand 100% conformance.

Striving for 100% conformance to valid requirements doesn't mean defects won't occur; it means that improvement will be continuous. When you and your management team become intolerant of defects and search relentlessly for the root causes of problems, dramatic improvement becomes the norm.

9. Assign responsibility for quality.

Because you can't know the details of every work activity, you must delegate quality control responsibility to employees. All employees should know the valid requirements for their work input and output and be held responsible for measuring and controlling them. Instruct employees not to guess or try their best. Teach them to stop, ask questions, suggest improvements, and tell their managers about any nonconformance.

10. Invest in education.
Your employees are your competitive edge in the quality improvement wars. Sharpen this edge by educating them in TQM. Show them how to solve quality problems. Ensure that their supervisors have been educated in the art of inspiring leadership. Make a commitment to long-term employee development at all levels.

11. Win employee commitment.
Many organizations have adopted one form of TQM or another. This means that a number of your employees have heard of the concept. As a result they also have a preconceived notion of its value. The typical objection you'll want to defuse is that a quality system adds to the responsibilities employees already carry. Explain to them that TQM *enhances* their work. It becomes enmeshed in their routine and soon makes their work more trouble free.

12. Create employee teams.
Quality improvement teams are essential to TQM. Ultimately, every employee should be on a team. Functional, cross-functional, supplier, and customer teams are all appropriate. A properly trained team brings the power of many minds to bear on quality issues. Teams serve as "learning laboratories" for personal interaction, planning, and managing skills. (56)

13. Install an employee suggestion system.
Employees who do the work know best what inhibits them from producing quality output and improving productivity. However, they often either don't know how to remove the inhibitors or don't have the authority to eliminate them. (40)

14. Establish a reward and recognition system.
When your employees fulfill their quality commitments and contribute to the achievement of your quality goals, provide appropriate rewards and recognition. Ask employees what they'd like to receive. (49, 50)

15. Communicate, communicate, communicate.
Tell your employees everything you know about your TQM process. Share your vision, the quality goals, the progress being made, and of

course the successes. Celebrate employee contributions, team milestones, improvements in customer satisfaction, and everything else that demonstrates the importance you place on quality improvement. Use all available media.

16. Make quality first.
You can be sure of one thing: your commitment to quality will be tested more than once. Be ready to walk the talk. When the inevitable struggle between short-term cost and long-term gain rears its head, put quality first.

81 | Twelve Considerations in Re-Engineering Your Company

You win in business when you come up with the idea first, design it quicker than your competition, and deliver it with total customer satisfaction. Of all the factors necessary for smart, quick, and nimble responsiveness, perhaps the most important is a lean organizational structure. Organizations are like people; as they get older and more successful, they put on fat. The remedy for fat people is diet and exercise; the remedy for fat organizations is *re-engineering*.

1. Continually remind coworkers whom you all work for.
Re-engineering is driven by one goal: *Satisfying the customer.* Any and all design decisions about reporting relationships or layers of management are made with the customer in mind. Your new organizational structure should bring everyone closer to the market. (96)

2. Draw organizational charts in pencil, not pen.
The structure is never finished. View re-engineering as a never-ending process. As your market and your competition change, so must you. Think re-engineer*ing*, not re-engineer*ed*.

3. Prepare for internal resistance.
Re-engineering challenges the status quo and moves employees beyond their comfort zones. Some will champion re-engineering; others will resist, both passively and actively. Show resisters how re-engineering will benefit them.

4. Think in-out, not up-down.
Most organizations are hierarchies reflecting power, status, and functional departments. That's up-down thinking. Forget about

hierarchy. Start focusing on your customer and design structures that push products and services out. That's in-out thinking.

5. Think processes, not departments.

Processes are groups of activities that help you meet basic customer expectations (e.g., fulfilling orders, maintaining equipment, invoicing). Departments are groups of employees who work in close proximity and have the same functional expertise (e.g., sales, finance and accounting, shipping). Employees should identify with the processes they maintain to satisfy customer needs, rather than the functional departments in which they perform those processes.

6. Think flat, not tall.

The more layers in your organization, the more internal lethargy, and the more bureaucracy experienced by customers. Removing layers of management pushes control down to the employees who get the work done and serve the customer.

7. Think team, not individual, leadership.

No act of re-engineering will change the fact that authority and responsibility rest at the top of every organization. What re-engineering can affect is how that authority and power are distributed. The person in charge should share with his or her senior staff the joint responsibility for many strategic operational decisions.

8. Think empower, not control.

When everyone works for the customer, control is in the customer's hand, not the management team. Managers have the role of empowering employees to respond to the dictates of "Boss Customer." Two ways to achieve this empowerment are:

- a leadership style that invests employees with a maximum of both responsibility and accountability
- using technology to create intelligent decision makers throughout the organization: shared databases, integrated PCs, and decision support systems

9. Think bridges, not walls.

Departments suggest rigidity, bureaucracy, tunnel vision, and parochial concerns. Department personnel work for the department head. By contrast, teams of cross-functional experts work for the customer. Create reporting structures that link cross-functional teams, rather than departments.

10. Think networks, not pyramids.

If you think about your organization as a collection of overlapping information networks (similar to the Internet), you'll have a more adaptive, responsive structure than if you see it as a pyramid. The former image focuses on information exchange, the latter on obedience and compliance.

11. Think time, cost, and customer satisfaction.

Improving a process ultimately means reducing the time and cost required to perform it, thus increasing organizational efficiency and customer satisfaction. Three questions dominate the discussion when re-engineering a particular process:

- How do we perform it in a shorter time?
- How do we perform it cheaper?
- How do we make the customer happier?

12. Think cultural change, not incremental improvement.

Re-engineering is rethinking the nature of what your organization does and how it does it. If you and your employees are prepared to change your culture from one of hierarchical control to empowered customer service workers, re-engineering will uplift you in the market. (76)

---

82 Twelve Ways to Turn Suppliers into Partners

Someone once described suppliers as friendly next-door neighbors. They maintain their own property but have a vested interest in seeing that your property also looks good. A supplier does indeed have a vested interest in making you look good. However, some companies have created strained relationships with their suppliers from not knowing how to turn a supplier into a partner.

1. Balance price and quality.

If your sole criterion for selecting a supplier is lowest price, you may pay dearly in the long run. Consider price, but not at the expense of such factors as responsiveness, delivery dates, shipping costs, quality of materials, training for users, and time required to create special orders.

2. Share your mission and vision statements with suppliers.
Your suppliers should know what you believe and why you believe it. Your values and beliefs help define the relationship you and suppliers develop over time. (74)

3. Ask to see your suppliers' vision and mission statements.
If they don't have one, suggest they develop one. Find out what they believe and why they believe it. You're their customer. How do they believe customers should be treated?

4. Help your supplier help you.
Think symbiosis—mutual interdependence. Find out what you and your employees can do to enable your supplier to serve you better. If you can help your supplier without jeopardizing relationships with your customers, do so.

5. Draft a statement of expectations.
Before you take on any new suppliers, share with them a detailed statement of the service you expect. Ask them for a reciprocal set of expectations—what they need from you and your employees to meet your service requirements.

6. Discuss issues of confidentiality and conflicts of interest.
If your supplier is also selling to your competitor, what guarantees can you get that your proprietary information will be protected? Before a supplier can expect to receive favored treatment from you, both parties must clearly understand this issue.

7. Share with trusted suppliers the results of strategic planning sessions.
This enables key suppliers to bid on how they can help you achieve the long-term goals of the company and it alerts them to your future resource needs.

8. Share letters of praise and complaints.
You live and die by satisfying customers. Similarly your suppliers live and die by satisfying you. Share the good news and the bad with suppliers involved in your products. You and your suppliers succeed or fail together.

9. Invite favored suppliers to company celebrations.
Integrate suppliers into your corporate culture. Let employees see them at picnics, parties, retreats, and ceremonies. Your suppliers

will feel like extended family and will try that much harder to satisfy you and your customers.

10. Take suppliers on a tour of your facilities.
Give your suppliers a behind-the-scenes view of how you do what you do. Suppliers need to understand fully what happens to their products at your facilities.

11. Ask suppliers for ideas on product or process improvements.
Suppliers bring a different perspective—a perspective that might greatly improve what you do and how you do it. Solicit their recommendations for any initiatives on which you suspect they have expertise. It's like hiring a free consultant.

12. Ask suppliers to provide technical training for your staff.
What are the most efficient ways to use that new software package? What are the safest ways to store a particular raw material? What new developments are on the horizons? Suppliers can answer questions like these and provide training on the best ways to use their products or services.

83 Ten Tips for Hiring a Consultant

A number of the checklists in this book recommend hiring consultants. Whenever you purchase anything for your company, you ask this crucial question: What's the return for this investment? Ask the same question when you hire a consultant. Because of the specialized knowledge that consultants possess and the intangible nature of much of their value, you might make the mistake of being less critical and discerning than you should be.

1. First specify your need.
If you don't clearly define the problem, you may buy a solution to a problem you don't have.

> If you can't fully identify the problem in advance, consider using one consultant to identify the problem and another to help you solve it. Here's one reason why. Let's say you know you've got serious morale problems but haven't figured out why. If you hire a human relations consultant both to pinpoint the cause and to recommend solutions, you're tempting that consultant to find the problems he knows how to solve.

2. Don't hire a consultant with prepackaged solutions.
Your problem is not generic. Your problem is unique because it's in *your* company, involving *your* people, and occurring *now*. Retain consultants with a reputation for studying organizations' problems and designing customized solutions.

3. Check with colleagues.
Hire someone who comes highly recommended by colleagues and friends in your industry. Find someone with a track record of producing satisfied customers among people whose judgment you trust.

4. Don't shop for bargains.
The best consultants don't come cheap. Their services are in great demand, so they charge high daily fees. But if you follow the advice on this list, the benefits you reap from their services will far outstrip their expense.

5. Meet face to face before you decide.
Except for those doing very small jobs or high-priced talent from out of town, prospective consultants should be willing to meet "on their nickel" for you to judge what they have to bring to your situation.

6. Search for "chemistry," "feel," and comfort level.
You're inviting someone into your company who may have access to private, sensitive information. You're going to trust the wisdom of some very critical advice. This may be the first date leading to a long-term relationship. Go beyond your five senses to evaluate a consultant's fit with you and your organization.

7. Ask for a proposal in simple, jargon-free language.
What exactly is the consultant proposing to do?

- How much will it cost?
- What are the expected benefits and measurable outcomes?
- How long will the project take?
- When does the consultant get paid?
- What happens if you aren't satisfied with the results?

8. Ask for an assessment of worst-case and best-case scenarios.
Any consulting project has a downside risk and may create unexpected problems. What are those potential problems? How likely

are they? What will the consultant do to prevent them and solve them? If your consultant won't or can't answer these questions, look elsewhere.

9. Find a consultant who will empower you.

Don't become dependent on a consultant. The best consultants are so good that clients never need them again. Make sure your consultant's dual goals are to help you solve your problem and to empower you to solve similar problems on your own.

10. If you hire a large consulting firm, insist on final approval over who will service your account.

Don't contract with a large consulting group based solely on its reputation. Put the individual consultant, or consulting team, the firm plans to give you through the rigorous scrutiny recommended in this checklist.

84 Ten Qualities to Look for in a Board Member

Membership on an organization's governing board carries significant status in our society, and rightly so. To be elected or selected for membership means that you possess qualities and talents that the typical citizen does not. What are these talents and qualities? When organizations search for individuals to replace a retiring or deceased member, or when they search for members for a newly composed board, what and whom should they be looking for?

1. Respect and visibility in the community.

Define community either locally, regionally, or nationally. The person should enhance the overall image and prestige of your organization.

2. Insight and intelligence.

The person should bring brainpower. Board members must be able to see the big picture and quickly reduce complex problems into manageable ones.

3. Talents and experience complementing the current board.

Don't look for someone who is exactly like everyone else on the board. Look for someone who adds variety to the existing talent.

4. Diversity.

Don't select minorities because of affirmative action; choose them because of the value they add. A portion of this value will be the perspective that many white, Anglo-Saxon, Protestant males cannot bring to the deliberations. (85)

5. A proven track record as administrator, leader, or business owner.

Look for someone who has "been there"—someone with experience making the tough decisions on which you seek counsel.

6. Integrity.

You need a board member who will keep you honest and make sure the company is a forthright, upstanding corporate citizen. A board member who will cut corners and engage in shady deals, regardless of how financially successful he or she may be, is not for your board.

7. Courage of one's convictions.

You don't want an observer or passive participant. You want someone to read the reports critically, listen to discussions intensely, and voice his or her views assertively. Don't pad your board with people who will rubber stamp your decisions.

8. The ability to be a team player.

Board members who want to work with other board members to ensure your success are the kind of people you want on your side. While you may need a few creative mavericks, round out the membership with those who work well with others.

9. Time to serve.

Don't get so taken with the credentials of potential board members that you end up with a group of winners who don't have the time or inclination to help *you* win.

> A good rule of thumb: If you have to twist someone's arm to serve, that person is unlikely to devote the time or the energy you need at the top of your organization.

10. A willingness to serve the organization, not use it.

Ego-driven people who want to use their position for the prestige it brings them or the perks they can extract should be on your competitor's board, not yours.

85 Thirteen Steps to Open Yourself and Your Organization to Diversity

Business is becoming more global, and our workplace more diverse. Today, being effective means knowing how to deal with the inevitable differences associated with gender, race, ethnicity, values, beliefs, physical abilities, and job classifications. These differences can result in serious conflicts when we don't understand or respect each other. These same differences also represent important opportunities. By learning to value each other and by learning how to manage interpersonal conflict bred by differences, you become better prepared to create high-performing work teams and to serve your diverse customers with distinction.

1. Acknowledge your biases and prejudices.
We all have prejudices. They were taught to us at an early age, and we develop new ones every day. That's part of the human condition. However, when your prejudices block others from making meaningful contributions, you fail yourself and your organization. Consciously work to manage your own biases so they don't become barriers.

2. Practice "reframing."
When you're in a situation where your biases come up, challenge them.

If John, an applicant for a management position, says he likes to spend as much time as he can with his children, your biases might lead you to conclude that he's a stable, family man, likely to work hard. If another applicant with the same qualifications, Mary, says the same thing, your biases might lead you to think she's probably going to be distracted and absent a lot to take care of her family. In this case, *reframing* involves seeing Mary just as positively as John for her dedication to her family, and perhaps even marveling that she has achieved so much while raising five children.

---

3. Look for opportunities to learn from others.
Seek the benefits that divergent perspectives bring to your work team. Practice walking in other people's shoes. Ask your colleagues in another department what their experience is like. Remind your-

self of a time when you felt isolated because you were abroad, or the only member of your gender or race at a large meeting. Use that memory to empathize with newcomers. Listen carefully to different people's perspectives. This enables you to make wiser decisions about how to improve your work team and serve your customers.

4. Create diverse decision-making teams.
If you want to invent a better mouse trap, you have to create a climate where you can get diverse ideas generated. Homogeneous teams give you limited perspectives. Make sure that your work teams represent a wide range of views and experiences. It will improve employee morale since your valued workers won't feel excluded.

5. Value your own difference!
Each of us is a culture unto ourselves. We have all had unique experiences based on our age, race, gender, job experiences, family background, the places we've been, and the beliefs we hold. Valuing and managing workplace diversity begins with understanding and valuing yourself. By understanding and prizing your own differences, you'll respect and welcome other people's uniqueness.

6. Check your policies for inclusiveness.
People do what's rewarded in their organizations. If you want to create a workplace where people are valued, your work policies must be inclusive.

- Is your scheduling of work hours sensitive to the needs of working parents?
- Do your products reflect the needs of consumers from different racial or ethnic backgrounds?
- Can people tell the truth at work without fear of repercussions?
- Are company menus planned with different ethnic groups on your workforce in mind (e.g., dietary rules, ethnic cuisine)?
- Are company events planned with everyone on your workforce in mind (e.g., games that many people can play, cultural outings many people would like)?

In short, do you treat people as they would like to be treated?

7. Challenge jokes, comments, and gestures that offend.
Creating a healthy, inclusive workplace means making sure that no group members are made to feel less than their peers. Remind people of the negative impact of jokes, comments, or gestures that may

alienate their colleagues or offend valued customers. State your expectations for company conduct clearly, then model the way yourself, by avoiding such behavior.

8. Get feedback on how your behavior affects those different from you.

Few managers have the good sense to regularly ask, "How am I doing?" Yet this feedback is absolutely essential for personal growth and managerial effectiveness. When in doubt about your behavioral choices in dealing with differences, ask! Then be willing to use what you learn the next time around. (34)

9. Mentor, or be mentored by, someone different from you.

People who mentor someone of a race, gender, or background other than theirs consistently report that they learn as much as the protégé. Move outside of your own comfort zone so you can gain and give new perspectives. (62)

10. Ask your customers for their needs.

Excellence in service begins with a commitment to diversity. Use customer feedback to become better at meeting the needs of many different kinds of customers. Your products and services will be sought by a wider range of customers. In addition, your organization will become the place of choice for a broader scope of talented employees seeking to make their fullest contribution. (94)

11. Be inclusive in your use of language.

Look for how your language and the language of your employees send exclusionary messages.

When businesswomen get mail addressed "Sir" or "Gentlemen," they're reminded of their difference from the norm and feel excluded because of it. The woman in the hard hat who broke barriers by getting on a construction team is told the same by a sign that says "Men at Work." The man in your hospital who happens to be a nurse, or the man in your office who happens to be a secretary, hears the same exclusionary message when he's identified as a "male nurse" or "male secretary." Consider the woman working to support her kids who is labeled "working mom," while her male counterpart is never called a "working dad."

12. Assume other people's experiences are valid for them.
Communicate in a way that sends the clear message "This is how I see things, and I want to learn how you see things." When you insist on getting everyone to see things your way, you miss opportunities to learn from others. Rarely is someone's perspective "right" and someone else's "wrong." It's usually a matter of different experiences leading to different perspectives.

13. Challenge the status quo.
The gift of valuing diversity is that it opens your mind to change. It empowers you to be more creative and more adaptive to your environment. Take advantage of these gifts by welcoming change in yourself and in others. Reward those who bring new ideas and perspectives to the table. Constantly look for opportunities to experiment, take risks, and empower others to act in new ways. Many of the secrets of innovation and excellence are rooted in diversity. (76)

86 Ten Ways to Improve Your Corporate Citizenship

You don't need an MBA to realize that people like to do business with organizations they respect. When this emotional attachment translates to the bottom line, it's called goodwill. When a company is audited to determine its market value, goodwill is one of the factors. Obviously it's in your best interest to be a good corporate citizen. It's good for you, your employees, your customers, and the larger society.

1. Never break the law.
Make it clear to every employee that actions in violation of local, state, or federal statutes will not be tolerated even if the crime goes undetected by authorities. Go one step beyond by striving to do even more than the law requires. (53)

2. Paint your building, mow your lawn, fix the fence.
Good neighbors take care of their property. This strategy is especially important if your facility is in an otherwise rundown section of town. You'll send a strong message to the community that you're proud of your company. Your facility could become the anchor of the neighborhood and a model for urban renewal.

3. Support employees who are active in the community.
You may have employees active in their church or synagogue, the United Way, civic groups, or other philanthropic organizations. Make it easy for them to continue their efforts. Make them heroes. Publicize them in the company newsletter. Don't make them feel like thieves if they use the copy machine.

4. Create an executive-on-loan program.
Some corporations provide sabbatical leaves for executives who work for philanthropic groups. Depending on the duration of the sabbatical, and the executive's salary, the philanthropic group may provide a portion of the salary. Look for a creative way to make it happen.

5. Choose a cause for the company as a whole to support.
Children's hospitals, tornado and flood victims, the Muscular Dystrophy Association, and other causes have reaped enormous benefits from corporate philanthropy. If you don't have a personal reason for selecting one cause, ask your employees to choose one that they as a group would like to support.

6. Start a company speaker's bureau.
Local groups are always looking for speakers. Make sure your message is instructional and uplifting, not a spiel for your product or service.

7. Fund a scholarship.
When you pay for someone's education, you invest in the future. A scholarship touches many lives. It's not only the right thing to do; it generates a good deal of favorable publicity.

8. Create a partnership with a local public school.
Schools are always looking for guest lecturers, benefactors to underwrite supplies, and successful role models to serve as aides or mentors. Today's students are tomorrow's corporate leaders.

9. Recycle corporate trash.
One man's trash is another man's gold. You may be amazed at the value groups would find in what your company throws away—from the copper in old wires to the uneaten food in your cafeteria. Assign this project to one of your most creative managers. The recipients of your largesse will be deeply appreciative.

10. If you downsize, do so with compassion and care.
Layoffs send a powerful message to the community. Don't effect them with an iron hand and callous disregard. (87)

87 Fifteen Ways to Handle Layoffs Effectively and Compassionately

If there is one lesson companies have learned in the last decade, it is this: No employee can be guaranteed a job for life. Even Japanese companies, long admired for their ability to provide lifetime employment, are no longer able to keep that pledge. Layoffs hurt. They hurt managers who must deliver the pink slips and they devastate the employees who receive them. Although it's impossible to lay off people without producing pain, it's possible to lessen that pain.

1. Don't promise or imply lifetime employment.
The pain of layoffs is heightened if employees believe that management has been dishonest with them, promising security but not delivering. This should be the message to all employees: The future is uncertain, but if you do your best we'll do our best to make sure you grow with us and thus appreciate in value both to us and to other employers in the marketplace.

2. Consider other alternatives for cutting labor costs.
Job sharing, shortened work weeks, benefit reductions, and across-the-board pay cuts are a few other options for cutting labor costs. Consider all alternatives before you reflexively choose layoffs. Also consider turning a full-time employee into a part-time, outsourced employee. Many employees find working for you on a part-time or as-needed basis an attractive option to no employment at all. (79)

3. Consider other alternatives for cutting costs.
What might happen if you convened employee focus groups throughout your organization with the following assignment? "Recommend cost-cutting measures sufficient to prevent us from having to lay off x number of employees at the end of the year. These measures must not reduce our ability to meet customer needs."

4. Consider ways to generate revenues.
What might happen if you convened employee focus groups throughout your organization with the following assignment?

"Recommended income-generating ideas sufficient to prevent us from having to lay off *x* number of employees at the end of the year."

5. Be as honest with employees as possible.

Rumors of impending layoffs spread through a workforce like wild-fire through dried brush. These rumors will affect employee productivity and morale. If layoffs are being considered, don't deny it. Disclose as much as you can within legal, operational, and competitive constraints.

6. Make sure your decision is nondiscriminatory.

Don't violate EEO and affirmative action guidelines or labor contracts in your decisions of whom to lay off and how. Check with your legal counsel even if you don't have doubts.

7. Inform employees privately.

Tell employees in private meetings, with no one who might be standing outside your office knowing the topic of the meeting. Don't inform employees in writing before the face-to-face announcement. If many employees are laid off, a larger group meeting to discuss the details and the implications of the layoffs may be appropriate *after* the initial in-person notification. Employees should never learn they have lost their jobs by seeing their name on a "hit list."

8. Consider timing.

Inform the person at the end of the work day. While there's no good time to announce job losses, you minimize the negative impact on other employees if you tell the person at the end of the day.

> If at all possible, don't announce layoffs or have them go into effect during or immediately after the holiday season. Not only will you look bad in the news, but employees may have just made gift purchases that they would have reconsidered had they known.

9. Prepare to console.

For many people losing a job is more than losing a paycheck; it's losing identity. This loss can be traumatic. Count on offering the employee a box of tissues, a cup of coffee, and a receptive ear. Also count on bearing the brunt of some angry reactions.

10. Offer outplacement help.

Contract the services of a respected outplacement firm that will help employees find employment elsewhere. If your firm is small and you're laying off just one or two people, offer access to your company's secretarial services and other administrative support in securing another job.

11. Negotiate a fair severance package.

Every decision you make during layoffs sends a message to remaining employees. Let them know that their employer is fair and reasonable. If at all possible, continued health coverage for some specified period should be part of this package. Get advice from your human resources officer.

12. If you expect trouble, have security guards available.

The compassion you have for terminated employees must be tempered by your responsibility for the security of the rest of the workforce and for corporate assets. If you think an employee or group of employees will seek revenge or act out in a violent manner, have security guards standing in the wings.

13. Escort the employee off premises.

Terminated employees should leave the premises as soon as possible. This is for the good of those terminated, for survivors, and for your organization. Security guards can provide the escort. If you don't have guards, do it yourself. Unfortunately, there have been too many cases of industrial sabotage perpetrated by outgoing employees. Escort with compassion. Don't treat the person like a leper or a criminal.

14. Conduct a meeting with survivors.

Remaining employees are the walking wounded. They've lost friends and are justifiably concerned about their job security. Talk about the future, answer questions, allay fears. But most important, listen. (37)

15. Avoid signs of extravagant spending following layoffs.

If you're cutting costs at the expense of human capital, make sure you don't alienate remaining employees with lavish supply orders, executive perks, and the like. When you bite the bullet during layoffs, you send an important message to employees. They know you're one of them.

88 Nine Tips for Creating a Succession Plan

If you've ever tried to secure a business loan, you're aware of the importance of a succession plan. Investors want to make sure that if anything happens to you, the business will still operate. Just as a will provides peace of mind for an individual, a succession plan provides security for the corporation. Create one not because you believe you *will* need it, but because you *might* need it.

1. Get a complete physical.
The best succession plan is one that keeps you healthy. Monitor your risk factors, control stress, follow your physician's advice.

2. Refer to your strategic plan.
Your strategic plan tells you what business you're becoming. Do you have the resident talent to take you there? The strategic plan is the starting point for the job descriptions you'll be writing in the future. (74)

3. Inventory the talents and skills of current employees.
If your performance appraisal system is doing what it should be doing, you already have an accurate assessment of what your employees can do versus what they need to do. Identify those who are closest to having the talent, skill, and vision to step into your shoes tomorrow.

4. Train, mentor, coach, delegate.
Develop your employees' talents and skills so that employees learn what they need to know to run the company in your absence.

5. Manage so that you are dispensable.
A well-run company is like a well-run kingdom. They both should endure regardless of how often a new king is enthroned. If you're indispensable, you're hurting your company, not helping it. Share information, power, and strategy. Your replacement should be on your payroll as you read this list.

6. Discuss succession planning with your board.
A good board will bring up the issue of a succession plan. If they don't, you must. A good CEO plans for the certainty that he or she won't be around forever.

7. **Select someone in the wings as an acting or interim replacement.**
Who would step in tomorrow if necessary? Who could provide transitional leadership while a full-blown search was conducted for a permanent replacement? What can you do right now to groom that person more?

8. **Keep abreast of the top talent in your industry.**
Who are the rising stars? What talent will soon be entering the market because of downsizing? Who out there might be a candidate for your seat?

9. **Purchase "key man" insurance for key executives.**
Consult with your insurance agent regarding the options for disability and life insurance. Negotiate with your board regarding who will be responsible for premiums and who will be the beneficiary.

89 Twelve Quotes Worth Quoting About Organizational Renewal

1. There is no more powerful engine driving an organization toward excellence and long-range success than an attractive, worthwhile, achievable vision for the future, widely shared. —*Burt Nanus*

2. Destiny is not a matter of chance, it is a matter of choice; it is not a thing to be waited for, it is a thing to be achieved. —*William Jennings Bryan*

3. Unless the company is endowed with . . . individuals who challenge old practices and, when necessary, violate company rules and policy, it won't be able to meet the difficult challenge of changing conditions. —*Thomas V. Bonoma*

4. The dogmas of the quiet past are inadequate to the stormy present. —*Abraham Lincoln*

5. One of the best lessons children learn through video games is that standing still will get them killed quicker than anything else. —*Jinx Milea & Pauline Little*

6. I skate to where the puck is going to be, not where it is. —*Wayne Gretsky*

7. If you don't know where you are going, you might wind up someplace else. —*Yogi Berra*

8. If you see in any given situation only what everybody else can see, you can be said to be so much a representative of your culture that you are a victim of it. —*S. I. Hayakawa*

9. The best way to predict the future is to invent it. —*Alan Kay*

10. I've never been satisfied with anything we've ever built. I've felt that dissatisfaction is the basis of progress. When we become satisfied in business, we become obsolete. —*Bill Marriott, Sr.*

11. The whittling away of middle management is further reinforcing the trend for companies to smash the hierarchical pyramid and adopt new people structures such as networks, intrapreneurs, and small teams. —*John Naisbitt and Patricia Aburdene*

12. It's real simple. If we're not getting more, better, faster than *they* are getting more, better, faster, then we're getting less better or more worse. —*Tom Peters*

7 STAY CLOSE TO THE CUSTOMER

Unless someone chooses to buy your product or service, you'll never be in charge of anything. This chapter is a self-contained training program for turning your customers into raving fans. You won't find hollow platitudes and "rah rah" slogans. You will find practical techniques for immediately achieving exceptional customer service.

90 Eighteen Principles to Guide Total Quality Service

In time of reduced resources and fierce competition, your best hope to protect your bottom line is to attract new customers and to keep your old ones. How do you perform this dual feat? By having a superb reputation for how you treat customers.

1. Establish a customer service vision.
Create an ambitious, inspiring, and widely accepted corporate statement of how you value your customers and employees and how you pledge to serve them. Plaster it throughout your organization: on wall plaques, on wallet cards, in your annual report, and so on. The other items on this list will give you some ideas of what might be included in the vision. (74)

2. Walk your talk.
Give your front-line service providers the time, facilities, equipment, and products they need to do a good job. Set a positive example to them in the way *you* treat customers. (54)

3. Hire the right people.
Recruit and choose employees with a knack for being courteous, pleasant, cheerful, and sensitive to others. Favor those who enjoy people, smile a lot, and love to serve others. (57, 61)

4. Orient and train employees to serve well.
Orient new hires thoroughly into your customer care culture with the help of your vision (see item #1). Train them to have outstanding product knowledge and the skills to apply that knowledge to serving customers.

5. State your customer service expectations.
Communicate your precise expectations for exceptional customer service to employees so they know exactly how they are to handle many situations. (93)

6. Put the customer second.
Customer relations mirror employee relations. Treat your employees even better than you treat your customers. Inspire them through your thoughtful and motivating leadership to *want* to serve customers exceptionally. Pay your people commensurate with what you ask of them. Dispense attractive benefits and bonuses. Provide job security, good working conditions, high status, fair treatment, and consistent company policies.

7. Serve through teams.
Build close-knit teams of employees to wait on customers and service their accounts. Don't force your customers to depend on one person to get what they need. (56)

8. Provide feedback.
Give employees regular, comprehensive performance reviews that measure their customer responsiveness. Recognize good effort with valued tangible rewards or enthusiastic praise. Criticize sub-par sensitivity to customer needs. (65–67)

9. Encourage ideas for improvement.
Ask employees for suggestions on how to serve the customer better, faster, and differently. Use the great ideas that result. (40)

10. Be paranoid; remain vigilant.
Act every day as though you are on the verge of losing each of your customers. Treat them warmly, excitedly, and appreciatively. Treasure them so they'll *feel* treasured. Be on the lookout for potential sources of customer dissatisfaction in your products, services, and facilities, and eliminate them before they cause trouble.

11. Be honest with customers.
Tell your customers everything there is to know about your products and services and the likely outcomes of using them. Don't mislead, manipulate, or deceive them.

12. Keep customers informed.
Describe up front all policies that affect your customers. Don't make them read the fine print. Don't let them be punished or upset by policies they didn't know to ask about. Give them clear directions and well-placed signs to follow.

13. Under-promise, over-deliver.
Give customers more than they expect, before they ask for it, without making them wait for it. Anticipate customer needs, rather than merely responding to them.

14. Swing into action.
Never permit customers to ask for something more than once. The first employee who learns of a customer need must accept the responsibility to guarantee that need is satisfied. Don't let your customers lift a finger to get exceptional service.

15. Stop providing products and services.
Start solving problems, meeting needs, easing pain, giving pleasure, improving lives, or helping your customers make more money. Get your employees to think this way so that they focus on the customer rather than just on what they give the customer.

16. Listen to customers.
Ask customers how you're doing through surveys, focus groups, follow-up calls, or manager-to-manager visits. Take action on what they tell you. (94)

17. Make it right.
When customers are dissatisfied with your service or your products, satisfy them quickly, happily, and generously. Thank them profusely for giving you a second chance.

18. Give superb customer service to insiders as well.
See that your service successes are achieved as much with internal customers as they are with external ones. Insist that your company's departments give maximum value to each other. (56)

91 Eleven Indicators to Measure for Total Quality Service

One of the central principles of total quality management is to measure everything. When you compare those measurements to what's going on in other companies, you discover the best places to direct your improvement efforts. Repeating the same measurements later tells you if you have improved and where you can improve further. Here are some of the most important internal measurements you'll ever make. They tell you how well you're pleasing the almighty customer.

1. Complaints.
Treat customer complaints like gold—mine them. Install a tracking system so that every service or product complaint is recorded by type and source and referred to a central location. Study these complaints regularly to uncover trends.

2. Service calls.
How does the number of service calls your representatives are making compare with industry averages and the number they were making six months or a year ago?

3. Customer satisfaction.
If you perform customer surveys that extract satisfaction measures, in which direction do they appear to be headed? What appears to be causing the change?

4. Behavior of customers.
Do the reports you get from the field suggest that customers are becoming more surly and demanding or more gracious and forgiving? Demanding customers are usually unhappy. Customers who love your service will cut you a lot of slack.

5. Quality of customers.
Are your customers highly prized by competitors? Are they at the top of the scale in your industry? If so, your employees must be doing some great things to earn them.

6. Attitudes toward customers.
Listen to your employees talk about customers. If they complain about them, avoid their phone calls, or ridicule them, you can be pretty sure they're not going out of their way to dazzle them.

7. Compliments.

Very few customers take the time to praise the service they receive, so an absence of compliments may not say much. But if you're hearing consistently nice comments about your operation or about one or two employees in particular, take great pride in them. Be sure to share the compliments with those who earned them.

8. Speed of service.

How long do your customers have to wait on average to be served? How does that figure compare with your closest competitors? How does it compare with six months ago? How does it compare with what you want it to be?

9. Repeat business.

This is the truest indicator that your employees are giving exceptional customer service. How high is your customer loyalty? Are you satisfied with it? How easy is it for your sales professionals to get more business out of existing customers?

10. Referrals.

When you track the source of a new account, how often does it turn out to be an existing customer? Do your customers send their friends, family members, and closest associates to you?

11. Relative growth of nearest rivals.

How does the level of your business activity compare with what's going on at your closest competitors? How much of that relative growth or decline is attributable to customer defections in either direction?

92 Six Training Programs for Total Quality Service

Exceptional customer service doesn't come naturally to most people. They need to be taught how to provide it. Here are six training programs you'll want to consider for your employees.

1. Orient new employees to your customer care culture.

Many companies miss out on the chance to impress employees with the importance of customer service before they get on the job and start to form bad habits. Orientation is the time to build loyalty to the company goals, including customer service. Intense, thoughtfully designed orientation programs immerse employees in your culture and make them feel they belong. Share your vision, values, and beliefs. Let them know that they're not merely employees, but vital members of a team dedicated to brightening the lives and advancing the fortunes of customers.

2. Teach people how to use the telephone.

Every time the telephone is answered, your company's reputation is on the line. The voice customers hear is the voice of your company. Be certain people are saying what you want them to say in the way you want them to say it. For example, when someone being called has left for the day do you want the receptionist to tell a customer, "She went home early today"?

3. Teach people how to meet your expectations.

Specify your customer service expectations. Explain them thoroughly. Give employees what they need to fulfill your expectations completely. (93)

4. Turn your sales professionals into customer service providers.

The best service organizations train their salespeople to stay with customers after the sale. Not only does this strategy retain customers, it also retains salespeople—especially the good ones.

As you sign the paperwork for a new car, the salesperson announces that whenever you need repairs he or she will be the one to schedule you in the service department. In addition, the salesperson sends a scenic postcard periodically to remind you of scheduled maintenance and calls you once a year with valuable maintenance tips. Where will you have your car serviced? Where will you buy your next car?

---

5. Equip employees to deal with difficult customers.

Train people in the different techniques that get best results from complainers, deceivers, negotiators, noncompliants, VIPs, and all other difficult customers. Use role-playing in the training so they can practice and be evaluated on the techniques you want them to use before they go out on the firing line.

6. Teach supervisors how to put employees first.

The most important customer service training you can provide is not for your front-line service people, but for their supervisors. The treatment employees give to customers is a reflection of the treatment they receive from the company. Yet in most companies workers are promoted into positions of leadership without being taught how to lead, and especially without being taught how to lead inspirationally. Don't do this to your supervisors, to your employees, and to your customers. For every dollar you spend on customer service training, spend two on leadership training.

93 Sixteen Expectations to Have of Your Customer Service Providers

How do you want your employees to treat customers? Ask that question of most people in charge, and they'll answer, "Treat each customer like a king." That's not specific enough to empower employees to provide exceptional service. They need far more clarity and precision. They need a statement of expectations much like the one below—revised, expanded, and customized to fit the requirements of your customers.

1. Speak clearly, correctly, and slowly.
Pronounce final syllables distinctly. Avoid using our industry jargon with customers. Clean up your communication act.

2. Use words and phrases that bond customers to us.
Examples: "May I help you?" "I'd be happy to take care of that for you!" "Your business is important to us." "I'm sorry to keep you waiting."

3. Say "we" or "our" instead of "they" or "their" when describing us to customers.
If a customer were to ask you why the company has decided on a new policy, begin your answer with the word *we*, not *they*.

4. Never use off-putting words and phrases.
Examples: "No." "You can't do that." "You're wrong." "You have to . . ." "We can't do that." "That's not my job."

5. Learn your customers' names—the ones *they* want you to use.
Use names when you greet them and when you thank them for the sale. Learn the correct pronunciation and spelling.

6. Treat all customers equally well.
Dazzle every customer with such thoughtfulness, courteousness, and warmth that you won't be tempted to react to their appearance, age, sex, race, nationality, accent, or the size of their account.

7. Treat every customer as though he or she is your first of the day.
Remain bright, energetic, and positive no matter what may have just transpired with another customer.

8. Anticipate the needs of your customers.
Don't sit around waiting for them to ask for what they need. Learn how they use our products or services and be there when they need us.

9. Never allow customers to ask more than one employee for what they need.
The first person to learn of a need has the responsibility to see that it's met. Never force a customer to restate a need. If you can't meet it, find the person who will.

10. Customers must never have to work to get exceptional service.
That's our responsibility. We'll make the call, fill out the form, check the records, correct the mistake, and otherwise go the extra mile to make them happy.

11. Remember that customers don't buy our services or our products.
They buy solutions to their problems and gratification of their needs. Your job isn't accomplished until their problems are solved and their needs are met.

12. Suggest ways we can serve customers better, faster, and differently.
You're in the best position to discover how we can best meet their needs. Suggest ways we can deliver the little things to customers that will make a big difference with them.

13. Listen to what customers are saying about us.
Report back what they like, what they don't like, and their requests for improvements.

14. Resolve customer complaints quickly, happily, generously, and appreciatively.
You don't have to check with upper management to make it right for an unhappy customer.

15. Pitch in willingly when your coworkers need your help with their customers.
Swing into action as a team whenever a customer need is identified.

16. Serve your internal clients as faithfully and as enthusiastically as you serve your external customers.
When you're not serving the customer, you're serving someone who is.

94 Seventeen Ways to See Your Business Through Customers' Eyes

A number of years ago a White House commission studied the state of customer service in this country. A startling statistic emerged in the report. Of every 27 dissatisfactions experienced by American consumers, only 1 is voiced in the form of a complaint to the company. But the 26 silent customers don't stay that way for long—they each tell another 10 about their unhappiness, who turn around and tell another 5. Worse than that, 91% of the mute malcontents will eventually shop around because of their unresolved dissatisfaction.

The clear message of this study for you is that you're not getting enough complaints. Do some muckraking. Find out what your customers are saying about you. Take off your blinders, change your perspective, and start looking at your business from the only perspective that matters, your customers.

1. Ask a question using the word *one*.
How did you respond to the last restaurant cashier who asked, "Was everything all right?" You probably said "yes" even if the coffee was weaker than you like it. Why weren't you more truthful and more helpful to the management of that restaurant? You were asked the wrong question! The question you and nearly every other customer in line would have answered more honestly is, "What's one thing we could have done to have made your meal a more enjoyable experience?"

2. Ask in the right way.

Another reason you don't tell service providers how you feel about their quality is that they don't seem to really want to know. If a cashier asks, "Was everything all right?" in rote fashion while looking down and counting out your change, you're not going to waste your energy to answer. Make sure your employees *want* feedback and that they ask for it in sincere tones while looking customers in the eyes.

3. Call on a client.

Executive-to-executive is one of the most important customer service encounters. Each week call on a high-ranking manager, perhaps the CEO, of a corporate client. Don't turn it into a sales call unless the customer insists. Just find out how you're doing and how you can do better from the person who makes the ultimate buying decisions.

4. Call on a colleague.

A peer or friend in another industry should be able to give you a reasoned, critical assessment of your operation. Listen without getting defensive. Offer the same service in return.

5. Form customer focus groups.

Each quarter invite a dozen customers to a two-hour lunch. This can either be a semi-permanent advisory panel or a different group each quarter. Ask them for their advice on making your product or service more attractive, valuable, and enticing. Get their reactions to your ideas for new product lines and services. Pay them for their time or provide them with valuable coupons.

6. Set up an 800 number.

Make it easy and inexpensive for customers to call you. Post the number on your products, trucks, invoices, and anywhere else in sight of the customer. Put a person, not a recording of one, at the answering end.

7. Hold a customer conference.

Conduct a yearly half-day customer conference. Bring in a popular speaker, update customers on useful information, and serve them a meal. Have your people circulate through the crowd listening. Poll employees afterward to find out what customers are saying.

8. Talk to your drivers, custodians, security guards, and maintenance crews.

These workers always seem to have strong feelings about what's good and bad about your company, but no one ever asks for their opinions. They hear from disgruntled customers, they see how careful and respectful employees are with company property—they're closer to the action than you are.

9. Administer paper-and-pencil surveys.

From time to time mail out surveys to customers or have them completed at the point of purchase. Without inundating them, get answers to your most important questions. Improve the rate of return by offering a coupon for their next purchase.

10. Print comment cards.

You often see these in hotel rooms and in restaurants. Unfortunately, their return rate is very low. Be creative to increase their use. For example, hotels could give them to guests at checkout while they wait for their bill to be processed. Waiters and waitresses could ask diners to write one comment about service or food quality on the back of the bill.

11. Make post-service calls.

A garage mechanic calls a car owner the day after working on her car to make certain repairs are OK. A nurse calls a patient three days after a doctor's visit to see how his sore throat is coming. The front desk clerk calls a guest who has just checked in to verify that the room is satisfactory.

12. Examine company policies from the customer's perspective.

Some policies are required by federal, state, or local statute (e.g., health, safety, employment). Other policies are written to help you run the business more effectively and efficiently. For all of these policies ask this crucial question: Does this policy help us serve our customer better or does it get in the way? (110)

13. Ask employees to conduct market research with friends and families.

This is a great way to involve your employees in the business and to get them to change their perspective. Develop an interview guide of five to six questions. Ask employees to report results to their supervisors along with recommendations for action.

14. Commission a customer research study.
The complexity and the volume of your service may justify hiring a firm to perform some combination of the services in this list and others that they may provide.

15. Interview lost customers.
Once-loyal customers are a gold mine of information. Over the phone or in person probe their feelings about your company. Why did they switch? What would it take to get them back?

16. Become a customer yourself.
Walk into your facilities as a customer would, imagining that you were there to buy, not to run the place. What do customers see and feel when they arrive? Have you ever called one of your service telephone numbers in a disguised voice to experience what your customers experience? Try it.

17. Hire a "mystery shopper."
A number of firms offer this service. A trained "customer" will interact with your employees and submit a detailed report on the results. Let employees know you're using this service and why you're using it. If you attempt to keep it a secret and they find out, they'll feel like you're spying on them. Besides, telling them that a "mystery shopper" might call at any time will keep them on their toes. Even so, use this technique as a last resort.

95 | Eight Inexpensive Ways to Do Market Research

Mortimer Zuckerman, successful investor and publisher, offers an irrefutable principle of marketing: "Before you build a better mousetrap, it helps to know if there are any mice out there." Regardless of how good your product or service might be, if there's no need for it or if it's not priced right, you'll simply be another executive with a great idea but no cash flow. Find out what your customers want, why they want it, and how much they're willing to pay. You can hire a market research firm to get the answers for you or you can turn to some less expensive alternatives.

1. Subscribe to *American Demographics*.
This monthly magazine is the Bible for marketers. It's written with a minimum of social science jargon and makes complex psychographics and demographics understandable.

2. Shop your competitors.
What are their best-selling items? How do they advertise? How do they merchandise? What kind of customer service do they provide? What are their pricing policies?

3. Establish a customer advisory group.
Bring together a panel of customers. Probe these issues with them: Are you getting value for your dollar when you deal with us? Are our products and services keeping up with your changing needs? What are our competitors doing better than we are? What do you wish we did that we don't do?

4. Focus your employees' attention on five basic questions.
Periodically call your employees together to discuss these questions.

- Who buys our product or service?
- Why do they buy it?
- How can we make it easier for them to buy it?
- What's happening in their lives that will affect their decision to buy from us?
- What new products or services are they asking for?

5. Offer free, no-risk trials.
If customers like the product, they pay. If they don't like it, they return it with an explanation of why. Use their comments to improve your product.

6. Contract the services of a marketing class at a local college or university.
Professors and students are always searching for case studies and research projects. You provide the case; they'll provide the time, effort, and expertise.

7. Start a marketing-oriented computer bulletin board with similar companies around the country.
Discuss marketing strategy, changing demographics, societal trends, pricing, and promotion. Ask for experiences with new products and services. Use one another as consultants.

8. Construct a database from current customers.
In exchange for filling out a questionnaire, offer customers a discount on future purchases. Build your database and start probing for trends and relationships.

96 Seven Easy Ways to Move Employees Closer to the Customer

Move your employees closer to the customer! The more they identify with customers, the more they'll be motivated to meet those customers' needs. Almost every person in your employ can be made to feel more connected to customers. Depending on the job they perform, one of these strategies should do the trick.

1. Take them on sales calls.
Employees fortunate enough to be present at sales calls will learn customer needs firsthand and will hear the promises that are made to fill those needs.

2. Tell them how their output is used.
Show employees how customers use what they do. Reveal how their work improves the lives of others. In a complex manufacturing process consider temporary job rotation as a way to demonstrate how the output of one employee becomes the input of another.

3. Let them serve the customer.
Bring behind-the-scenes employees (telephone operators, warehouse workers, secretaries) out front periodically to meet and actually serve customers.

A consultant was brought into a metal fabricating plant to train first-line supervisors. One day he was out in the plant yard talking with hourly employees. Just then a trailer pulled out the front gate loaded with billets those same employees had produced. He asked, "Where might that shipment be going?" None of the employees had any idea. Do you think those employees had as much pride for their output as they would have had if they knew that truck's destination?

---

4. Let them work for a day for the customer.
In some cases it's both possible and desirable to have a worker exchange program with customers where employees spend a day or more gaining empathy for "the other side."

5. Let them sign their work.
Employees whose names appear somewhere in relationship to their work (in the pocket of a shirt, on the name badge of a nurse, on the box packed by a warehouse crew) often feel more connected to the customer.

6. Let them make post-service calls.
Imagine an appliance repair technician whose job involves calling clients the day after a repair to confirm that it was effective. How sensitive do you imagine that technician would be to homeowners?

7. Arrange with customers to offer purchase discounts to your employees.
Find ways to encourage your employees to use the very products they produce or the very services they provide.

97 Ten Steps to Resolve Customer Complaints

One of the most difficult challenges for your employees is how to handle complaints, especially when customers get upset. Very few people have been trained in mastering this delicate skill. Use this list to teach your customer service providers what to do when something goes wrong. Call on it when you find yourself on the firing line.

1. Listen.
Listen carefully to calm the customer, to understand the mistake, and to learn the customer's perception of the problem. Allow the

---

If you have difficulty listening, try this technique. Pick up a pencil. Turn it into a "listening stick" by squeezing it in your hand with your thumb pushing on the eraser. Imagine your thumb on the eraser as keeping your mouth closed. When it's finally time to speak, let up on the eraser.

person to vent completely. Don't interrupt even if you have a quick and easy solution. Show interest and concern on your face and in your eyes. (31)

2. Remain calm.

Don't let people push your buttons. You can't reason with them if *you* get angry. Try these anger-controlling techniques.

- Count to ten.
- Take a deep breath.
- See any outbursts as a reflection on them, not you.
- Tell yourself you'll succeed only by staying in your head, not dropping into your stomach.
- Picture something pleasant that you've been looking forward to.
- Remember that angry people are either afraid or in pain. The more you can empathize with that fear or pain and even pity the person, the less attacked you will feel.

3. Acknowledge that you listened.

Once the customer has finished speaking, paraphrase what he or she said to show that you cared enough to listen and that you understand the problem well enough to resolve it. If you missed something, ask the customer to repeat it.

4. Ask questions.

Ask whatever questions will help you fully understand the circumstances. Do so in a calm, nonaccusatory voice and only after the customer has stopped talking. Seek clarification and amplification, not justification. "What makes you say that?" is an attack. Try instead, "What happened that caused you to feel that way?" (33)

5. Validate the customer.

Empathize by saying something like this: "I think I understand why you feel that way." Note that this is not the same as agreeing with the customer's assertions. It shows you have listened and affirms that the customer's feelings are legitimate, which they always are. The purpose of this step is to fix the customer as you fix the problem.

6. Apologize.

Customer service statistics show that a complaining customer is justified about two-thirds of the time. When that's the case, say so. Apologize for the inconvenience, but don't feel the need to fix blame.

Say something like, "We really let you down on this one. Please give us a chance to make it right for you."

7. When customers are wrong . . .
When you believe customers' claims to be mistaken or untrue, take one of these three approaches:

- Double-check the facts in the customer's presence to allow the truth to settle the matter. "Let's go over that invoice to see where it may have led you astray."
- Get to the bottom of their assertions. If what was said sounds untrue, it may just be that customers are not explaining themselves very well. "You may be right about that, but I interpreted the message from your assistant differently. Please tell me again why the situation occurred."
- Without being patronizing seize on a teaching opportunity. "I'm glad you pointed that out to me. The information you needed was included on the third page. Next time your new secretary will know that and I'm sure we'll avoid this kind of misunderstanding."

8. Deliver.
When you have wronged the customer, make it right quickly, happily, and generously. Make sure your front-line employees have make-it-right strategies at their disposal.

9. When the customer is unreasonable . . .
When nothing you offer satisfies the customer, ask this question: "What would you like me to do; what will make you happy?" Then either comply with the customer's request or say why you can't comply.

10. Thank the customer.
Express appreciation for the opportunity to make the correction. No matter how negative the interaction was, end it on a positive note.

98 Ten Commandments of Exceptional Consultants

Some of your employees may work in a consulting relationship with clients: public accountants, lawyers, computer software experts, and so on. The client-consultant relationship brings a particular set of issues to the business setting. Use this list as a teaching tool to be sure your consultants understand these issues and practice these tips.

1. Remain client-centered.

Enter each consultancy with an open mind, believing that you don't know what clients need until they tell you. Never enter with a specific tool to sell regardless of the client's needs.

2. Diversify and broaden your knowledge.

Develop as wide a repertoire of capabilities as possible so that you can offer a broad and rich range of services.

3. Listen.

Let clients explain their needs to you before you describe your capabilities to them. Ask your clients what you can do to serve them and listen to their responses. Ask clarifying questions and test that you hear what they say.

4. Exceed expectations.

Under-promise and over-deliver. Give clients more value than they expect.

5. Don't demean or criticize clients.

Don't belittle clients with words such as: no; you've been doing it the wrong way; that's not the way to do it; that's not possible; that won't work; let me put this in terms you'll understand.

6. Don't foster dependency.

Avoid being seduced into making decisions for clients. The job of a process consultant is to empower clients to:

- see themselves accurately and assess their current situation clearly
- understand the forces that got them where they are
- express their goals and priorities
- see the choices open to them to achieve those goals
- understand the implications of each choice
- implement their choices
- evaluate the outcomes of the implemented choices and take corrective action to improve results

7. Stop providing products and services.

Start solving problems, meeting needs, easing pain, giving pleasure, and helping your clients be more successful.

8. Get evaluation data from your clients.
Find out how well you're meeting their needs. For unhappy clients make it right quickly, happily, and generously.

9. Maintain the highest ethical standards.
Guard client confidentiality. Avoid discussions of your client's business with other clients or anyone else without a need and a right to know. Be scrupulously honest and trustworthy. Minimize client cost, while maximizing the value clients receive.

10. Work yourself out of a job.
Teach your client to flourish in your absence.

99 Twelve Quotes Worth Quoting About Customer Service

1. There is only one boss—the customer. And he can fire everybody in the company from the chairman on down, simply by spending his money somewhere else. *—Sam Walton*

2. Whenever a customer enters my store, forget me. He is king. *—John Wanamaker*

3. You can have everything in life you want if you will just help enough other people get what they want. *—Zig Ziglar*

4. Treat the customer as an appreciating asset. *—Tom Peters*

5. Natural talent, intelligence, a wonderful education—none of these guarantees success. Something else is needed: the sensitivity to understand what other people want and the willingness to give it to them. *—John Luther*

6. People spend money when and where they feel good. *—Walt Disney*

7. Expectations are critical when you serve customers. Meet them to satisfy the customer. Exceed them to make the customer love you. Set unrealistic expectations—promises you can never hope to keep—and your customers will hold you beneath contempt. *—Robert A. Peterson*

8. You can't promise your customers sunny weather, but you can promise to hold an umbrella over them when it rains. *—Sign in a telephone service center*

9. Customer service isn't about satisfaction. It's about dazzlement. —*Chip R. Bell*

10. Rule 1: The customer is always right!
Rule 2: If the customer is ever wrong, reread Rule 1. —*Sign in front of Stew Leonard's Dairy Store*

11. We don't desert you after we deliver it. —*General Electric commercial*

12. If I pick up a ringing phone, I accept the responsibility to ensure the caller is satisfied, no matter what the issue. —*Michael Ramundo*

8

CONTROL YOUR ORGANIZATION

This chapter advises you on how to stay in touch and in control of what goes on in your organization. You'll learn the forms and logic of financial statements and ratios and how to use and interpret them. You'll also learn how to set formal policies, order a computer system, and get the most from outside professionals. You may have experts on your senior staff or on retainer to handle these tasks, but as the person in charge you have to know the basics, too.

100   Fifteen Financial Ratios You Should Know

A financial ratio is simply one accounting number divided by another. At the end of each accounting period (usually quarterly), numbers from your firm's balance sheet and income statement are combined into various financial ratios. These ratios—commonly called "the language of business"—reveal the strengths and weaknesses of your organization. They're a useful way of looking at, and thinking about, your work. Ratios can be grouped into five major types.

LIQUIDITY RATIOS TELL YOU HOW SOLVENT YOUR
ORGANIZATION IS OR IS NOT.

1. Current ratio (= current assets/current liabilities).
This shows how well short-term cash inflows (as generated by current assets) are covering short-term cash outflows (as caused by current liabilities). In general, the higher the current ratio, the better, assuming you don't have excessive current assets.

2. Quick ratio (= current assets minus inventory/current liabilities).
This shows how well the most liquid current assets (which are all noninventory current assets) are covering current liabilities. The quick ratio is also called "the acid test." Again, the higher this ratio is, the better, assuming no excessive current assets.

DEBT RATIOS (SOMETIMES CALLED LEVERAGE RATIOS) TELL
YOU HOW EXTENSIVELY YOUR ORGANIZATION USED DEBT
(INSTEAD OF EQUITY) AS A SOURCE OF FUNDING.

3. Debt ratio (= total debt/total assets).
This tells you what portion of assets has been obtained with borrowed money, instead of your own money. Creditors and investors don't like to see this ratio become too high.

4. Debt/equity ratio (= total debt/total equity).
Another way of expressing the debt ratio. A debt/equity ratio of 1.0 means that the owners borrowed one dollar for each dollar they put up of their own money.

5. Times interest earned ratio (= earnings/interest payments).
The TIE ratio tells you how well your earnings are covering your interest payments, which you're legally required to pay. A TIE ratio of 1.01% indicates that the organization is barely earning enough to pay the interest on its debt—a dangerous position.

6. Fixed charge coverage ratio (= earnings/fixed charges).
Like the TIE ratio, but this includes all other fixed expenses (rent, utilities, insurance, and so forth) in the denominator. In general, the higher this ratio, the better, assuming fixed charges are reasonable.

PROFITABILITY RATIOS INDICATE HOW PROFITABLE
THE ORGANIZATION IS.

7. Profit margin on sales ratio (= net profit/sales).
This tells you what percent of sales is pure profit. The higher, the better.

8. Return on assets (= net profit/total assets).
The ROA tells you how much pure profit a dollar of total assets generates. For example, if the ROA is 15%, then you know that each dollar of assets has generated 15 cents of pure profit. The higher, the better. Also referred to as the return on investment (ROI).

9. Return on equity (= net profit/total equity).
The ROE tells you how much pure profit accrues back to each dollar of equity. For example, if the ROE is 20%, then investors are receiving $1.20 back from the firm for each dollar they invested. The higher, the better, of course.

ACTIVITY RATIOS (SOMETIMES CALLED ASSET-MANAGEMENT RATIOS) MEASURE HOW ACTIVELY THE FIRM IS USING ITS ASSETS.

10. Inventory turnover ratio (= sales/inventory).
Also called "turn," this measures how many times the firm has sold out or turned over its inventory. You can also apply the inventory turnover ratio to specific product lines to see what's selling best. The higher, the better.

11. Total asset turnover ratio (= sales/total assets).
This measures how many times the firm has sold or turned over its total assets. The higher, the better.

VALUATION RATIOS (SOMETIMES CALLED MARKET-VALUE RATIOS) MEASURE HOW VALUABLE THE FIRM IS TO OUTSIDE INVESTORS.

12. Earnings per share ratio (= net profit/shares of stock outstanding).
The EPS ratio reveals how much in earnings each share of stock can claim. For example, an EPS of $2 means that each share of stock has a claim on two dollars of the company's earnings. In this case, the company could pay one dollar of dividends for each share and retain the other dollar of the investor's earnings for future expansion. The higher, the better.

13. Price/earnings ratio (= market price per share/earnings per share).
The P/E ratio reveals how much investors are willing to pay for a one-dollar claim on the firm's earnings. For example, if a share of stock is trading at $30 and has an EPS of $2, then its P/E ratio is 15. Of course, the higher, the better.

14. Book value (= equity/shares outstanding).
Book value is a simple measure of each investor's claim on the entire company.

15. Market-to-book ratio (= market price per share/book value per share).
Market-to-book indicates how many times the market price of the stock exceeds its book value. The higher, the better.

101 Seven Warnings About Using Financial Ratios

In relying on financial ratios, managers must be very careful about how those numbers are calculated and interpreted. If used incorrectly, financial ratios can lead decision makers to unjustified conclusions.

1. Look at the trend.
In assessing the health of your company with financial ratios, it's more valuable to compare yourself today to yourself five years ago than to simply judge a percentage.

2. Compare your firm to your industry.
Compare ratios to the industry average or to particular competitors. Is an ROA of 5% good or bad? It depends. If you're in the banking industry, it's phenomenal. If you're in manufacturing, it's the pits.

3. Watch out for consolidated data.
Be wary of averaged ratios computed across divisions of a company. Ratios calculated from a consolidated financial statement are often meaningless. For example, if a company that makes dog food and golf balls consolidated its two divisions' balance sheets into one, how could you assess either division separately? What would success in one area tell you about the state of the other division?

4. Use comparable accounting systems when comparing firms.
Compare the ratios of one firm to those of another only if they use comparable accounting systems.

5. Adjust for seasonality.
If you're analyzing a firm whose activities are very seasonal, it's best to use average figures instead of end-of-period figures. Otherwise, a particular ratio in May could be misleadingly different from the same ratio in November.

6. Watch out for window dressing.
Window dressing is any technique that makes ratios look healthier than they actually are. An unethical firm might use such techniques, for example, to fool your firm into granting them trade credit; it could increase its year-end current ratio (an indicator of its solvency) by taking out a two-year loan on December 30 and repaying it on

January 2. A sharp financial manager should be able to detect such subterfuge. (109)

7. Know your industry.
Each industry embraces different ratios. In judging your company's performance, stay focused on the ratios of your industry's leaders.

102 Seven Quick and Rough Estimates of Your Company's Worth

People in charge need to know how to measure the value of their firms. Knowing relative values of divisions, subsidiaries, and other distinct operations enables you to compare their relative worth, recognize where you need to improve, and make better strategic decisions. Executives must also know firm values in order to successfully negotiate mergers and acquisitions. Here are some useful estimates.

1. Capitalize the cash flow.
Find the present value of the company's future net cash flows and discount it at an interest rate that reflects the riskiness of the company. This is the proper method to find the value of a company. Unfortunately, cash flows are tough to estimate, especially for outlying years, and it's hard to pinpoint the correct interest rate. That's why many other techniques have been developed.

2. Eyeball your net worth.
One quick way to estimate your company's value is to look at the net worth or equity on your balance sheet. This gives the "book value" of your company—a good starting point, although not a true measure of your company's worth because it's not the market value.

3. Set a lower limit on market value.
A lower limit to a company's market value is its *liquidation value* (i.e., the net amount realized from selling a company's assets and retiring its debt). Note, however, that this doesn't reveal the much fuzzier *going-concern value:* the value of the company when it's operated "as is" by current management.

4. Calculate the value of your stock.
The best quick estimate of a public company's going-concern value is to calculate the market value of its outstanding stock. If the company has X shares outstanding at $Y/share, then the company

has a value of X times Y. This technique is quick and easy. It also dovetails nicely with the number one objective of a public corporation: to maximize value to the company's shareholders.

5. Review purchase offers.

For either public or private companies, offers from prospective buyers are a good indication of your company's worth, especially if you receive several in the same price range. Ridiculously low offers should be readily apparent; ignore them. Ridiculously high offers? Take them.

6. Identify a typical year.

If none of the above techniques are applicable, identify a typical year for your firm and calculate firm value assuming that most years will be typical. Find the present value of the cash flows from operations, discounted at the average interest rate the firm pays on its debt, and subtract the dollar value of the firm's total debt.

7. Remember the importance of perceptions and expectations.

In all cases, market values are ultimately driven by perceptions and expectations. You may manage the most efficient firm in the country, but if you're manufacturing buggy whips your company won't have much market value. However, a poorly managed company that just patented a cure for cancer could have enormous market value based on its future prospects.

103 Seven Logical Steps for Understanding an Annual Report

As its name implies, an annual report is a year-end report issued by an organization. It contains basic descriptive data about the firm, several key financial statements, the management's opinion of the health of the firm, and the auditor's opinion of the validity of the figures in the report. Shareholders, creditors, government grantors, donors, and others use your annual report to help them make decisions about your organization. And you'll use annual reports to make decisions about another firm. Here's how to make sense of one.

1. Read the auditor's letter.

A clean and unqualified auditor's letter tells the public that the data comprise a fair picture of a firm's activities. If not, the letter will state which figures aren't in conformance with generally accepted accounting principles (GAAP) and why.

2. Analyze the descriptive information.
The descriptive information about the firm summarizes its products or services, its key personnel, its markets and strategies. This section typically contains lots of photographs, charts, and direct quotes.

3. Study the key financial statements.
The key financial statements in an annual report are:

- the balance sheet
- the income statement
- the cash-flow statements
- the statement of retained earnings

4. Review the retained earnings.
The retained earnings statement shows the earnings left over from the previous year, the current year's retained earnings (i.e., the current year's net income less dividends paid out), and the new total accumulated retained earnings.

5. Read the letter from management.
The letter from management is usually from the chairperson, although it could be from the CEO, president, or some grouping of the firm's top officers. It gives management's opinion of the present and future health of the firm. Naturally, the letter tends to be optimistic.

6. Look for "red flags" in the footnotes.
Footnotes provide the details such as method of depreciation, dates of loans, etc. Although boring to many, the notes can be highly illuminating.

7. Remember what's being reported.
An annual report describes the *past* behavior of a firm and is no guarantee of its *future* behavior.

---

104   Nine Steps for Putting Together a Balance Sheet

A balance sheet is a set of two lists. One shows an organization's assets; the other shows where the firm obtained the money to buy these assets as liabilities (borrowed money) or equity (shareholders' money). Hence, the two lists must balance at all times. Normally your accountant is responsible for summarizing and presenting the data in your balance sheet. However, you need to understand the logic behind the accountant's decisions.

1. Split the assets.
Assets are always divided into current assets (items that will generate cash for less than a year) and fixed assets (items that will generate cash for more than a year).

2. Rank the current assets.
Current assets comprise the working capital of a firm. They're listed in decreasing order of liquidity:

- cash
- marketable securities
- accounts receivable
- inventory

3. Depreciate the fixed assets.
List your fixed assets at their original purchase price, and then subtract the total depreciation accumulated over the years of their usage.

4. Split the liabilities.
Like assets, liabilities are divided into current liabilities (those that will be paid off within a year) and long-term liabilities (those whose payments will continue for more than a year). Your firm's current and long-term liabilities constitute its "total debt."

5. Break down the current liabilities.
Current liabilities consist of:

- accounts payable (trade credit)
- notes payable (short-term loans)
- accruals (primarily wages and taxes)

The difference between current assets and current liabilities is called the "net working capital" of your firm.

6. List any preferred stock.
Preferred stock (if any) is usually listed after total debt. Preferred stock is a hybrid between a bond and common stock; it has features

of both. Most analysts categorize it one way or the other and group it with either debt or equity for analysis.

7. Add up the equity.
Equity, also called "net worth," consists of common stock and retained earnings. It's listed after total debt and preferred stock. The common-stock entry shows the number of shares and dollar value of all stock sold. If shareholders paid more for the stock than its face value, the excess is shown as "paid-in surplus."

8. List your retained earnings.
Retained earnings are the accumulated portions of profits not paid out to shareholders as dividends but retained by the firm for future expansion.

9. Check that the two lists balance.

105   Eight Steps for Putting Together an Income Statement

An income statement summarizes an organization's revenues and expenses over a given period of time, usually quarterly or yearly. While a balance sheet can be likened to a snapshot of the firm at a given time, the income statement measures the *flow* of a firm's activities over a given interval. Here's how your accountant puts one together.

1. Start with your total revenue for the period.
Total revenue (or sales) reports the total income for the period resulting from the sale of your firm's products or services.

2. Subtract operating costs.
Operating costs include all normal costs associated with producing and selling the products or services (such as materials, labor, and overhead) but exclude depreciation and interest expense.

3. Then subtract depreciation.
While depreciation is actually an operating expense, it's treated separately because it's not an out-of-pocket expense. Subtracting operating costs and depreciation from total revenue reveals your net operating income.

4. Add (or subtract) other income (or losses).
To net operating income is then combined with other income or losses on a net basis. Other income might include income earned from marketable securities, royalties, and so on. The result is Earnings Before Interest and Taxes (EBIT).

5. Subtract interest.
Interest expense is then subtracted from EBIT to give Earnings Before Taxes (EBT).

6. Pay Uncle Sam, the governor, and the mayor.
Finally, taxes (federal, state, and local) are subtracted to reveal net income (the firm's profit) for the period.

7. Pay your dividends.
A portion of net income may be paid out to shareholders as dividends, and the residual amount will be the period's "retained earnings."

8. Remember that income is not cash flow.
Remember that an income statement only reports accounting income and does not reveal a firm's cash flow. (106)

106 Seven Logical Steps for Understanding a Cash Flow Statement

The cash flow statement shows the actual cash inflows and outflows for an organization over a given period, such as a quarter or a year. For a business, cash is defined as currency plus checking accounts— and for most businesses, cash is overwhelmingly the latter. More and more firms today are focusing on cash flow instead of their accounting income because cash is what's used to pay dividends and buy assets. Here's the logic your accountant uses in drafting a statement.

1. Identify the cash inflows.
A cash inflow results from any activity that generates hard cash, such as selling goods or services, taking out a loan, or selling an asset.

2. Identify the cash outflows.
A cash outflow results from any activity that requires an actual cash outlay, such as buying an asset, repaying a loan, or paying dividends.

3. Break down your cash inflows and outflows into three groups.
Cash flows are generally grouped into three areas:

- operations
- investing
- financing

4. List the cash flows from operations.
Cash flows from operating activities show the inflows and outflows from the firm's normal operations (cash received from customers, paid to suppliers, etc.).

5. List the cash flows from investing.
Cash flows from investing activities show capital expenditures: the cash paid out for fixed assets such as plant and equipment.

6. List the cash flows from financing.
Cash flows from financing activities show the results from raising and repaying money, such as borrowing from a bank or paying dividends to shareholders.

7. Net out the cash flows.
Total all three groups of cash flows and add them to the organization's cash at the beginning of the period to arrive at the cash figure at the end of the period.

107 Ten Questions an Investor or Creditor Will Ask You

At some time in your career you'll have an unexpected opportunity to close a potentially lucrative deal, spin off a new company, or enter into a joint venture. If you have enough cash, you can underwrite the opportunities yourself. If you don't, you'll have to seek outside financing. Regardless whether you talk to a banker, an independent investor, or a venture-capital firm, you should expect the following questions.

1. What's your credit history?
Don't expect a loan if your suppliers, employees, dissatisfied customers, and other creditors are waiting for you to make good on what you owe them.

2. What's your collateral?

The old joke still holds true: The best loan applicant is the one who proves he doesn't need the money. What assets can you put on the table in exchange for the investor's financial risk? Expect an independent appraisal of that collateral.

3. Am I investing in you or in a business plan?

Some deals are structured on basis of the talent, drive, and imagination of the deal maker. Others are based on the objective merits of the deal itself. And some deals involve a combination of both. What exactly are you asking the investor or creditor to bet on?

4. Where's your business plan?

If you can't document how you'll spend the money, your projected cash flow, the competitive advantage you expect to meet, the problems you anticipate, and your methods for solving those problems, don't expect to get the loan. Do your homework. Show the numbers. (108)

5. What are your major competitive threats?

This question provides the foundation for further probes:

- What product or service weaknesses are your competitors likely to leverage?
- How likely is it that new competitors will enter the market?
- How vulnerable are you to new, aggressive competitors?

6. How sure can we be that you and your team will be able to perform?

This question targets three concerns: management talent, management commitment, and management succession. Who will lead the project if you or other key players pull out? (88)

7. What kind of "key man" insurance will you provide?

This insurance pays off if pivotal individuals die or are physically unable to perform their duties.

8. What has been your personal financial status for the last five years?

Expect the investor or creditor to scrutinize your most recent tax statements and personal net worth statements.

9. What has been your corporate financial status for the past five years?
Cash flow for this year is only part of the picture. Expect the investor or creditor to get as full a picture as possible.

10. Are you willing to have an investor sit on your board?
Some investors will only put up the money if they have a hand in how the investment will be managed.

108   Seven Components of an Effective Business Plan

A business plan is a blueprint for building your business. It gives you a picture of what you intend to do and the resources necessary for doing it. Even if you've personally had a questionable credit history, a good business plan may be enough to secure loans and investments. The following components should be in your plan.

1. Executive summary/overview.
In one page or less summarize what you intend to sell, why a market will buy it, your projected cash flow, and when you project bringing your business on-line.

2. A discussion of the product or service.
What exactly are you bringing to the market? Is it new or modified? What research has gone into developing it? What's the status of copyright/patent applications?

3. Competitive analysis.
What's the current size (people and dollars) of the market? What's the projected market growth? What's the profile of the industry you will compete in? What are the industry trends and profit potential? Who will be your major competitors? How do you differentiate your product or service from the competition?

4. Marketing strategy.
What segment of the market are you aiming for? What are the characteristics of your niche market? How will you advertise to your potential customers? What is the expected cost of the advertising? What is your pricing strategy?

5. Manufacturing and distribution.

What are your manufacturing, warehousing, and logistical requirements? What is the current and projected production capacity?

6. Finances.

What are the assumptions underlying the forecasts? What are the projected sales forecasts? What are the projected cash flows? Cost of sales? Debt/equity ratio? Inventory turnovers? Profits? Are there any pending lawsuits involving the company?

7. Management team.

Who are the key members of the management team? What experience and talent do they bring? What is their projected compensation? How committed are they to the company?

---

109 Nine Expectations to Have of Your Business Manager

In a large corporation the chief financial officer has the primary responsibility to help you maintain operational control in your organization. In a smaller organization or department, the business manager serves the same function. Because of this unique assignment and because of the nature of many of those educated in accounting and finance, people in charge should have a few extra expectations of their CFOs and business managers. Tell your business manager to:

1. Educate the entire staff about financial accountability.

See yourself as a coach, not merely a referee. Teach them how to use financial concepts to be more productive and increase quality. Conduct seminars and remain accessible.

2. Tell me the fiscal implications of my ideas and initiatives.

Warn me when I venture onto thin ice. Give me detailed financial impact statements on proposed plans. Never let me be surprised by a financial outcome.

3. Know when to back off.

Be assertive with your warnings, but when I've listened and choose to proceed against your advice, support me fully.

4. Don't limit yourself to a "watchdog" role.

Don't tell me just what we *can't* do. Be an innovator. Show me how we can make money, not just save money.

5. Don't preach gloom and doom.

Don't be unrealistic, but don't see just the downside of every pro-posal. When our economic picture is bleak, don't forget to point out the bright side of the picture if there is one.

6. Exchange expectations with other senior staff members.

Other staff members depend on you for vital input into their deci-sions and for realistic assessments of the financial impact of their actions. You need their cooperation as well. Spend some time learn-ing what they need from you and pointing out what you count on from them.

7. Exchange performance feedback with other staff members.

Find out how well you're meeting their expectations and tell them how well they're fulfilling yours. In response to the feedback do everything you can to enhance the role you play in the fiscal aspects of their processes.

8. Supervise your employees like people, not numbers.

Be a model of fiscal accountability and stringency in your depart-ment, but don't go overboard. Be considerate of your employees. Show your appreciation for them.

9. Remember, you serve in a staff position.

Don't mistake your control function for a leadership responsibility. I may ask you to advise managers directly of the financial implications of their actions, but it's ultimately my responsibility to say yes or no.

---

110 Nine Questions to Ask Before You Implement a Corporate Policy

As a person in charge, you'll invariably wrestle with company policies. A policy is a course of action or a set of rules selected to guide present and future actions. The questions to answer about policies are: How many should we have? What's the purpose of each one? Is it possible to have too many? Is it possible for policies to have negative effects? Each of these questions will help define your philosophy and shape the policies you implement. Although we can't tell you the specific policies you need in your company, we can help you make sure you write the best policies for your specific needs.

1. What problem are we trying to solve?

Policies are written because of a perceived problem. If you don't have a problem, you don't need a policy. Don't be tempted to overact with a policy every time some little thing goes wrong or one employee does something that upsets you.

2. Will the policy create a more significant problem?

Consider the problems the policy itself may create. For example, companies that forbid employees to date one another find that it's tough to fight sexual attraction and Mother Nature; these companies' employees may feel cheated or demeaned, and their job satisfaction and productivity may be lowered.

3. How much will it cost to implement this policy?

All policies have both apparent and hidden costs. Make sure you fully understand how much it's costing you to solve your problem with a policy. If the cost is greater than the costs incurred with the problem, you don't need the policy yet.

4. Is the policy in any way discriminatory?

Even the best laid policy can have unintentional consequences, possibly resulting in a charge of discrimination. For example, companies that provide day care for employees' children often hear complaints from employees without children, who feel cheated because they aren't given a comparable benefit. Convene a diverse panel of employees. Get their input before you draft any new policy.

5. Is the policy legal?

If there's even the slightest question that a policy may infringe on employees' constitutional rights, check with an attorney before you implement it. (115)

6. Is the policy unequivocally clear?

If you have a policy that states, "Employees will have a clean and neat appearance," make sure you define "clean" and "neat." If you have a policy that states, "Employees will be compensated for reasonable out-of-pocket expenses," make sure you define "reasonable." When policies contain ambiguous language, you create problems for the managers who must enforce them.

7. Does management broadly support this policy?

If your managers won't get behind a policy, you're not going to have much luck with either compliance or enforcement.

8. Are policies internally consistent?

Consider these two policies: (1) We believe in dignity, respect, and affirmative action; and (2) The customer is always right. What does a manager do if an important customer treats an employee in a racist or sexist manner? How will you handle situations where policies may contradict each other?

9. Do we really need it?

Oftentimes common sense, personal coaching and counseling, and careful recruitment and training have greater positive impact than long, detailed policies. Get a reality check from a colleague whose opinion you trust before you implement your next policy.

111   Seventeen Guidelines to Control Employee Theft

Most employees are scrupulously honest and would never consider stealing corporate assets. Unfortunately, some employees under the right circumstances will be tempted to embezzle or steal. Police professionals are fond of saying, "Locks are for honest people." In other words, a thief will steal from you regardless of your security system; an honest person with access might steal, but would think twice if you had adequate security. The tips in this list are intended to provide the "locks" to maintain honesty among your honest employees and put your dishonest employees on notice.

1. State your theft policy clearly and emphatically.

Employees should know that stealing is illegal and unethical. Employees should also know they'll be terminated if caught and may be prosecuted.

2. Enforce your policy.

Out of compassion you may opt for giving a thief a second chance. Fight this temptation. If you don't terminate (or prosecute), you'll waste needless energy worrying about whether this employee will steal from you in the future. Worry about pleasing your customers, not about whether an employee is rehabilitated.

3. Carefully screen job applicants.

It's easier to prevent a problem than it is to solve one.

> Background reference checks are worth the time and money you spend on them. A candidate who lies on an application or on a résumé should be dropped. If someone calls you while doing a background reference, answer questions as honestly as you'd want your own questions answered.

4. Consult with your insurance carrier.

Your insurer has a vested interest in not paying a claim. Experienced agents and their companies are willing to devote significant time and energy to help you maintain security over corporate assets. Get your money's worth from them.

5. Vary your daily routine.

Security consultants advise clients that the best protection against kidnapping is to make the kidnapper guess at your itinerary. Similarly, if your employees are able to predict what their managers do, when they'll do it, and where they'll do it, you increase your vulnerability to theft.

6. Get out of your office and open your eyes and ears.

Managing By Wandering Around (MBWA) can be a deterrent to theft. When you do it, vary your schedule and route from day to day. (45)

7. Double-check the cash flow.

Accounts payable and accounts receivable should not go through the same person. Internal controls should place these functions in different hands. Don't assign foxes to guard henhouses.

8. Monitor travel accounts closely.

Claims for travel costs are often inflated by unnecessary expenses or outright fraud. Set controls in place that hold your business travelers accountable for their claims.

9. Double-check inventory control.

The person in charge of purchasing should not be in charge of maintaining or auditing inventory.

10. Warn against illegal deals with suppliers.
Make it clear both to your suppliers and to your employees that you won't tolerate even the slightest hint of shady dealings. Constantly be on the lookout for employees who might be extracting kickbacks for contracts.

11. Maintain healthy skepticism.
Don't look for crooks, but don't shut your eyes either. People are basically honest, but pressure and stress can force them to do things they might not do otherwise.

12. Forget stereotypes.
Anyone could steal from you—including your model employee and your most trusted advisor. There's no demographic profile of the employee most likely to steal. There are only two things consistently true of corporate thieves: (1) they need money; and (2) they have access to assets.

13. Consult your accountant.
An experienced accounting firm will have specific recommendations for increasing the security of corporate assets. Ask your accountant to make surprise audits of key documents from time to time. (116)

14. Guard your assets.
Valuables (money, information, inventory, equipment, supplies, medications) should be locked, secured, and in some cases guarded. Keys and access codes should be carefully monitored and periodically changed.

15. Employees should secure their personal property.
Employees are as likely to steal from each other as from the company. Car doors should be locked. Offices, desk drawers, and file cabinets should be secured when they contain personal property. If you have a security force, put them on alert every payday.

16. Establish an employee hot line.
Some companies have had success with an internal anonymous hot line that employees can use to report unethical or illegal activities, including theft and embezzlement.

17. Design computer systems to monitor theft and embezzlement.
Today vital information, and even cash, is computerized, so computer security is as important as physical security. Have your system designed with this in mind:

- It should be very difficult for employees to gain access to information they don't need.
- You should have quick and easy access to files highlighting inventory or cash flow discrepancies. (106, 114)

112 Eleven Qualities of the Best Management Audits

From time to time you'll want to take a close look at the operation of one of your units, departments, or divisions in the form of a management audit. For example, you might want to measure how well a department is adhering to sound financial management principles. The purpose of a management audit is to discover ways to improve the unit and enable it to meet its goals more efficiently and effectively. This is most likely to happen when the following conditions are met.

1. The organizational climate is favorable to the conduct of audits.
Over the years management audits have developed a reputation in some quarters as witch hunts. Before you advance them in your company, dispel that image. Make management audits so clearly a benefit to recipients that your managers clamor for them.

2. The audits are focused on a specific opportunity or problem.
A management audit shouldn't be a fishing expedition. Before you go in, decide what opportunity for improvement you hope to realize or what problem you need to solve. Focus the audit on that opportunity or problem.

3. Goals are clear.
Everyone involved—you, the auditors, those being audited—should agree on the rationale for the audit, the potential opportunities, the nagging problems, and the variables to be measured.

4. Crack audit teams are assembled.
Choose auditors appropriate to the task and to the culture of the unit. Assemble an interdisciplinary and experienced team that is professional, objective, credible, sensitive, and armed with exceptional analytical and communication skills. Organize them flexibly and give them inspirational leadership.

5. Audits are culturally sensitive.
See that the conduct of audits is sensitive to the political, social, economic, and cultural realities of audited units. Audit teams can

eliminate much of the threat and gain the confidence of unit employees with these actions:

- Introduce the audit team in a friendly environment.
- Maintain a servant attitude.
- Involve unit employees in planning.
- Respect the norms and traditions of the unit.
- Post the audit schedule.
- Ensure confidentiality.
- Guarantee no reprisals.
- Promise and deliver preliminary reports.

6. Audits meet scheduled deadlines.
Even the most professionally conducted audit is a disruption. See that all audits are completed within the promised time frame so that people can turn their full attention back to the work of the unit.

7. Auditors use sound methods.
By working closely with unit personnel, the audit team will ensure that the tools it uses to collect data are appropriate. Team members should also be expert at data analysis, synthesis, and reporting.

8. Audits stay within budget.
Some audit teams have the mistaken idea that their work is so important and their discoveries so unpredictable that they should spend whatever it takes to get the job done.

9. Audits are worth their expense.
If the results of an audit can't be shown to save more money or make more money over the long haul than it cost to conduct the audit, there was insufficient reason to carry it out.

10. Results are reported quickly.
Opportunities for improvement uncovered by the audit should be seized immediately—on the spot if possible. Preliminary versions of the final report should be revealed as they become available. The final report should be published as soon as the ink dries.

11. Results are practical.
Recommendations should be consistent with the vision of the company and with the goals and priorities of the unit. They should provide practical and customized solutions and suggest the pursuit of realistic opportunities. (74)

113 Eleven Steps to Effective Benchmarking

Benchmarking is a process of identifying, collecting, and analyzing information from various sources (either internal or external) for comparison. "Best practices benchmarking" is obtaining information from successful departments or world-class organizations in order to design and implement programs that improve quality in your organization. The comparisons possible as a result of benchmarking enable great companies to stay great and aspiring companies to achieve greatness.

1. Decide why you want to invest in benchmarking.
What was the trigger for your decision? What do you hope to accomplish? What internal processes are you hoping to improve? What evidence exists that benchmarking will actually help you improve those processes?

2. Form a diverse benchmarking team.
Gather a group of employees from cross-functional departments to work together throughout the benchmarking process. This team approach provides diverse perspectives and accumulated expertise. Select team members for their credibility in your organization and their ability to develop rapport with staff at the outside organization providing the information.

3. Plan your benchmarking process before you leap.
Decide on the what, who, where, how, why, and toward what end. What type of information will you request from which departments or organizations, by what date, through whom, and in what form? Information may be requested by telephone, through paper-and-pencil surveys, or in face-to-face interviews.

> Telephone interviews are great for getting immediate benchmarking results. Return-mail surveys are convenient for the company being benchmarked since they can be completed at will; however, they may be completed improperly, submitted late, or ignored. Face-to-face interactions are best for collecting confidential information; they're also the best way to gather detailed information, but they can be expensive when they require out-of-town travel.

4. Collect only information that improves your organization.
There's plenty of information out there. Collecting it all is neither feasible, useful, nor cost effective. Ask yourself, "What type of information will lead to action plans that will improve our organization?" Too often benchmarking teams collect information voyeuristically ("I was just kind of curious about . . .") or to reveal an interesting statistic that has no decision-making value.

5. Take stock of your current situation.
Assign the team to perform an organizational self-assessment to reveal all the information on all the topics that will make the benchmarking effort worthwhile. The importance of the information you need to collect should be understood fully by the team and within your current organization prior to benchmarking.

6. Obtain benchmarking data from internal sources.
Internal data is often overlooked as a potential source of valuable information. Many times organizations have procedures in place that are taken for granted, go unnoticed, or are viewed as not applicable to other parts of the company. Before investigating external sources of information, consider the possible value of benchmarking internally.

7. Obtain information from direct competitors, as well as from industry leaders.
Find out whether your competitors perform critical functions consistent with the best practices in the industry. This may reveal the causes of any competitive advantages or disadvantages you currently experience in the marketplace.

8. Identify the best practices of organizations in other industries.
There's much to be learned from the practices of successful organizations regardless of their industry. Conventional wisdom suggests that functions in other industries have little relevance to yours. To the contrary, the best practices have been transferred between diverse industries with great success.

9. Share results of benchmarking projects with those who provided information.
Sharing a summary of benchmarking results with those companies that gave you information is a way of saying thanks, promoting goodwill, and increasing your credibility. When more than one

company is involved, provide only an overall summary, and maintain the confidentiality of each company's results.

10. **Use the information obtained through benchmarking to customize practices.**
Too often organizations attempt to imitate complete processes from best practice organizations without regard to other factors that may influence those organizations' success. Learn from the best practices of others, but customize your resulting actions to your organization's strategy, structure, corporate culture, processes, and people.

11. **Commit to benchmarking as an ongoing process.**
Use benchmarking to remain in constant touch with the best practices available to you, but don't overdo it. Sources of benchmarking information aren't limitless. Don't wear out your welcome. When others request benchmarking information from you, provide them with the same courtesy that you expect from them.

114 Fourteen Rules for Selecting a New Computer System

Computers are an increasingly important part of the workplace at every level. Organizations with a long history of centralized computing are putting smaller units on people's desks, and computers are appearing in operations that have historically been people intensive. While it's hard to generalize rules that are applicable to all environments, the following checklist should help you to ensure your organization is moving in the right direction.

1. **Get advice.**
Information technology changes rapidly. New computing hardware appears on a daily basis, and computing practices are in constant flux. The larger your organization, the more likely you are to have an information services group committed to its computing traditions. Get an outside consulting firm to review recommendations made internally. Smaller firms will want to find an experienced consultant to take them through the remaining steps in this list.

2. **Think information, not computers.**
It used to be that organizations purchased hardware and then asked what might be done with it. Now we have shifted from thinking about computers to thinking about the information they provide:

- Focus on the information you wish to manipulate, with a particular goal in mind.
- Next, search for the software you need to achieve the goal.
- *Only then* identify the hardware needed to run the software.

3. Re-engineer business processes.

Many of the recent gains in business productivity using information technology result from management redefining work in light of the new technology. Don't simply automate existing practices with a new computer system before considering whether those practices should be modified first. (81)

Business procedures that involve the application of clearly defined and generally invariant rules can be handled by a computer program. For example, once a product has been ordered and delivered, your company should pay for it. While there are exceptions, the majority of orders are filled as requested. A program can be written to make payment in the standard cases, leaving humans free to deal with the few cases in which there is some problem.

4. Think information integration, not specialization.

Information technology is best used to integrate information so that the human worker can be more of a generalist, rather than a specialist. Thus, while traditional division of labor might suggest that a loan be processed by ten people, each with a particular expertise, information technology turns over the routine analysis to a program, allowing the human worker to act as a customer advocate. How might a computer system enable *you* to provide more information to workers, empowering them to take a more complete view of their job and provide better service to your customers?

5. Decentralize with control.

It's now possible to put enormous amounts of power on individual desktops or in departments rather than having it centralized on a single mainframe. This puts information closer to the people who need it, making it easier to input and maintain the data, and it reduces costs. At the same time, it gives responsibility for security, backup, and maintenance to staff. Thus, while decentralization has financial advantages, it's a potential time bomb if you don't plan for security, backup, and data integrity.

6. Plan for migration and conversion of legacy data.

Whether you purchase a single PC or a complex system, consider your existing data, software, and hardware. The plan for any new system must include a way to move from the existing system. People need to be trained and checks need to be run to make sure the new system produces the same (or better) results as the old. Plan for a phased migration and for converting existing files. Factor the costs of these tasks into your investment and set a realistic time frame for them.

7. Plan for growth.

As your people use new computer systems, they'll discover new applications. In your plans for computerization include the possibility of this type of growth.

> Several companies that have invested heavily in information technology have seen the electronic information stream become an auxiliary business in and of itself. The simplest example is the mailing list. Many retail businesses that obtain electronic information on their customers find not only that they can sell their products more easily, but also that they can generate revenue by selling the information about their customers.

8. Consider the total enterprise.

Too many organizations exist as "computing islands." They may be proficient at moving information within their structure, but fail to look beyond their corporate boundaries. In the next decade, computing will be increasingly concerned with the interconnection of computing islands. One outcome of this shift will be the need to standardize the form in which organizations share information. Plan for a computer system that will include the following:

- a networking plan that includes outside e-mail gateways
- standards for Electronic Data Interchange (EDI), so you can share data with other enterprises
- standards for Electronic Funds Transfer (EFT), so you can collect payments through e-mail

9. Use standards whenever possible.

The PC made it possible to move data from one place to another because of standard disk sizes, formats, and applications. There are a growing number of standards that you should consider in your computing system. Ask yourself, "In our computer system applications, how are we addressing the emerging standards in the field? If we're choosing to ignore them, what's our justification?"

10. Consider the impact on your people.

Some portion of your staff is likely to be computer-phobic. Don't take for granted that they'll uniformly see the need for a new system. Involve them in the planning from the beginning. Give them a chance to air their concerns and have their questions answered. Ensure adequate training.

11. Purchase a computer system that enhances human performance.

Computer systems are being used by an increasing percentage of the workforce. In this role, computers can either enhance or detract from the human work effort. The more highly paid your staff and the more they depend on the computer system, the more important it is to ensure that your system provides an interface that adds to their work effort.

> Consider an electronic mail interface that slows down the reading of mail an average of four seconds per message. In an organization of 100 people making an average of $25,000 per person annually, in which people read ten messages a day over a 250-day work year, the inefficiency caused by that four-second delay adds up to $3,500 per year. Saving $1,000 or $2,000 by buying the less efficient system isn't really a savings.

12. Eliminate duplicate systems as soon as possible.

It's estimated that organizations commit somewhere between five and ten percent of their budget to information systems. As you increase the amount of electronic information in your organization, there should be some decrease in the amount of paper-based information. If you continue to spend the same amount on paper file cabinets while expenditures for electronic files increase, or if you institute a comprehensive electronic mail system and your physical mailing costs continue to increase, there may be a problem.

13. Send several suppliers a request for proposals (RFP).

Invite several computer system suppliers to propose their best system for the needs you describe. Many suppliers would like to be your sole source, but you want continual access to the best systems and the best prices. An RFP will scare away the incompetent and ensure low bidding by qualified providers.

14. Work from contracts.

The larger your system, the more certain you can be that there will be many problems in the installation and tailoring of the system. Once you decide on a supplier, develop a contract that specifies:

- what is to be delivered
- the speed with which problems are to be addressed
- the financial responsibility for fixing various kinds of problems

115 Eleven Tips for Using Your Lawyer More Effectively

Someone once said that the two purposes of a corporate attorney are to tell you what you can't do and then get you out of trouble when you do it. This aphorism ignores much of the value of legal counsel. Your lawyer can be a powerful ally and a valuable resource if you apply a bit of common sense to the relationship.

1. Choose a lawyer (or law firm) wisely.

Most lawyers and many law firms specialize. Select one that has demonstrated both interest and a successful track record in your business or in the branch of law most vital to you. Get references and ask past clients these two questions: "What one thing do you like best about their work?" and "What one thing do you like least about their work?"

2. Agree on a billing structure.

Have your lawyer explain fee arrangements ahead of time. If you think alternative arrangements would be proper and helpful, discuss these possibilities up front. If you have a budget problem exacerbated by legal fees, ask your lawyer to help you solve it.

3. Educate your lawyer about your business.

Be sure your lawyer knows how you function, appreciates the environment in which you work, and understands what your business is about. Share your vision of the company and your strategic plan. Introduce your lawyer throughout the organization.

4. Educate your staff.

With the help of your attorney clarify for your management team the role he or she plays in your organization. Have him or her train your staff in the application of the law to their work.

5. Err on the side of asking for too much counsel too soon.

Executives who consult their lawyer too soon run the risk of being told, "We'll talk later." Executives who ask for too much advice run the risk of paying higher attorney fees. But executives who ask for too little advice too late run afoul of the law and lose lawsuits.

6. Explain your problem fully.

When seeking legal advice regarding a problem, a lawsuit, or a deal, explain fully all aspects of the situation. Assume your lawyer needs all the information you're sitting on. The time to save on lawyers' fees is not during your explanation of the situation. A lawyer operating in the dark may not get you the results you hope for.

7. Listen.

Heed your lawyer's advice regarding the legality of your actions, understandings, forms, documents, and agreements. Don't hear only what you want to hear.

8. Make your lawyer explain.

Insist that your lawyer explain the options for your business activities and the legal consequences of each. Make sure you understand your legal exposure and potential risk. Insist that your lawyer's advice is explained simply, clearly, and fully. Advice, no matter how astute, is worthless if you don't understand it. When your lawyer uses jargon or recommends strategies you don't understand, it's your right to say without embarrassment, "Please explain that to me." A lawyer who doesn't welcome your questions is falling short.

9. Manage your lawyer like an employee.

Make your lawyer understand that he or she is a necessary, respected, and vital member of your business team. Compliment exceptional performance; criticize poor performance. If your lawyer is not a satisfactory member of your team, retain a new one.

10. Minimize billable hours.

Lawsuits and deals can take a lot of time. If your employees can cut the time your lawyer spends by gathering background documents and providing explanations and information, have them do it.

11. Choose one lawyer from a firm as a liaison.

If your legal advice comes from a firm, designate one lawyer whom you trust there to provide you with the right people to handle your work. Let that person know that you're relying on his or her judgment in staffing your legal work with the firm's most effective people.

116 Nine Ways to Use Your Accountant More Effectively

An accountant's role can range from an employee to an independent outside auditor, and everything in between. No matter what the role, the accountant can be an invaluable resource. It's often said that an accountant can be the most necessary and trusted counselor in your sphere of advisors. Follow these guidelines to achieve a successful and prosperous relationship with your accountant.

1. Understand what an accountant can do for you.

An accountant inside your organization will generally be adept at preparing a general ledger or an internal financial statement; an internal accountant might also work in cost accounting or finance. Public accountants provide financial statement and tax services and business advice from outside.

As a result of fulfilling stringent licensing and continuing education requirements, Certified Public Accountants (CPAs) can also provide these services: tax planning for individuals and businesses; financial, retirement, and/or estate planning; attestation services (audits); consulting on management information systems; helping clients secure financing; assisting in business acquisition, disposition, or reorganization; litigation support services including damages calculations; and business valuation services (including divorce matters).

2. Get more out of your accountant.
Ask your accountant what he or she can do, in addition to the services already provided, to help you make more money.

3. Define the role of your accountant on your advising team.
There are many advisors at your disposal. You may deal with attorneys, bankers, insurance agents, financial planners, or brokers. Each advisor defines his or her services in a certain way and will mark territory accordingly. Be certain you set boundaries in the appropriate places. Your advisors should work in harmony with distinct responsibilities that overlap only when you desire.

4. Match the right tool to the right job.
If a problem falls outside the expertise of your accountant, he or she should acknowledge the limitation and refer you to an appropriate expert. This may be another accountant or someone in another field entirely.

5. Make your requests early.
If you've already executed a document or consummated a transaction before calling an accountant, you waited too long. Unfortunately, accountants are often called after the deal is struck, and the cost can be enormous. The same rationale applies for recurring work like tax return preparation. Send your information early so your accountant can process it before the tidal wave hits.

6. Provide your information in an organized manner.
Use your accountant cost effectively. Most accountants charge by the hour or fraction of an hour. The more organized you are, the less time the accountant will spend sorting through your information. At times, however, there may be value in having an accountant sort through the gory details. This is a cost-benefit decision only you can make.

7. Provide information at one time, not piecemeal.
An accountant will be most efficient if all of the information he or she needs is available from the beginning. Take a little time now to save more time later.

8. Provide sufficient information.
Accountants, as with most advisors, will render the most accurate and useful advice when given all the information. Don't make the

mistake of releasing information to your accountant on a "need-to-know" basis. Explain what you've got and let your accountant make that decision.

9. Discuss fees in advance.
Reduce the possibility of "sticker shock." At the same time, recognize that it's nearly impossible to predict the cost of any job with certainty. Requesting a fixed fee isn't always the answer. In nearly every fixed fee arrangement there's a loser; when you ask for one, expect to receive a bid that makes it nearly impossible for the accountant to lose.

117 Twelve Quotes Worth Quoting About Operational Control

1. Here's a piece of advice
   That's worth a king's crown:
   To hold your head up,
   Hold your overhead down. —*Ruth Boostin*

2. The only things that evolve by themselves in an organization are disorder, friction, and malperformance. —*Peter Drucker*

3. Expenditure rises to meet income . . . Individual expenditure not only rises to meet income but tends to surpass it . . . [and] what is true of individuals is also true of governments. —*C. Northcote Parkinson*

4. Deals usually aren't blown by principals; they're blown by lawyers and accountants trying to prove how valuable they are. —*Robert Townsend*

5. I don't want a lawyer to tell me what I cannot do; I hire him to tell me how to do what I want to do. —*John Pierpont Morgan*

6. A computer will not make a good manager out of a bad manager. It makes a good manager better faster and a bad manager worse faster. —*Edward M. Esber*

7. [Computer] programs do not merely substitute brute force for human cunning. Increasingly, they imitate—and in some cases improve upon—human cunning. —*Herbert A. Simon*

8. By a small sample we may judge the whole thing. —*Miguel De Cervantes*

9. If you can't measure it, you can't manage it. —*Anonymous*

10. My experience of the world is that things left to themselves don't get done right. —*Thomas Henry Huxley*

11. Look beneath the surface; let not the quality nor its worth escape thee. —*Marcus Aurelius*

12. If you refuse to accept anything but the best, you very often get it. —*W. Somerset Maugham*

9

FIND YOUR BALANCE

This chapter is written with a simple premise: It's hard to stay in charge when you're hooked up to a respirator. The lists in this chapter include advice for your physical, emotional, and even financial well-being. Your family, friends, and coworkers will be delighted when you follow it.

118 Eleven Possible Prices You Pay When in Charge

Leadership comes at a price. Many who have risen to the top didn't anticipate the sacrifices of that position. If you haven't yet assumed command, you'll want to anticipate these possible costs and consider what you might do to prevent them. If you already experience one or more of them, you can at least be assured that you're not the only one feeling pain at the top.

1. Your reputation is on the line.
The person in charge of an organization gets the credit when it succeeds and takes the heat when it fails, almost in scapegoat style.

2. You're accountable for the success of others.
One of the most difficult responsibilities of any leadership position is to be accountable not only for your own performance but for that of employees over whom you can never have complete control.

3. You become the object of high expectations.
Living up to the ideal picture of the person in charge is difficult. You'll be expected to have the wisdom of Solomon, the patience of Job, the decisiveness of Napoleon, the compassion of Mother Theresa, and the human relations insights of Dale Carnegie.

4. You have to make wrenching choices.
You can expect to have a hand in decisions that will have a direct impact on the lives of others. You'll turn down management applicants, determine titles and salaries, discipline or fire nonperformers,

and possibly have to lay off good employees in bad times. You'll be faced with choices that raise issues of values, ethics, and propriety. You'll find it necessary to commit yourself to initiatives that are bound to generate criticism from someone, somewhere.

5. You're called upon to manage massive egos.
Your senior staff is likely to consist of high-energy, strong-willed, difficult-to-control professionals. Such people have a tendency to disagree and to work at cross purposes to each other. You'll be called on to act as referee. (52)

6. Long days are the norm.
Someone once defined a boss as the person who comes early when you're late and late when you're early. In fact, most bosses both open and close the office, and this says nothing about the miles, piles, and files of work they take home each night.

7. Grueling travel schedules may be inescapable.
Few executives spend all their time in the office. When the company is large and geographically spread, they may spend days or even weeks on the road each month.

8. Emotional stress is likely to result.
The demands on top leadership are enormous and stressful. Owners insist on profits; customers want special service and premier products; staff members need support and nurturance; the community asks for your time; the media demands information; your family begs for more attention.

9. Little time is left for you.
You never stop being the top dog. The constituencies identified above have few qualms about catching you wherever they can to have their needs met. Your evenings are fair game; your vacations may never be the same.

10. You lose your privacy.
The person in charge operates in a fishbowl. Your background, habits, values, beliefs, and tastes become everyone's business.

11. Your spouse and family may feel neglected.
Perhaps the biggest price of executive leadership is felt by the family. Your spouse and children suffer during the weekends you work, the

evenings you spend buried in paperwork, the family events you miss, and the vacations you can't quite get into.

119 | Six Red Flags of Burnout

When you're in charge, the pressure can be debilitating. It can affect your health, your family's well-being, and the financial health of your company. You're probably well aware of the potentially devastating effects of pressure from seeing friends or colleagues succumb to it. However, you may not be aware of an even greater problem: the power of denial. The desire to show strength, self-control, and leadership may make you discount or distort the symptoms of burnout apparent to everyone around you.

1. Chronic fatigue without a medical basis.
If you're always tired and lack energy but your physician can find no organic reason, your body is telling you something. Excessive focus on work may have you drained.

2. Depression.
You go to work, come home, spend time with family and friends, and nothing really turns you on. You go through the motions as if you were on autopilot. You sleep a lot more. You can't remember the last time you felt excited about anything.

3. Deterioration in work performance.
You're forgetting details you never forgot before. You're missing deadlines you never missed before. You're not following through on commitments you always honored. You don't seem to be able to do nearly as much work as you once did.

4. Detached, uncaring attitude.
In the past whenever you made a mistake or disappointed someone, you felt that you let yourself and other people down. These days it's not as important to you to get things right, and you care far less about how others are counting on you. Your general attitude is "So what?"

5. Cynicism and hopelessness.
You see plenty wrong in what people are doing, and very little right. You can't remember the last time you said "thank you" and neither

can anyone else. You're starting to see the downside of everything. Your pet phrases have become "We tried that before" and "That'll never work." You're losing faith in the people around you.

6. Impatience, irritability, and anger.
You no longer tolerate other people's idiosyncrasies that you once accepted and perhaps even enjoyed. You blow up at things that used to roll off your back. You'd just as soon work alone and eat lunch by yourself.

120 Eleven Tips to Reduce Your Stress

When you're in charge, you have a stressful job. That's the bad news. The awful news is that researchers estimate that 75% of all illnesses are stress related. The good news is that stress can be managed. You don't have to become a candidate for an early heart attack, a walking billboard for Valium, or an intimate friend of Jack Daniel. Rather than succumb to the debilitating consequences of stress, you can combat stress in your life. Manage stress and you'll enrich your life and the lives of those who love you and care about you.

1. Get a complete physical.
The first step in managing your stress is to get an accurate assessment of your health. What's your cholesterol count? What's your blood chemistry? What are your risk factors for heart disease? How much weight (if any) should you lose? If you're currently experiencing symptoms of stress, your physician will assess their significance and prescribe a treatment. Follow that advice.

2. Begin the journey towards a healthier lifestyle.
Health is a buffer against stress. Increasing your physical stamina through diet, exercise, and rest will help you combat the stressors in your life. Remember, you're embarking on a journey. Don't expect to run a marathon or do fifty push-ups immediately. If you're terribly out of shape, follow your doctor's advice before you start your exercise program.

3. Take a time management course.
Get control of your calendar and your watch. Stress increases as other forces gain increasing control of your agenda. The more you can control the pace of your day, the more you'll control your stress. (8, 9)

4. Stop expecting perfection.

You have a right to expect excellence; you don't have a right to expect perfection. Perfection, because humans are incapable of achieving it, is a goal that will only frustrate you and those around you. Stop beating yourself and others for failing to achieve goals that can't be achieved.

5. Learn to juggle multiple assignments.

Delegate, work with teams, plan more effectively, use information and technology more intelligently. Find the one thing you do routinely that has the least utility and eliminate it.

6. Learn when to say no.

You can't be all things to all people. Pick and choose the projects to complete, the assignments to fulfill, and the causes to support. Saying no at first is better for you and the person who asked than saying yes and feeling guilty because you haven't delivered what you promised.

7. Take energizing breaks.

Take short breaks during the day. Close your door and take an invigorating cat nap. Go for a walk during lunch. Carry a book of poetry or affirmations that you can quickly scan when you feel depressed or pressured.

8. Practice relaxation techniques.

Close your eyes. Focus on peaceful thoughts. Inhale and exhale deeply and slowly two or three times. Do this whenever you feel an anxiety attack coming on or whenever you feel the stress is overbearing.

9. Find balance in your life.

Perspective and balance are essential for physical and psychological health. Spend time with your family, religious groups, clubs, hobbies, sports, recreation, or any other activity that removes you from the daily grind. (125, 126)

10. Release pent-up stress.

Find an appropriate time and place when you can scream. Let out the nervous energy, pressure, or anger you're feeling. When something is bothering you, talk about it with close friends, confidants, family members, or counselors.

11. Shield yourself from destructive relationships.
Certain people can make you sick if you let them. When you've done your very best to work through a difficult relationship and it continues to be a source of pain for you, break away for a while. Do it with remorse, not guilt.

121 Thirteen Behaviors of Successful People

This book prescribes effective behavior for leaders. The purpose of this list is to personalize that advice even more for you. It presents actions that set the most successful people apart from those who don't quite get the same results. The wisdom contained in it is vital for all phases of human experience. Use it and share it with everyone in your life—subordinates, peers, friends, and family.

1. Bring your behavior in line with your values, beliefs, and desires.
The most fulfilled and satisfied people are those whose daily behavior reflects what's important to them. Are your actions consistent with your convictions? Here's how to find out. First, list on a sheet of paper the values, beliefs, and desires you hold in these fifteen areas of life:

- faith/religion/spirituality/worship/prayer
- spouse/family/children/parents
- friends/affiliations/alliances/teamwork/partnerships
- finances/wealth/possessions
- health/fitness/energy
- hobbies/recreation/free time/relaxation
- achievement/accomplishment/ambition/career/work
- courage/risk taking/standing up for beliefs
- excellence/beauty/perfection/accuracy
- persistence/commitment/follow through
- service/generosity/charity/humanitarianism
- integrity/honesty/ethics/law
- quality of life/pleasure/sensuality
- happiness/optimism/positive outlook
- contentment/inner peace/harmony/agreement

Second, put your statements in priority order. Third, consider whether you've been living your life consistent with your statement

---

Consider each area listed on the previous page one by one. Do you have one strongly held value, belief, or desire in it? If so, write it down and move on to the next area. You may end up with one or two dozen statements. These are best when written out as sentences. ("I believe my life and the lives around me will be improved by a positive, optimistic, and noncritical outlook.")

---

of values and beliefs. Fourth, take actions to increase harmony between what's important to you and what you do. (*Warning:* Think carefully before making major changes in your life, even if you're sure they'll bring your actions into harmony with your beliefs. Be sure to consider the impact that sudden changes in your behavior might have on those around you.)

2. Endure the pain of feedback in order to secure the joy of growth.
There are two important views of you as a leader: how you see yourself and how others see you. The second perspective is more important. How others see you determines how they respond to you and, in the case of leadership, what they *do* for you. The best way to find out what others think of your behavior is to ask them and to be genuinely thankful when they tell you the truth. One feedback-soliciting question that gets good results is, "What's one thing I could do to help you be more effective?" This will be far more successful than the more general and threatening "How am I doing?" (34)

3. Abandon hope for a better yesterday.
One reason some people never have happy and successful todays is that they continue to relive or to whine about unhappy yesterdays. Don't waste time revisiting the pain of the past when you can be making plans for a fantastic future. You *can't* erase earlier injuries or injustices. You *can* get on with life. You can summon the energy, commitment, and knowledge to ensure a better tomorrow.

4. Stop waiting for a better tomorrow.
Have you ever told stressed-out employees that if they'd just hang in there with you things will eventually calm down? Have you ever thought that once you can get through a trying time, you'll have the chance to enjoy yourself? Have you ever looked ahead to a next

phase of life for better circumstances? There are three problems with waiting for a better tomorrow:

- It's an excuse to function in suspended animation while waiting for improvements to materialize.
- You're in effect wishing away a part of your life and might ignore the happiness, excitement, and satisfaction present through all phases of life—both the good and the bad.
- The time of greater calm, less struggle, and ease of life you hope for may never materialize. Experience the joys of today!

5. Reject failure.
When some people don't get the results they hope for, they brand the experience a failure. Others come away feeling, "I just learned one more way not to . . ." The latter group examines what went wrong and resolves not to repeat any mistakes. They persist and nearly rejoice in the so-called failure, knowing that it's a path they'll never let themselves walk again.

6. Reject negative thinking.
Do you tend to see the glass as half empty or half full? What you see in your mind is what you create, and what you think is what you get.

> You may have heard the story of the shoe company looking for new markets that decided to send two salespeople into the bush country of Africa. Not long after arriving, one salesperson got to a phone and called the home office to say, "I'm leaving on the next plane. There's no market here. These people aren't wearing shoes!" A few days later the second salesperson called and reported this: "Sorry I haven't called before now. Business has been great! When I got here, these people weren't wearing shoes."

7. Reject limiting language.
If what you think is what you get, then what you speak is what you become. Speak in positive terms.

- Replace the weakly stated "I'll try" with "I will!"
- Kill *shoulds, ought-tos, have-tos* and other stress-building and guilt-creating intentions.

- Replace "I can't," "I don't," or "I won't" with "I haven't up until now."
- Never say, "I'm too [inexperienced, busy, disorganized, conservative, stupid, fat, out of shape, weak, afraid] to . . ."
- Start accepting compliments with "thank you" instead of protesting that you don't deserve them.
- Accept offers of help instead of shooting back an automatic, "No thanks, I can handle it."
- When asked how you feel, say "great" or "marvelous," not just "fine" or "okay."

8. Remain physically fit and energetic.

How many successful people do you know who are unhealthy and tired all the time? Exercise a minimum of twenty minutes at least every other day. Don't smoke. Get a complete physical yearly. Follow your doctor's advice. Ask about the wisdom of taking vitamins. Eat a low fat diet. Drink plenty of water. Get the amount of sleep you need—probably about seven hours. Schedule refreshing breaks into your workday. Relax in the evenings. Take your vacations.

9. Make the best use of your time.

Successful people spend the bulk of their time strategically—setting plans, making critical decisions, coaching employees, and meeting customer requirements. They've learned how to minimize the time spent fighting fires (fewer fires burn in their organizations), the time spent doing routine tasks (they're great delegaters), and the time that gets wasted (they're organized). (8)

10. Study successful role models.

An executive serving as a mentor was approached by one of his young protégés with this question: "What does it take to become CEO of this company?" The one-sentence response was, "Think like a CEO, talk like a CEO, and act like a CEO." Don't be misled by the glibness of the message. It's perhaps the best answer the mentor could have given. If you aspire to success at a higher level, look to people who have done well at that level. Find something in their styles that you might profitably emulate.

11. Communicate more precisely and more powerfully.

Leadership is a process of influence. Influence is exerted through your communication skills. Very few successful CEOs have difficulty expressing themselves. (15–26)

12. Listen even better than you speak.
Dean Rusk once said, "The best way to influence others is with your ears, by listening to them." Give people your ears. Not only will you influence them—they'll tell you everything you need to know. (31)

13. Serve those around you.
Do you give as much value as you can to subordinates, peers, superiors, customers, family, friends, and others, with little regard for what you receive in return? If you do, you've discovered what few people know: such selflessness pays two enormous benefits in the form of self-satisfaction and returned service.

122 Nine Ways to Manage So Your Employees Have a Home Life

Today's employees enter the workforce with expectations and needs distinctly different from those of their parents and grandparents. In the recent past, employees were committed to the company, even if that meant sacrificing family life. They were happy to have the job and were loyal. Today's employees define success differently. They may be just as committed to their profession as earlier generations, but not at the expense of hearth, home, and hobbies. Their loyalty is less to an employer than to a lifestyle. Once another employer appears willing to be more supportive, they're gone. Manage your employees so that careers are in harmony with home life.

1. Invest in information technology.
Workers who manipulate information can work almost anywhere. State-of-the-art information technology will help you serve your customers better, improve your bottom line, and provide mobility for your employees. They'll be able to meet your goals and spend more time with people other than coworkers.

2. Rethink the five-day, 40-hour week.
Flex time, job sharing, telecommuting, and the four-day, 40-hour week are ideas whose time has come. Check with your chamber of commerce or local business groups to research how other companies have implemented these new work configurations.

3. Meet your employees' families and friends.
Invite families and friends to social functions. Support company-sponsored family outings. When you meet who's waiting for your

employees at home, you may be less likely to expect outrageously long hours from them. (6)

4. Don't make your work habit the norm.
You may enjoy being a workaholic and have a TGIM (Thank Goodness It's Monday) sign on your desk. Unfortunately, you may find greater satisfaction in your office than in your home. But don't impose those values on your employees. You hurt your employees and your company by establishing a corporate culture of workaholics.

5. Use teams to schedule work assignments.
Team members will negotiate among themselves for weekend assignments. Some may be able to put in the extra work, others may not. They'll trade with one another for extra work and weekend assignments. They'll also set up their own time debit and credit systems. Over the long run equity will prevail, employees will have a home life, and your company goals will be met.

6. Manage so that crises are the exception, not the norm.
Most reasonable employees (and most employees are reasonable) realize that an occasional "all nighter" at the office is necessary. However, when employees are consistently breaking commitments with their families because of an emergency at the office, you're failing to manage effectively. The best manager prevents crises and manages so that employees are able to write in ink on their personal calendars.

7. When an employee sacrifices family for the company, send a gift to the family.
Employees and their families do indeed sacrifice when the company comes first. Show your appreciation. Send the family a plant, tickets to the movies, or a gift certificate for dinner on you. You'll encourage their continued support of your hard-working employees.

8. Invest in dependent day care.
Employees with dependents can't give their total commitment to their work if they're worried about their children's or parents' care. Consider providing dependent care as a fringe benefit. Another option is to start a consortium with other employers in your area and share the cost of dependent care.

9. Invest in time management training for your employees.
It's possible to juggle multiple projects and succeed at all of them.
And it's possible to achieve in a 40-hour week what others do in 60
hours. Teach your employees time management techniques. (8)

123 Nine Steps to Change Yourself

We intentionally placed this checklist near the end of this book. If
you've read each page up to this one, you've been bombarded with
nearly 2,000 ideas for more effective leadership. You may already
be practicing some of them, and you may have rejected others for
one reason or another. The rest stand before you as challenges.
Now the question becomes: How do you do it? The advice may be
perfectly clear, but after years of behaving otherwise how do you
change?

1. Accept imperfection in yourself.
Will Durant once said, "Sixty years ago I knew everything; now I
know nothing. Education is the progressive discovery of our own
ignorance." What a wonderful attitude to have—especially to believe that you may be ignorant about yourself and the impact you're
having on the people around you. This attitude is the prerequisite to
personal change.

2. Overcome the fear of change.
When you resist the idea of getting feedback from others, ask
yourself why. People fear change—in this case, learning something
about yourself that you didn't already know—because they fear
losing something as a result. What do you fear losing? Control?
Security? Prestige? Self-esteem? Relationships? Acknowledge your
fear of feedback and discuss it with someone in whom you can
confide. (2)

3. Ask for feedback.
Very few people will volunteer personal reactions to someone in
charge. You'll have to ask—and ask in a way that convinces people
you really want the truth. They have to be convinced that the
feedback will hurt neither them nor you. One question that may
resolve both of these concerns is, "What's one thing I could do to
help you become even more effective than you are right now?"

4. Listen to feedback nondefensively.

View yourself as a work of art in progress. Each piece of feedback you receive adds one more important brush stroke to the canvas. Even when you die, you may not be a finished masterpiece, but neither was *The Mona Lisa*. (31)

5. Find out the problems caused by your behavior.

Once you learn what you're doing, or not doing, that others wish you'd change, find out what the negative impact is on them and on you. Someone once said that to know ourselves diseased is half our cure. Awareness of our dysfunctions may not be half of the solution, but without it we'd never be able to proceed to the next and most critical step of all.

6. Hate the problem caused by your behavior.

The only way to muster the motivation you need to change a long-standing behavior is to hate what it's doing to you or to important people in your life. Until you mount this step, it makes little sense to go ahead with any plans to change.

The chain smoker who says, "I think I'll take a crack at giving up cigarettes this week" is unlikely to succeed. However, the smoker who says this is on the right track: "I hate cigarettes. I hate the way they make me smell. I hate the secondary smoke my children inhale because of them. And I hate losing two minutes of life every time I light up."

---

7. Devise a plan.

Now that you know the problem and realize what you need to do to solve it, what's your plan—or better yet, your *vow*? What will you do? When will you do it? Whom will you ask to help you?

8. Take action.

Do it!

9. Let assimilation do the rest.

Soon after you embark on a new behavior, the twenty-one-day rule takes over. That is, it takes about twenty-one days for any repeated behavior to become a habit. Let's say, for example, that neglecting to praise your employees has been the problem. Your plan might be to write a reminder in your planner to catch at least one employee each day in the act of doing something right. After about three weeks you can stop writing the reminder.

124 Thirteen Tips for Managing Your Career

To paraphrase Forrest Gump, a career is also like a box of chocolates—you never know what you're going to get. But although careers are filled with uncertainty, you needn't throw up your hands and cry that planning is for naught. To the contrary, you *can* create a blueprint for professional success. In this list we provide strategies for setting goals and planning your career so that the surprises in your box of chocolates will be pleasant ones.

1. View your career as a journey, not a goal.
Your career evolves over time and through many experiences—some are positive and some are negative. You learn from each if you're open to the lessons they teach. Each company you join, each assignment you fulfill, and each person you work alongside will educate you.

2. Keep on top of trends.
Opportunities knock at the door, but are you listening? When you anticipate and recognize changes in technology, markets, competition, and cultural forces, you'll hear the knock. (35)

3. Understand the criteria by which you'll be judged.
Find out what the expectations are of the board or the boss that you serve. Never fail to achieve because you didn't know what was expected.

4. Don't rely on others to manage your career.
The only person responsible for your career is you. The only person responsible for making you smarter is you. Consume continuing education and professional development opportunities. Soak up knowledge like a dry sponge. Each year vow to add value to your leadership skills.

5. Maintain an up-to-date résumé.
You'll never know when a head hunter will call, or when your boss or board of directors will say your time is up. Periodically update

your résumé by adding new skills you've acquired, new courses you've completed, and new goals you've reached.

6. Always bring more money into the company than you're paid.
Whenever you return more to your employer than you're paid, you increase your value to your present employer and all prospective employers. View your salary as a yearly debt you plan to return with interest. Look for opportunities to increase sales, reduce costs, improve products, and satisfy customers.

7. Choose mentors wisely.
Select a star higher in the sky than you with insight, personal integrity, and a strong power base. (62)

8. Get wiser before you get older.
There will be times in your career when you fail to produce stated goals or you simply make an honest but stupid mistake. Don't waste time and energy in denial or scapegoating. Just make sure you understand what you did wrong so you won't do it again.

9. Never burn your bridges.
In the process of being a success, you'll undoubtedly make enemies. Nevertheless, do what you can to make every peer and every associate a lifelong ally. You never know who might someday be in a position to advance, or set back, your career. Leave every job in a way that would allow you to come back into open arms.

10. Maintain balance.
Will your career be a success if you can't share it with anyone? Manage your career so that your professional responsibilities harmoniously coexist with family and personal responsibilities. Don't sacrifice one for the other. (125)

11. Set personal development goals.
Each year write down three personal enrichment goals that you plan to achieve.

12. Value your values.
Once you start rationalizing unethical behavior, you start a downward slide from which you may never recover. If you can't hold your head up with pride and dignity, you've cheated yourself and your employers. When all is said and done, a principled life will always be the most rewarding.

13. Train your replacement.
Never get into a position where you become indispensable. Executives who are indispensable are sometimes not offered new responsibilities because they can't be replaced. Start grooming your replacement today. (88)

125 Eleven Ways to Balance Your Work and Personal Life

In the words of Jackson Brown, "No one on his deathbed ever said I should have spent more time in the business." It's easy for the person in charge to lose perspective and allow the balance of professional and personal life to tilt completely in favor of work. If you fear that outcome for yourself, consider one or more of the following actions.

1. Take your vacations.
Take every day of vacation coming to you each year. Take it in big chunks rather than in dribbles. Most executives work so intensely that they need three or four days away from the office before they can unwind fully.

2. Find a retreat.
Find a spot within a few hours of your home—perhaps a beach house or a mountain home if you can afford it. Get away for as many long weekends and holidays as you can.

3. Don't take work home.
Many people in charge take two to three hours of work home with them every evening. Cut that amount down or black out certain nights of the week for other things you want to do.

4. Stay active in a hobby.
Mental and physical diversions are vital for people who work as hard as you do. Read, become a collector, ski, play golf, or develop another hobby that you enjoy enough to turn away from your work for a while.

5. Escape for one hour each day.
Reserve the same hour each workday for yourself. You might read, pray, or engage in your favorite form of exercise, relaxation, or inspiration. Except when you're interrupted by travel or emergency, that time always belongs to you and possibly someone very close to

you. One way to find this hour is by waking up one half hour earlier (after going to bed one half hour earlier) and going to the office one half hour later.

6. Take maximum advantage of technology.
Hire a telecommunications consultant to study your workday and recommend ways you can automate more of what you do. Don't just take on more work with the time you save. Divide that time up equally between work and personal life. If you estimate you save thirty minutes a day, go home fifteen minutes earlier.

7. Delegate greater responsibility to subordinate managers.
You shouldn't be the hardest working person in the office. Spread out the workload among your senior staff with you taking no more than your share. Divide the time you save equally between work and personal life. (46)

8. Limit travel.
Travel as little as you can. Experiment with conducting more long-distance business over the telephone. Take the last flight out for early morning meetings. Take morning flights for afternoon meetings. Spend as few nights as possible in hotel rooms. (9)

9. Settle for less.
Big title and big money usually go with big responsibility. In many cases people who accept high-paying jobs are expected to sacrifice their personal life. No one holds a gun to your head and demands you to take the money. The choice is yours. (118)

10. Ask your spouse for feedback.
Talk about the balance between work and family with your spouse. Get his or her ideas about what you can do to be more available both physically and emotionally.

11. Reserve time each day for children.
The number of minutes the average executive spends daily in meaningful communication with children can often be counted on the fingers of one hand. Shoot for the same time each day when you'll seek out your children and share thoughts, feelings, and emotions. Ask them about their day and tell them about yours. Don't forget your responsibility to teach them.

126 | Fifteen Movies to Help You Find Your Balance

Maintaining balance in your life is easier said than done. Your need to achieve and your talent have brought you to a position of leadership, control, and power. Yet you also realize that achieving financial or corporate success at the expense of a fulfilling personal life can be a hollow victory. Periodically, we need to find a message that shakes us up. The videos on this list provide that message. So gather your family, get a bowl of popcorn, put the tape in the VCR, sit back, and learn.

1. Almost any movie Frank Capra directed.

2. Any of the great musicals based on Broadway plays.

3. Any movie that made you cry as a child.

4. The last movie that made you cry.

5. A movie that made you laugh out loud and still brings back pleasant memories.

6. A movie that helped you and your spouse learn something about your relationship.

7. Your children's favorite movie.

8. A movie that sent you out of the theater with a smile on your face and a lift in your step.

9. A movie that forced you to look at a problem through other people's eyes.

10. A movie that helped you learn an important lesson about the relationship between happiness and success.

11. *Forrest Gump.*

12. *Flight of the Phoenix.*

13. *Lorenzo's Oil.*

14. *Pride of the Yankees.*

15. *Cheaper by the Dozen.*

127 Nine Steps to Take Toward a Happy Retirement

Almost no one is neutral on the issue of retirement. You either can't wait for the freedom and excitement, or you insist they'll have to carry you out kicking and screaming. However you feel about the prospect of no longer being in charge, you'll find the information on this list helpful.

1. Begin financial planning early.
From the time you earn enough to support yourself, you should fund your retirement plan. Set a retirement income goal and make a resolute commitment to the arrangements necessary to achieve it.

2. Pick an age.
By the time you're 50, you should have a retirement target age in mind.

3. Consider phased retirement.
Jumping into a cold swimming pool is far less painful than gingerly descending the steps like a tea bag. Retirement is quite the opposite. Whether your target age is 50 or 70 (average in the United States is 62), consider sneaking up on it slowly through gradually reduced work weeks and longer vacations.

4. Plan now for the emotional adjustments.
Retirement will force you to recognize how much you depended on work.

- Your company has met your need to belong. What will replace it?
- Your business achievements have sustained your self-satisfaction. What will fill in the gap?
- Your identification needs were met by your building, your office, your title, and your business reputation. What will take their place?
- The goals that have motivated your behavior over the past decades were tied to your business and your profession. What goals will fill in for them?
- You're in charge *now*, but how will you deal with no longer being the top dog? Will you start acting like the CEO of your family and make them wish *they* could retire?

5. Don't allow work to become the reason for your existence.
Too many executives fail to survive the first year of their retirement; their lives became indescribably empty when they left the office. Others continue to work beyond a sensible retirement age, and as a result miss out on so many of the joys that life has in store for those with the time to celebrate it.

6. Develop hobbies and interests to carry you into retirement.
Play those rounds of golf you've always dreamed of. Take up cross-country skiing. Travel with your spouse to those places you've never seen. Volunteer with some of those worthy community organizations that need you. Dedicate yourself to a social cause. Telephone and write letters to all the friends you never had time to keep in touch with. Teach a class.

7. Plan to enjoy the simple, beautiful, and precious things in life.
Spend more time with your grandchildren. Plant a garden. Start a collection. Read the comics. Stroll through the woods. Read the spiritual text of your choice.

8. Attend preretirement seminars.
Get some preretirement counseling. Learn about and anticipate both the joys and pitfalls of beginning this new phase of your life.

9. Stay healthy.
Eat well and exercise. Keep an active body and mind. Poor health will make retirement miserable.

128 Eleven Tips for Selecting and Using a Financial Advisor

You may manage a seven- or eight-figure financial portfolio for your company with a high degree of competence and rationality. Unfortunately, it's difficult to manage your own investments with the same aplomb. Besides, your intense work schedule may not leave the time you need to devote to them. What's the best way to find a good financial advisor? The answer is to select him or her the way you would a doctor or lawyer—with care and caution. Do your homework and prudently select the one most qualified to help you reach your financial goals.

1. Ask around.
Seek recommendations from friends and associates whose judgment you respect. Your lawyer, accountant, and banker are good sources for information about financial advisors.

2. Narrow the field.
After making a list of prospects, interview them. Time your appointments for the afternoon, following the close of the market. If you're new to investing, make certain that you look for someone willing to help you learn the fundamentals.

3. Reveal your financial personality.
Explain in detail your current and anticipated financial status and needs. Discuss your attitudes about risk and make sure you're comfortable with the advisor's investment philosophy and strategies.

4. Ask about fees.
Some advisors will charge on a per-transaction basis; others charge based on a percentage of an investor's total portfolio. What are the percentages? Is there a custodial fee for IRAs?

5. Check references.
Ask candidates for the names of clients with whom the advisor has worked for at least two or three years. Call these clients and ask how the advisor has handled their business and how accessible he or she is. Ask about the advisor's track record over a range of market conditions.

6. Check for a match of values and beliefs.
Finding a talented financial advisor is only part of the task; comfortably working with him or her is equally critical to the success of your investment program. You're looking to develop a solid, long-term relationship that's mutually rewarding.

7. Probe and listen.
Ask questions about anything that concerns you. Find out what services you can expect. Get a sense of the advisor's investment strategies: ask about three of his or her recent recommendations, the information behind them, and the rationale for them.

8. Understand the basic security transactions.
Make sure you fully understand the mechanics of buying, selling, or any other action that your advisor may recommend. Ask him or her for a pamphlet or to recommend a book on the subject.

9. Update your portfolio.
Periodically review your securities, assets, and overall financial picture with your advisor.

10. Don't misuse your financial advisor.
Don't rely on your financial advisor for legal advice any more than you'd trust your lawyer for financial advice. Keep a team of professionals including a lawyer, accountant, and financial advisor at your side to help you to cope with diverse financial, investment, and tax matters. (115, 116)

11. Keep your vision prominent.
Perhaps the most important key to working with a financial advisor is for both of you to completely understand your investment goals, especially as they change. As you mature as an investor, the service provided by your advisor is also likely to evolve, from providing direction when you're starting out to more complex investment management services when you acquire substantial assets. Your advisor will be best able to meet your changing needs if he or she knows precisely where you want to be at each stage.

129 Six Crucial Records in the Event of Disaster, Disease, or Death

None of us wants to think about the worst scenario, yet living in an uncertain world we must. There are many people at work and especially at home who depend on you. If you aren't around to make decisions about your assets, they must. Will they have the skills to make all those decisions? The documents in this list will provide the help they need and will give you peace of mind.

1. An up-to-date will.
Stop procrastinating. Make an appointment with your attorney and draw up that will. If you have a will but it's outdated because of changes in your life, get it changed. Show your spouse or trusted friend where it's located.

2. Living will.
Do you want your physician to take extraordinary steps to keep you alive? What medical procedures do you want him or her to employ if you're in a vegetative state? If you're terminally ill or permanently unconscious, this document will tell family and friends how you

wish to be treated medically. Your physician should have a copy of this document. Show your spouse or trusted friend where the original is located.

3. Power of attorney.
Authorize a spouse or trusted individual to make financial decisions on your behalf. Make this decision very carefully. A power of attorney is a potential license to steal. If you have large investments at various brokerage firms, check on the power of attorney forms they prefer. Show your spouse or trusted friend where this document is located.

4. A registry of your insurance agent, accountant, attorney, and financial advisor.
Who currently advises you in legal and financial transactions? List all these professionals, their names, phone numbers, and addresses. Keep this list current. Show your spouse or trusted friend where this list is located.

5. An inventory of financial assets.
List deeds, stock certificates, jewelry, coins, antiques, insurance policies, bank accounts, money market accounts, and other valuable assets on this inventory. Provide names of accounts, location, and approximate market value. Show your spouse or trusted friend where this list is located.

6. A video expressing your good-byes to friends and family.
The previous items on this list are designed to prevent protracted litigation. This one is designed for the heart and soul of those left behind. What are the final thoughts you want to leave with them? Again show your spouse or trusted friend where the video is located.

130 Twelve Quotes Worth Quoting About Balance

1. By working faithfully eight hours a day you may eventually get to be a boss and work twelve hours a day. —*Robert Frost*

2. Do not take life too seriously. You will never get out of it alive. —*Elbert Hubbard*

3. There are an enormous number of managers who have retired on the job. —*Peter Drucker*

4. It is seldom that an American retires from business to enjoy his fortune in comfort. . . . He works because he has always worked, and knows no other way. —*Thomas Nichols*

5. One ought, every day at least, to hear a little song, read a good poem, see a fine picture, and, if it were possible, to speak a few reasonable words. —*Johann W. von Goethe*

6. If I'd known I was going to live so long, I'd have taken better care of myself. —*Leon Eldred*

7. Live in each season as it passes, breathe the air, drink the drink, taste the fruit. —*Henry David Thoreau*

8. Never allow your sense of self to become associated with your sense of job. If your job vanishes, your self doesn't. —*Gordon Van Souter*

9. A man is ethical only when life, as such, is sacred to him, that of plants and animals as well as that of his fellow man, and when he devotes himself helpfully to all life that is in need of help. —*Albert Schweitzer*

10. By the time you rise through the ranks, the culture of homogenization has bred the spirit and imagination out of you. —*Ralph Nader*

11. Energy enables a man to force his way through irksome drudgery and dry details and caries him onward and upward to every station in life. —*Samuel Smile*

12. Seek out the struggle that will toughen you up. Negativism is a sin; so is self-indulgence. Bad times, such as depression or a state of war, should be a challenging test. Real men tighten their belts, throw full weight into the harness of their daily activities, and pull with all their might and main.—*J. C. Penney*

INDEX

This index is keyed to list numbers, not page numbers. If the index cites several lists for one topic, the numbers in boldface indicate the most basic advice.

ACKNOWLEDGMENTS

Two groups played giant parts in the creation of *Smart Moves for People in Charge*. First come all those people in charge whom we've worked with over the years—particularly those in the past year or so who told us what they wanted to see in this book. Second are those executives, entrepreneurs, and consultants who wrote certain lists in this book better than we could. We thank the following distinguished team of experts for their smart moves:

Al Borowski for lists 15 and 16, on writing accurately and persuasively. Al designs and delivers workshops on business communication with a focus on business writing, customer service, telephone skills, listening, and training trainers.

> Al Borowski
> Profit Margins Inc.
> 281 Arden Road
> Pittsburgh, PA 15216

Bernard R. Kuzma for list 68, Eleven Ways to Respond to a Problem Employee. Bernie is vice president of a community hospital. His professional experience spans fifteen years in hospital administration and twenty years in human resources.

> Bernard R. Kuzma
> 2322 Patterson Street
> Pittsburgh, PA 15203

J. Robert Graham for list 80, Sixteen Steps to Install a Successful TQM Process. Bob is a corporate executive, consultant, speaker, and trainer with specialties in executive development, leadership, and the creation of world-class Total Quality Management systems.

> J. Robert Graham
> 4057 Little Spring Drive
> Allison Park, PA 15101

Delorese Ambrose for list 85, Thirteen Ways to Gain Value Through Diversity. Delorese is a practitioner, author, and motivational speaker who leads a multicultural team of professionals in diversity training, leadership development, and team building.

Delorese Ambrose, Ed.D.
Ambrose Consulting and Training
1 NorthShore Center, Suite 210
Pittsburgh, PA 15212

Russ Ray for lists 100 through 105, all about understanding organizational finance. Russ teaches corporate finance, banking, investments, financial markets, derivatives, and international finance at the University of Louisville. He also conducts seminars in corporate and personal finance, time management, peak performance, and futurism.

Russ Ray, Ph.D.
Professor of Finance
University of Louisville School of Business
Louisville, KY 40292

Frederick J. Slack for list 113, Ten Steps to Effective Benchmarking. Fred is a Certified Management Consultant who has led more than 500 benchmarking, customer satisfaction, and employee opinion survey projects over the past twenty years.

Frederick J. Slack, Ph.D.
Box 326, Route 380
Saltsburg, PA 15681

Michael B. Spring for list 114, Fourteen Rules for Selecting a New Computer System. Michael is on the faculty of the Department of Information Science at the University of Pittsburgh, with research interests in interactive systems, office automation, large scale document processing, and information technology standards.

Michael B. Spring, Ph.D.
School of Library and Information Science
University of Pittsburgh
Pittsburgh, PA 15260

David B. Fawcett for list 115, Eleven Tips for Using Your Lawyer More Effectively. Dave has over 35 years of trial and appellate experience as a civil litigator in state and federal courts. He also serves as an arbitrator and mediator.

David B. Fawcett, Esq.
Shareholder/Director
Dickie, McCamey & Chilcote
Two PPG Place, Suite 400
Pittsburgh, PA 15222

Lawrence J. Sipos for list 116, Nine Ways to Use Your Accountant More Effectively. Larry is a partner at Kaplan Sipos & Associates with expertise in tax and business planning for individuals and closely held businesses.

Lawrence J. Sipos, CPA, JD
Kaplan Sipos & Associates
Suite 2650, Two PNC Plaza
Pittsburgh, PA 15222

Michael J. King for list 128, Eleven Tips for Selecting and Using a Financial Advisor. Mike is an experienced financial consultant in the private client group at Merrill Lynch.

Michael J. King
Vice President
Merrill Lynch
Liberty Center, 14th Floor
Pittsburgh, PA 15222

ABOUT THE AUTHORS

Sam Deep taught at the college level for twenty years, most recently in the Communication Department of the University of Pittsburgh, where he also served as an administrator. In 1986 he expanded his part-time consulting practice into a full-time career. He now helps organizations empower their employees by enhancing the interpersonal, communication, and leadership skills of their managers.

Lyle Sussman is Professor of Management in the School of Business, University of Louisville, Kentucky. Previously he was affiliated with the University of Michigan and the University of Pittsburgh. He received his Ph.D. in Communications and Industrial Relations from Purdue University. He serves on the faculties of several state and national banking schools.

Deep and Sussman conduct seminars and give speeches for a variety of organizations from the *Fortune* 500, the health industry, public school systems, colleges and universities, professional associations, and government agencies. A few of their recent clients include: Alcoa, American Bankers Association, Austrian National Bank, Bahamas Ministry of Tourism, Bayer, Blockbuster Video, Brown Williamson Corporation, Carnegie Mellon University, Dean Witter, Deloitte & Touche, General Electric, Hallmark Cards, Humana, Kentucky Fried Chicken, Ketchum Communications, Kraft Food Service, Mellon Bank, Merck & Co., National Cattleman's Association, National Park Service, PPG, Pittsburgh Symphony, Paradise Island Resort & Casino, Presbyterian-University Hospital, Puerto Rico Hotel and Tourism Association, Rally's, Rockwell International, South-Western Bell, Union Switch & Signal, U.S. Foodservice, U.S. Postal Service, Veterans Administration, Westinghouse, and Xerox.

Their ideas about leadership and communication have appeared in the *Chicago Tribune, Cosmopolitan, Self, USAir Magazine, Working Woman, Working Mother, Ladies Home Journal, Boardroom Reports*, and *Executive Report*, to name a few. Their taped programs appear on USAir's Inflight Audio Entertainment. They have been interviewed on countless radio and television stations throughout the United States and Canada. Their management columns have been carried by four newspapers. Their management best-seller *Smart Moves* has been published in twelve languages.

SEMINARS BY SAM DEEP AND LYLE SUSSMAN

Sam and Lyle give seminars and motivational talks and conduct retreats on many of the topics covered by the lists in this book. Each seminar is carefully crafted in length and in focus to the needs of your organization or group. The seminars below use *Smart Moves for People in Charge* as a textbook.

As Time Goes By
Building Teams that Win
Building a Unified Board
Communicating with Confidence
Criticism and Praise: Giving and Getting Them
Dealing with Difficult Employees
Four Secrets of Leadership
Getting the Best of Stress
Getting Your Employees to Give Great Customer Service
Hiring Top Performers
Making Change Happen
Making Meetings Work
Presenting Yourself with Impact
Resolving Conflict, Anger, and Hostility in the Workplace
Selling Your Ideas to Others
The Servant Leader
Seven Secrets of Highly Effective CEOs
The Smartest of Smart Moves for People in Charge
Strategic Planning that Works
SuperVision 2000
Ten Secrets of Personal Success
Yes, You Can!
You're Not Listening!

For more information on any of these programs, write or call:
Sam Deep
1920 Woodside Road
Glenshaw, PA 15116
412-487-2379